T0197019

PREPARE YE THE WAY OF THE LORD!

THE SIGNS OF THE TIMES SIGNAL THE SOON
RETURN OF SATAN, FROM THE BOTTOMLESS
PIT, TO START THE TRIBULATION PERIOD THAT
WILL SERVE AS THE PRECURSOR TO JESUS'
SECOND COMING!

DOUGLAS AHO

WESTBOW
PRESS®
A DIVISION OF THOMAS NELSON
& ZONDERVAN

WestBow Press books may be ordered through booksellers or by contacting:

WestBow Press
A Division of Thomas Nelson & Zondervan
1663 Liberty Drive
Bloomington, IN 47403
www.westbowpress.com
1 (866) 928-1240

ISBN: 978-1-5127-3526-0 (sc)
ISBN: 978-1-5127-3527-7 (hc)
ISBN: 978-1-5127-3525-3 (e)

Library of Congress Control Number: 2016904605

Print information available on the last page.

WestBow Press rev. date: 06/22/2016

A LAYMAN CRYING IN THE WILDERNESS:

"WHERE ARE MY FATHER'S CHOSEN?"

- Do you know only the chosen are eligible for salvation?
- Do you know if your name is written in the book of life?
- Do you know if your church is teaching false doctrine?
- Do you know that there is only one source for truth?
- Do you know who the Father sent to reveal truth?
- Do you know the role of work's righteousness in salvation?
- Do you know you are solely responsible for your salvation?
- Do you know you must be led by the Spirit to be a child of God?
- Do you know there is no pre-tribulation rapture?

A chosen has the right to know the truth! Where you spend eternal life depends on Jesus' Great White Throne Judgment that offers only two verdicts: The lake of fire or the Father's family. Both are eternal.

NOTE

Given the importance of biblical truth, your pastor should conduct an open congregational forum on the veracity of this Record. Prior to the forum, church members should be given time to study the Spirit revelations contained in this record. This would allow the Chosen member participants to receive counsel, from the Holy Spirit resident with their spirit, prior to and during the comparison of church doctrine with the revelations in this Record. Of course the Father would bless and endorse any forum seeking biblical truth.

CONTENTS

FOREWORD

The origin of this Record began in the Fall of 1974, when the Father gave me Matthew 6:33, told me I would never worry about my salvation while arranging a nursing home ministry lasting 35 years. Then in December, 2009, He told me to get into the Word because I couldn't preach the truth, if I didn't know the truth. There were two doctrines of the church I have always adamantly rejected: Isaiah 53 and John 3:16. They are violated by false church doctrine that denies understanding of the Father's salvation plan. They don't limit prayers pleading the blood of Jesus to the soul nor limit the number of John 3:16 gift opportunities to the Chosen. Both scriptures are the product of false doctrinal exegesis to promote prosperity theology.

Do I deserve the right to salvation? NO! Everyone comes into this world with a death legacy caused by Adam's sin. His sin required two types of death to all descendants, whether Chosen or unchosen. The first death is the death of the flesh for all descendants. The second death is the spirit of death judgment when the Books of the dead are opened. The second death affects all unchosen since they were never offered the Spirit of Life that departed from Adam when he sinned. But what about the Chosen? Adam was also their earthly father which required the second death like the unchosen. This is where the Father manifest His Salvation Plan that withholds Satan's second death rights over the Chosen until judged by access to the cross. The Father allows the Spirit to be resident in all of His Chosen's beginning with the Spirit baptism until being judged by the Spirit for access to the cross. Those Chosen denied access to the cross will lose their Chosen status, their names removed from the Book of Life and join the ranks of the unchosen to await the second death. When the Book of Life is opened, those Chosen whose names remain written in the book will join the Father's family. The unchosen reap the second death of the Lake of Fire.

The Spirit is become resident in all qualified Chosen at Spirit Baptism. Most church members have not been taught scriptures relating to the Elect/Chosen and the fact that their Names may be recorded in the Book of Life. It begs the question, 'How can I ascertain whether if I am among the Chosen?

1. Seriously pray to the Spirit and ask that He quicken your spirit with a sense of His presence. If your heart desires to know Him and you experience a hunger and thirst for righteousness, then follow the approach I used when the Father gave me Matthew 6:33 in 1974, 'Seek Ye first the Kingdom of God and His Righteous.' I strongly recommend you start a daily communion that grows your discernment of and fellowship with His presence. An opportunity for Joy and Peace with the Trinity can be yours!

2. Toward the end of my walk, I asked the Spirit what is available to those not exposed to biblical truth. The answer was knowing the only one unimpeachable source of Truth. You are responsible for your salvation and the only true source of truth is the Spirit. What you need to do is cut out the middle man and go to the true source. Now you can follow the counsel in '1' above.

I believe in the church, as your best source of Christian fellowship where you can enjoy sermons and bible studies while developing your spirit led discernment to weed out false doctrine.

PREFACE

In December 2009, the Father spoke to my spirit: "YOU NEED TO GET INTO THE WORD! YOU CAN'T PREACH THE TRUTH, IF YOU DON'T KNOW THE TRUTH." Early in my walk with the Spirit, I embraced the application of hermeneutics to gain biblical exegesis of scriptures. However, based on widespread denominational doctrinal differences in exegesis, one could easily conclude that the application of hermeneutics was controlled more by man's intellect than by the Spirit. My Father was right about my ignorance of truth and the fact that my truth malady was rampant in the church was of no comfort. Since His admonition, my walk with the Spirit has opened the mind of God portrayed in the bible vastly different than that reflected in church doctrine.

This is a personal record of a scribe recording revelations received from the Holy Spirit. When the Father told me I couldn't preach the truth, if I didn't know the truth, I quickly recalled the scripture of Jesus telling his followers, that it was important that he return to the Father and request Him to send the Holy Spirit, who would lead them into all truth. The Father's mind, as expressed in the truth of His Word, can only be accessed through Spirit revelation.

This record is designed for God's Chosen, often referred to as the Elect, to alert them of their Chosen status and prepare them for Spirit led service. The Chosen were named in the Book of Life before creation and in Revelation's description of the Great White Throne Judgment. There is very a limited discussion of the Chosen in today's churches and little or no witness to being Chosen. This Record is a 'come to Jesus' call for all Chosen, who don't know they are among the Chosen, but love Jesus and would like to find some answers.

Today, Sunday, August 16, 2015, almost six years after my commission, the Spirit quickened my spirit to one of the most profound revelations I have received. He just said one word 'SOVEREIGNTY' and my spirit came alive. It was the answer to understanding the spiritual decay in the church and the Father's SOVEREIGN right to choose a Family. My Record of Spirit led truths will cause much confusion and anger. Whether we agree or not, the Father has the Sovereign right to control everything in His creation. That includes our mind, spirit and body. He has the absolute control over dispensers of church doctrine.

The Father has given Satan the limited right, controlled by Jesus, to chastise His Chosen. This means all actions of the church hierarchy will conform to the purpose and glory of the Father. This includes control of denominational hermeneutics. The resulting false doctrine is used to separate the church's wheat from their chaff, by allowing only the Chosen the right to access Spirit revealed truth. These Chosen names were written in the Book of life, are the 'world' of John 3:16 and received the gift of the Holy Spirit as counselor and teacher.

The Father is a sovereign deity, who has the absolute right to exercise his purpose and glory, in accordance with his will.

PROLOGUE

Nearing completion of recording Spirit revelations, I continue to marvel at being honored by the Father's commission to record and share the truth. Considering the word's 'Find and Share,' I knew the Father was commissioning me for scribe duty to record Spirit revelations of His Word.

The last few years, I have pondered over how to share the results my Record. I understand that no one knows the mind of God but believe that much of the Father's mind is presented in His Word.

Since the Holy Spirit was sent to reveal biblical truths to the Father's Chosen, we could conclude that the bible was intended to provide a salvation plan for the Chosen. But why did the Father partake in the long suffering associated with a plan starting in the Garden of Eden, through centuries of disobedience, to the sacrifice of His Son, followed by additional centuries of disobedience to the Great White Throne Judgment. There are some 6000 years revealed in the 66 books of the bible. During some six years of fellowship with the Trinity and accepting total sovereignty, I would like to share a layman's thoughts regarding the bible:

1. The bible's goal was to provide a plan to fulfill the Father's desire for a family.
2. The bible was designed to shield truths from unchosen intellects subject to Satan's counsel, leaving access to biblical truth to Spirit led Chosen.

3. The bible is designed to strengthen the beliefs of the chosen and confuse the egos of the unchosen.
4. The size of the bible reflects a history covering the first souls in the Garden, to the last soul dying at the end of the coming tribulation period.

The total number of souls, including the souls Chosen for the Book of Life, is not provided by the Father. The U.S. Census Bureau's living world population estimate for 2015 was 7,256,490,010 souls. When thinking about the narrow gate and the few that enter therein, we have to look at the meaning of 'few.' We can think about the size of the universe plus the new Jerusalem and conclude that there is room for a big family. One percent of the 2015 census is 72,565 million living souls at the end of the year. It does not include occurring deaths. It all comes down to the sovereignty of the Father whose Will established the number in His Salvation Plan before the foundations of the world. I believe the number Chosen and unchosen will not be known until the Great White Throne Judgment, when the books of the dead and those in the Book of Life are opened. I believe the Father deliberately withheld these numbers, to confuse the theological elite during their application of ego controlled hermeneutics. For example, their exegesis of 'world' in John 3:16 means every soul. Yet we know that only the Chosen have an opportunity to be led by the Spirit on the salvation path. We can only conclude that all unchosen were destined to hell because Adam sinned. How can the love of God be applied to those He predestined to hell? It begs the question, 'what prompted the false exegesis?' Are we, like the early church selling indulgences, any different when we increase our coffers and membership by offering salvation to anyone who asks? What do you think would happen to the Church's coffers and membership, if they preached on the Chosen and the Book of Life? Have you ever heard a sermon being preached on the Father's Chosen and the Book of Life? Likewise, have your ever heard sermons preached on the effect of Chastisement and Work's Righteousness on your salvation? If not, your pastor is not preaching the full counsel of God nor is led by the Holy Spirit.

6. I believe the Father wanted to purge His Kingdom of Satan and his angels. Satan was sent to the Garden to chastise Adam. This

action restored full righteousness to the Father's Kingdom. The sin element had been removed.

7. I believe the Father wanted and deserved a family of righteous children for His purpose and glory. Righteousness can only be achieved through Spirit counseled works righteousness that glorifies the Father and leads to Spirit approval to access the cross.

8. I believe the Father provided a Bible that confused the egos of men, in understanding biblical truths, since they are Spiritually discerned. Only the Chosen have access to biblical truth.

Whose names are written in the Book of Life? Most, if not all, main line denominations, refrain from addressing this issue of 'WHO' from the pulpit or their bible classes. Most churches have no idea about the correct exegesis of John 3:16 and the doctrine of election. This Record was commissioned to share biblical truth understandings to answer such questions.

My Father's commission is to prepare an epistle to the Chosen as a primer for finding and teaching the Father's Chosen, by leading them to the Holy Spirit. The Spirit knows all of the Chosen named in the Father's Book of Life. He will examine the hearts of all Chosen He meets, inviting those who have a hunger and thirst for righteousness to enter the narrow gate that leads to the cross and salvation. The scope of this Record is the same as the Jesus' Great Commission focusing on reaching the Chosen, all over the world.

I expect many will call me a blasphemer for the truths in this record. I don't expect the church hierarchy to cut me any 'live and let live' slack, like they do for hundreds of others with differing denominational doctrines. I can understand their hesitancy in accepting a Chosen layman who says he learned his theology from the Holy Spirit. My response to the naysayers is simply that I am totally committed to Jesus and will stand on His Word of Truth until martyrdom or death.

What grieves me most is the truth I am sharing may cause angst to many. Like Jesus' disciples said of his teachings in the 6ᵗʰ Chapter of John, 'these are hard sayings!'

+ 6:64 "But there are some of you that believe not. For Jesus knew from the beginning who they were that believed not, and who should betray him." His followers included the Chosen and those 'that believed not,' the unchosen. He was with the Father, in 'the beginning,' when the Father recorded the names of His Chosen in the Book of Life. In fact, the soul of Jesus as True Man was also in the Book. Note: A soul in the soul pool is inanimate. Divinity is not inanimate, but the soul of Jesus as True Man in the soul pool is!

+ 6:65 "And he said, 'Therefore said I unto you, that no man can come unto me, except it was given unto him of my Father." The souls that the Father gave to His son were from among Chosen members recorded in the Book of Life. The Father's Salvation Plan uses the Spirit to draw only His Chosen through the narrow gate.

+ 6:66 "From that time many of his disciples went back and walked no more with him." Because of Jesus' hard sayings, the unchosen departed.

The number 666 has a sinister biblical reference to the Anti-Christ. Verse 6:66 suggests that when the hard truths from Spirit led exegesis of God's word is preached, the Father will use the great deceiver to separate the wheat from the chaff.

Christian history is replete with martyrs who gave their lives for truth, including many pastors burned at the stake. Martyrdom began with Jesus giving His life for the Father's Chosen. We are called to be living sacrifices to bear witness to God's Son.

The Churches, ignoring the Book of Life and Chosen issues, may have misled countless Chosen, by preaching and teaching false doctrine that may have denied access to the Spirit and the Narrow gate.

A few scriptures for you to keep in mind as you read this Record:

> Hebrews 4:12 "For the word of God is quick, and powerful, and sharper than a two edged sword, piercing even to the dividing asunder of soul and spirit, and of the joints and marrow, and is a discerner of the thoughts and intents of the heart." Since the 'word' is truth, false exegesis is a serious problem for the Chosen seeking access to the gate.

> II Timothy 2:15 "Study to show thyself approved unto God, a workman that needed not to be ashamed, RIGHTLY dividing the word of truth." Words to heed and embrace since salvation is a personal responsibility.

I was commissioned to find the truth under tutelage of the Holy Spirit. I fully realize I am culpable, if I blaspheme the Holy Spirit by non-truths recorded in this epistle. My spirit is committed to serving the Trinity, regardless of the personal cost inflicted on me, for what I believe is Spirit led revelations of truth.

My Record is offered, as my Spirit led truths, for independent comparison with denominational doctrines. They can accept or reject my Record as led by their spirits. Like Luther, I will stand on the truth I know. It is a random selection of gathered truths that at times will include other issues. It reflects a process, in which the revelations received focus on how they support John 3:16 by weaving a mosaic of truths in the Father's Salvation Plan. This of necessity, is required to link supporting truths. It also provides a plus of giving you a mosaic that adds clarity. There are two ways you can read my Record:

1. If you are a journalist applying a studied application of journalese to shoot the messenger and ignore the message, be my guest! It is highly unlikely you are among the Chosen for whom this epistle applies. I know you will have a field day! Please enjoy with my complements!
2. With an open heart and a desire for a spirit to Spirit revelation that provides access to the Narrow Gate.

My approach is based on:

+ Six years of fellowship with the Spirit gathering exegesis for this Record.
+ Not only was I was gathering exegesis to compare with church doctrine, but I was growing in an increasing awareness of the Trinity presence wherein the understanding of scripture, when reading and writing, was being monitored in real time.
+ The more I got into the exegesis I was recording, the more I could see the pattern of the Father's Salvation Plan revealed. I began to view a mosaic of tentacles which are the tenets of the Father's Salvation Plan based on John 3:16. There is a linking of these exegesis tentacles to resemble a spider web that focuses tying together all of the tenets in support of the source of truth found in John 3:16. If your doctrine on John 3:16 is wrong, your tenet doctrines are based on faulty exegesis.

MY APPROACH: When I noticed the linking of truths of the tentacles and links, I decided to include the exegesis links that supports the tentacle exegesis. I believe these supporting links will quicken your understanding of the relationships between the key doctrinal truths. I have found repetition to be a good learning tool, especially when used to tie scriptures together.

11/12/15: An afterthought from the Spirit. I have been thinking about sin, work's righteousness and the cross. We have been conditioned to accept false understanding of the roles these issues play in salvation. We accept salvation as a right earned by accepting an alter call that assures us that "Jesus Paid It All!" So sinning is no 'BIGGIE' for a God who just wants to hold our hand as we sin daily, because He has a Son who will be crucified to cover our indiscretions. This is the crowning jewel of prosperity theology. It is Satan's counsel to church leadership lacking a moral and chutzpah. Sadly, it is a malady that is widespread in Christian churches. I am concerned about the impact it has on the Father's Chosen. Please consider the following promise:

> II Chronicles 7:14 "If my people, which are called by my name, shall humble themselves, and pray, and seek my face, and return from their wicked ways; then I will hear from heaven, and will forgive their sin, and will heal their land." An Old Testament promise. The thought that just entered my mind was "The prayers of a righteous man availeth much.!" As I remember, a few decades back, there was a major outcry from Christians invoking this scripture for our nation. Realty set in and the status quo returned. Witnessing Jesus' return is the order of the day! It is not sin that prevents you from accessing the cross, it is your failure to glorify the Father. Glorifying the Father is only accomplished by work's righteousness that demonstrates a heart accepting His will. The cross provides a cleansing of a sin nature leading to the righteousness required to access the Father's Kingdom.

There is one observation you should keep in mind. Sovereign control of every action in God's creation demands conformance with the Father's purpose and glory. In effect, everyone and everything falls under the Father's Will. As an example, the Salvation Plan's uses of Satan counsel that results in the church's false application of hermeneutics to establish doctrine.

MY MOST EXCITING REVELATION

Sunday, November 1, 2015

The most worrisome issue that followed me throughout my walk with the Spirit was the abuse of hermeneutics in their application for exegesis and the importance of truth in the salvation process. I knew my record would cause a lot of angst in the Christian community. I expressed my concern to the Father last evening, asking if I was missing something in my discernment of Spirit revelations. The Spirit responded the next day. I watched two Christian TV sermons from pastors who I knew embraced much of prosperity theology. I couldn't shake the feeling, that there were likely a number of chosen ones in good standing, who were being subjected to false doctrine and not aware of their chosen status. I then proceeded to church to listen to a young pastor whom I respected for his preaching. There was evidence of his strong desire to serve Jesus. Now as I look back, I can recall other pastors with similar qualities who served Jesus while preaching false doctrines based on hermeneutics lacking Spirit-led exegesis.

It begs the questions: Is there more to the salvation process than just knowing the truth? And can there be salvation for those who preach false doctrine in the church?

In my record, I share revelations that show how the path to salvation involves two separate actions:

1. This is the first step that provides access to the cross. In the salvation process you will be subjected to works that the Father had

ordained for you to walk in. If your works reflect glory to the Father, they will be counted, as Abraham's were, as works righteousness. The Spirit considers your work's righteousness in His aye or nay decision to access the cross. THIS IS A RIGHTEOUSNESS TEST OF WORTHINESS TO ACCESSS THE CROSS.

2. The cross's cleansing action for sin is secured by paying the ransom needed to achieve righteousness. This righteousness guarantees retention of your name in the Book of Life. IT IS THE TESTED BLESSING OF JOHN 3:16

As I was sitting in my pew, the Spirit shared two Scriptures with my spirit.

The first was Matthew 21:28–31:

> "But what think ye? A certain man had two sons; and he came to the first, and said, go work today in my vineyard. He answered and said, I will not but afterward he repented, and went. And he came to the second, and said likewise. And he answered and said, I go, sir: and went not. Whether of them twain did the will of his father? They say unto him, the first."

My understanding of this passage was that two sons knew the works of the father. One son refused the works, but later accomplished the works. This pleased the father. The second son accepted the works bur did not accomplish them. Scriptures tell us that we are created in Christ Jesus for good works that the Father has prepared beforehand, and they tell us that we should walk in them. These are works of righteousness that bring glory to the Father.

The second Scripture the Spirit shared with me was found in James 1:22–25:

> "But be ye doers of the word, and not hearers only, deceiving your own selves. For if any hearer of the word, and not a doer, he is like unto beholding his natural face in a glass: For he hath beholdeth himself, and goeth his way, and straightway forgetteth what manner of man he was. But whoso looketh into the perfect law of liberty, and continueth therein, he

being not a forgetful hearer, but doer of the work, this man shall be blessed in his deed.'

These Scriptures rebuke the most damaging of the false doctrines found in many churches—the pre-tribulation rapture; once saved, always saved; and the lack of works in the salvation process, to name a few. It appears that many denominations ignore these passages out of fear of their effects on their greatest recruiting tool: false witnessing or offering free salvation to all who ask, without any conditions, while joyfully singing, "Jesus paid it all!"

There is only one salvation path for Abraham's covenant and Jesus's covenant of grace. Both involve a forward look to Jesus and the cross. And both require walks of work's righteousness as a chosen vessel counseled by the Spirit. The Spirit counsel for Abraham's chosen people came from the Father in heaven, while the Spirit counsel for the Christian was the indwelling Spirit. The scenario requires the use of the chosen vessel to perform works provided by the Father to test worthiness. If the works brought glory to the Father, they were imputed as work's righteousness for his account. Righteousness and work's righteousness are not the same! Work's righteousness is the Father's last screening program to weed out those unworthy to access the cross. Access to the cross provides righteousness to access the Father's kingdom and provides permanent residence in the Book of Life.

Why am I so excited? These revelations limit the influence of false doctrine on salvation. However, the Book of Life remains as a limitation to salvation based on the size of His desired family. Before my 2009 commission to get into the Word, I shared in the feelings of most Christians who believed that the Father was unfair in selecting the chosen for salvation. Understanding the total depravity of man and the right of sovereignty to insure all actions conform to His purpose and glory, I recognized and accepted the right of the potter to exercise His will over my clay, as He desired.

So what are the issues that shine a new light on our chosen status?

- Sin is the vehicle needed to establish the screening program.
- The Father's screening separates the wheat from the chaff by Satan's chastisement and Spirit's counsel to determine work's

righteousness that brings glory to the Father. If approved by the Spirit, access to the cross is granted.

- Jesus provides righteousness with the blood cleansing of sin.
- Work's righteousness brings glory to the Father providing access to the cross.
- Work's righteousness is imputed righteous credit to access the cross.
- Without work's righteousness, there is no cross access and no salvation.
- False doctrine is a screening tool used by the Father, to expose a chosen one to the counsel battle between Satan and the Holy Spirit, in a flesh vs. spirit battle for his or her soul.
- The battleground is the preordained works of the Father, and the enemy is the counsel chastisement of Satan. If your response to Satan brings glory to the Father, it is imputed to your work's righteousness account.
- The role of the Holy Spirit is widened to compensate for false doctrine. This is *huge* because it uses the churches, with both chosen and unchosen members, to provide an opportunity for the Spirit to draw the chosen through the narrow gate. Do you comprehend the significance of this revelation? This suggests that the work of the Holy Spirit is not limited by any particular religious organization. How about the scope of the Great Commission? Putting down any religious group is contrary to the Great Commission.

You will notice in my record that I voice increasing concern over the narrow gate becoming more constricted with increasing revelations. With this revelation, the narrow gate has widened and the angst I felt for my record's adverse effect on Christians has been markedly reduced.

While I don't have the foggiest idea of how many chosen there are, we can speculate that, a two million square miles by six-hundred-thousand-stories high New Jerusalem should, provide ample space for a large family. In addition, we would have the universe for a playground.

More Understanding

Added November 15, 2015: Sunday Church Service

I was thinking about the influence of false doctrine on the Father's elect when the Spirit quickened my spirit to go back and review this greatest revelation. When I finished, I recalled sharing a revelation of the heart that excited me.

The revelation shared was the role of the heart in being the final test, before access to the cross, is a Spirit examination of your heart's desire, displaying a hunger and thirst for righteousness accepting the Father's will and giving Him glory! We have a salvation where false teaching can be overcome by reaching out to the Holy Spirit. There is a Scripture that tells us that we shall know the chosen by their fruits. Looking on the positive side, I believe this Scripture can be applied to many in the church, who are blessed with peace and joy in the Lord but who do not recognize that they been chosen.

It's a good feeling to remove the roadblock of false doctrine and provide an understanding that the Father desires to confirm your name in the Book of Life with the Spirit; you will then be able to join the chosen and His servants to announce the return of Jesus.

INTRODUCTION

In recent months, I have felt a special sense of the Father's love for our whole family when seeing His presence manifested in the witness of those being chastised. We know that the Father will bless those whom He will bless, but He will also chastise those whom He loves. It is chastisement that molds the character and strength of witness, displaying a work's righteousness that brings glory to the Father. It identifies you as among the chosen who are the "world" of John 3:16. It is my prayer that you will follow Jesus's example of steadfastness in your faith walk to the cross. The gift of John 3:16 is given only to the Father's chosen people, who are created in Christ Jesus for good works.

The following is my understanding of chastisement as revealed to me by the Spirit. There is one very important given: you must have acceptance regarding any action, good or bad. All actions are in accordance with the Father's will, and their results are controlled by Jesus. Never lose sight of the fact that you house the Trinity.

Chastisement: An Important Truth to Understanding Salvation

For the past five years, I have been a scribe to the Spirit, recording revelations of biblical exegesis. In our Christian denominations, we can assume that all know of the Holy Spirit, but we can't assume all are being led by the Spirit. There can be only one Record of biblical truths and they can only be revealed by one Holy Spirit. We find ourselves in a serious conundrum involving Spirit Led and Intellect Led Doctrines.

The lack of doctrinal unity among Christian denominations can only be explained by the lack of Spirit led exegesis. "And ye shall know the truth and the truth shall set you free!" In my walk as a scribe to the Spirit, I am counseled by revelations received during exchanges between my spirit and the Holy Spirit. As we opened up is the exegesis of the scriptures together, several thoughts jumped into my mind: 1) I have a new bible! 2) No one knows the mind of God! and 3) Most church doctrine reflects intellect driven hermeneutics. Instead of focusing on the Truth that sets one free, denominations have elected to exclude Spirit Led exegesis in favor of an intellect controlled hermeneutics that attracts the sheep and ignores the Shepherd. Denominations compete with each other for a limited sheepfold. The power of the intellect has ignored the power of the Spirit in their search for acceptable doctrine.

My family has experienced serious chastisements which prompted me to seek the counsel of the Spirit. My study, to date, has led me to conclude that Satan's Weapon of Mass Confusion is hermeneutics. The design and application of hermeneutical standards are controlled by and, for the most part, internal denominational politics.

The hermeneutics standards are designed to intellectually achieve an exegesis process that favors a church - man and not a God - man theology. The key to destroying the church is through the Intellectual Elite. I suspect most doctrine come out of seminaries, where a number of the elite decide on an acceptable set of hermeneutical guidelines that favor prosperity theology, to gain consensus on the exegesis of a scripture. Considering the widespread doctrinal disunity among church denominations, Satan's success, since the garden, has been outstanding in replicating Adam's fall from grace. Let's go back and track the evolution of Adam's sin.

Before the foundation of the earth, the Father knew He needed a salvation plan for His children, who were the purpose for His creation. Since the December 2009 call, the Father has been revealing His Family Plan. In the beginning, during my first spirit to Spirit meeting with the Father, my spirit understood that any new family member would need to demonstrate a hunger and thirst for righteousness, while under the counsel of the Spirit and a heart filled with unconditional love. The Father's salvation plan began with the Father choosing a random selection of souls in His soul pool. The names of these souls, His Chosen, were entered into The Book of Life. The remaining souls in the pool were also named.

It didn't take the Father long to exercise His will and engage Satan as His head of chastisement. It was an arrangement like the one with Job, except death was not excluded for the Chosen. However, Jesus controlled all chastisement against a chosen. In both cases, the enforcer of the Father's will is Jesus. We all agree the Father is omniscient, so we can agree the entire Will of the Father shall be accomplished from the soul pool to the Great White Throne Judgment. Satan and a third of his angels were kicked out of the Kingdom of Heaven to chastise Adam, by convincing his intellect to sin leading to the spirit death of all of his descendants. This was Satan's first chastisement service call for the Father. This chastisement led to the first sin and loss of eternal life. It is at this point that everyone was consigned to hell and the Salvation Plan was set in motion.

The following thoughts are designed to show how chastisement can be the greatest deterrent to a successful salvation walk. The Father's giving Satan access to His Chosen is designed to refine the metal of His future children. It is difficult to put a number on the Chosen who will be removed from the Book of Life. That number will be determined by the Spirit's enforcing the father's Salvation Plan's screening plan.

Yes, church, James was right, salvation without works is dead! Here is the Father's screening plan for salvation:

+ First Screen: Separation of the unchosen and the chosen randomly Selected for the Book of Life.
+ Second Screen: Satan talks Adam into sinning, thereby consigning all of his descendants to hell. The unchosen are those screened out while in the pool. The Chosen were given a future John 3:16 escape option.

+ Third Screen: The Chosen were offered access through the narrow gate. Some Chosen elect to stay in the world and remain consigned to Satan. Their names were removed from the Book of Life.
+ Fourth Screen: Jesus teaches the Word. Those lacking a hunger and thirst for righteousness, were consigned to Satan and their names were removed from Book of Life. The rest were Spirit baptized and began their walk of faith, under the counsel of the Spirit.
+ Fifth Screen: Chosen will be evaluated, by the Spirit, on work's righteousness during chastisement performances. Access to the cross is judged by the glory the Father receives. Those found worthy accessed the cross and salvation. The remaining Chosen were consigned to Satan and their names were removed from the Book of Life.

My RECORD, when published, will go into depth on major errors in doctrine. If we can agree that biblical truth is revealed solely by the Spirit, then it follows that we can only discern truth as a Spirit led Christian. Looking back, I can't remember many pastors or bible class teachers that displayed a discernible hunger and thirst for righteousness. Early in the first year of my Father's commission to ferret out biblical truth and building a sizable reference library, I activated my scribe services to the Holy Spirit. Since then, the revelation of error in church doctrine appears pandemic.

I have watched a son singing hallelujah as he died of cancer, a wife being ministered by the Trinity through the valley of dementia and finally taken home in her sleep. Satan continues to chastise members of our family as the Trinity continues to use Satan's actions to strengthen our faith.

BEGINNING THOUGHTS

In early December 2009, the Father placed a call on my life saying I needed to get into the Word because I couldn't preach the TRUTH if I did not know the TRUTH - this was about a week after He provided a replacement for my 35 year nursing home ministry. Seeking source material for my search, I was introduced to Cross TV's DVD series on "The Sovereignty of God" and "A Workman Approved of God." These two series blessed me with the excitement of finding a living Word and a growing closeness to the Trinity, that fueled an increasing "hunger and thirst for righteousness" and desire to be an active servant of the Holy spirit.

After two years of getting to know the Trinity and their Word and reflecting over my best approach to share God's truths as a layman, I decided on an approach which recently I sensed the Holy Spirit desired. It is based on a basic premise of understanding "who" is and not "what" is biblical TRUTH. Jesus said "I am the way, the TRUTH, and the life and no one comes to the Father but by me. We must keep in mind that each member of the trinity enjoys majesty coequal. Jesus said He and the Father are "one." He told His disciples that the Father would send the Holy Spirit who would lead His elect into all TRUTH. The concept, of a Trinity with "one in three" and "three in one," is not well understood and will be addressed in detail later. Suffice it to say that scriptures teaches those led by the Spirit of God are children of God and have the Trinity residing within them. We know that there are two thrones in heaven occupied by the Father and His Son. When Jesus was glorified and assumed His throne at the right hand of the Father, the Holy Spirit was sent to select and draw the ELECT of the Father and lead (teach) them into all TRUTH. John 4:24 - "God is SPIRIT and those who worship Him must worship in SPIRIT and TRUTH." It is the Spirit that stands as the door to GRACE and only the elect/chosen can enter therein.

When I think about the trinity and how it functions, I am reminded of Jesus and His miracles and His acknowledging, that He sees the Father performing His will (miracles) when He prays. In the role of "true man," He was divorced from His glory as the Son and provides us an example of praying in the will of the Father. We petition the Father, but not with direct access. We access the Father by invoking the name of Jesus as we pray through the SPIRIT. Romans 8:14 "For as many as are led by the Spirit of God, they are the sons of God." It is the Holy Spirit that is the key to our benefits as a child of God. When one thinks about the Trinity within us on an individual basis, the Father and Son on their thrones and the Spirit within us as our personal intercessor providing access to the Father through Jesus, we can only come to the conclusion that we serve an awesome God. The more I study the Word and understand the gulf between my sin and my Father's righteousness, I find I have no merit basis on which to qualify for God's grace. This is the reason that I am so excited!

There is no way you can please and serve God, without accepting the servitude required to be a vessel of the Spirit.

There is no way you can understand and accept the sovereignty of god, without understanding and embracing the truth of scripture as revealed by the Spirit.

There is no way you can discern the truth of biblical teachings without being guided by the Spirit.

The rational conclusion is that the key to salvation and being included in the Book of Life is the Holy Spirit. If we accept the scripture of Romans 8:14, "For as many are led by the Spirit of God, these are the sons of God," and, as I believe, chosen by God before the beginning of time. Since GRACE dictates you have no say in your salvation, we can conclude that there is a GRACE GATE that cherry picks the ELECT from the

"MANY." The Father's sovereign election was introduced prior to Adam being introduced to the Garden of Eden! I know that scripture states "many are called, but few are chosen" which lends itself to the environment of alter calls in churches and evangelist alter calls. These "come to Jesus" invitations, which generate donations, do not include the limitation of Romans 8:1 above that requires being led by the Spirit. In addition, they ignore "being led into the TRUTH by the SPIRIT" and being "born again in the SPIRIT" before the faith walk to Jesus.

The election of the Chosen is not readily accepted by the vast majority of Christians based on their feeling that it wouldn't be fair. "How could a loving God send people to hell." I would invite you to consider the garden and Adam's sin which purchased a one-way ticket to hell for all of his descendants and how about the flood? Who are we to condemn Adam for sinning against God when all he did was eat an apple as compared to the sin we commit daily. Scripture is clear, "All have sinned and fall short of the glory of God." All of us deserve to go to hell! To question God's decision to elect a family to share eternity with the Trinity, is to question His sovereignty. I personally believe anyone denying the Father's right of election is denying His Sovereignty. You can't study Sovereignty without addressing Election. I believe that grasping GOD'S SOVEREIGNTY is the linchpin to understanding the TRINITY, the TRUTH and the SALVATION FAITH WALK TO GLORY! In my humble opinion, these issues are the major contributors to the cornerstone of our faith.

In addition, I would like to share my precursory understanding of other issues, like those shared above. These understandings were developed during a two-year search of available biblical exegesis. These two years have been the most exciting of my life as God's Word came alive with power, when sharing thoughts with members of the trinity which was very gratifying and a real blessing. During this time, it was a special blessing to take a Finnish sauna several times a week with my new Trinity friends. As I typed the word "friends," it struck me how privileged I was to have been honored with a call to serve the living Trinity. It also sparked a memory of driving to the nursing home in the mid-1980s following an argument with my wife. I asked the Lord how He could use me after what happened.

In one of the rare times wherein the Spirit addressed a direct personal question by speaking to my spirit: "I use you because you make yourself available. "When I built my home, I installed a sauna and it became a fellowship retreat several times each week. I would share thoughts and questions with the Spirit and He would quicken my spirit recall scriptures I had memorized, including a large number learned but forgot during a bible study course I took almost 40 years ago. One of my first quandaries was trying to figure out which member of the Trinity was talking to me. I was certain the Father was the lead during my two ministry calls, one in the fall of 1974 for my first commission leading to a 35 year nursing home ministry, and in December 2009, my second commission to prepare for a new ministry. The Father's second call was pretty direct: "Get into the Word, because you cannot preach the TRUTH if you don't know the TRUTH. Since the Spirit is the teacher member of the Trinity, I assumed He was my counselor following the second call. During the period between the first and second calls, I never sensed a real presence of the Spirit, although I had a strong desire to serve my Father. While the Spirit was in me during this period, I was teaching and preaching from what I was exposed to in bible studies, Sunday school and from the Pulpit. The Father opened my eyes to the error of my Christian training, by providing a replacement for my nursing home ministry and telling me I needed to get into the Word if I wanted to preach the TRUTH.

2/12/2012 Sauna Time: I recently ran across a scripture that talked about having one's name erased from the Book of Life. It raised the predestination question of "once saved - always saved and the doctrine of election, the Book of Life and how can an elect be removed from the Book. My thoughts considered King David and the magnitude of his sin, his excited dancing around the Arc and his repentance, followed by Paul and his discourse on the sin in his body and the confidence in his salvation and believing there is no condemnation for those who are in Christ Jesus. My thoughts then turned to the stalwarts of God's servants; Abraham, Job, John the Baptist and the apostles. Since all have sinned and fall short of the glory of God, it would appear that it is not the sin of the flesh but grieving of the Spirit that removes one's name from the Book. It also appears that the Spirits role as the gate keeper who draws/allows only the elect to enter, does not guarantee a clear path to salvation in Jesus. The Book question came to my mind the next morning and I thought about the path leading from the Grace Gate. Passing through the Gate is not a born again experience wherein the Spirit takes up residence with your spirit. The Spirit must lead an elect into the truth followed by examining his heart, to determine if worthy enough to be born of the Spirit (Born Again). Now the elect is equipped with the Spirit, a measure of faith and the full armor of God for the walk to the cross.

We have been taught that by Grace alone are we saved and that election is a sovereign work of God. But can the Doctrine of Election be abused? Is election and "once saved, always saved" synonymous? Are we home free after the born again experience or can we stumble in our faith walk and be erased from the Book? Is there much more to James admonition to demonstrate our faith by works, than has been and is accepted by the church. Read Rev 3-5 about the church in Sardis' "works" and the few who had not soiled their garments; "and they will walk with me in white: for they are worthy." I am reminded about Jesus telling his Father that he had not lost any of those He gave him except to son of perdition. Does the blood of John 3:16 cover those who have soiled their garments whether or not they are of the elect?

BILICALTIME LINES

MONDAY, SEPTEMBER14, 2015. The Spirit quickened my spirit to include a time line of key Biblical truths, that are inherent in the Fathers Grand Plan for the salvation of His Chosen. It begins before time with the creation of the Soul Pool.

BEFORE FOUNDATIONS OF THE WORLD

SOUL POOL: A Pool containing all of the souls needed to cover the period, from Adam to the last person to die at the end of the coming tribulation period, ushering in the Second Coming of Jesus. These souls were inanimate, named and numbered sequentially as needed for conception. The pool also included Jesus, to qualify Him as True Man and the second Adam. Both Adam, before his sinning and Jesus possessed the seed of the Father at conception, both being without sin.

BOOK OF LIFE: When the Father completed the soul pool, He randomly selected souls from across the entire spectrum of the pool and wrote their names in the Book of Life. They were called the Elect or the Chosen. This Book will be opened at the Great White Throne Judgment. It separates the Chosen from the unchosen. Only the Chosen will get an opportunity to demonstrate their worthiness to remain in the Book for it's opening on judgment day. The souls of the unchosen will face two deaths, flesh and spirit, because of Adam's sin.

THE TWO DEATHS: The FIRST DEATH is the death of the flesh for everyone. This is the physical death. The SECOND DEATH is a spirit death that is decided at the Great White Throne Judgment, when the books of the dead and the Book of Life are opened. It is an eternal judgment of souls. The souls of the unchosen will be judged according to their recorded works. They will be cast into the Lake of Fire. The Chosen souls, in the Book of Life, were judged righteous when granted access to the cross. Their names remained in the Book of Life. The names of the Chosen, denied access to the cross based on lack of work's righteousness, were erased from the Book of Life and cast into the Lake of Fire.

THE FATHER'S GRAND PLAN: The plan was conceived and executed before creation. Remember the Father's Kingdom is without time considerations. He knew every action in His plan would conform to His will, in accordance with His purpose and Glory. The plan was accomplished before time but executed through real time, starting with creation.

CREATION TO NOAH

THE GARDEN OF EDEN: During the creation of the world, the Father set aside a special paradise for His children, called the Garden of Eden. Here the Father created Adam and Eve. In the Garden were the Tree of Life and the Tree of Knowledge of Good and Evil. The Garden provided for all of their needs and desires, except their self-controlled ego, controlled by free will. This was the destination of Satan and his angels when the Father kicked him out of heaven.

CONCEPTION: The soul is received from the soul pool at conception. This soul has the breath of life and free will from the Father. This soul will have a spirit of the flesh and a spirit of Life. They also received the Spirit of Life which provided a holiness that lasted until Adam sinned.

At this point the Spirit of Life was withdrawn. So we can say Jesus was like Adam until Adam sinned. It then follows that Jesus was not of the seed of Adam thereby not losing the Spirit of Life. This allowed Jesus to maintain Spirit communications with the Trinity. When we are baptized in the Holy Spirit, we too, can communicate with the Trinity because we, like Jesus, are True Man without Divinity.

SATAN AND HIS ANGELS KICKED OUT OF HEAVEN: Subject to the sovereignty and Will of the Father, Satan and his angels were kicked out of heaven at the beginning of time. This action restored righteousness to the Kingdom of God, which was needed to receive His Chosen, cleansed by the blood of the Son. Satan was sent to the Garden, where his actions were limited by the Father's Will and enforced by Jesus.

SIN: Sin caters to the mind which caters to the flesh and ego. The Father sent Satan to test Adam. Satan counseled Adam's ego to be like God. Adam sinned leaving a legacy of death for his descendants, including the spirit of the flesh and the spirit of life. Adam was the target of Satan's Weapon of Mass Deception.

CHASTISEMENT: Satan is the Father's primary provider of chastisement services. Within the scope of His Sovereignty, the Father's Will controls everyone and everything, including Satan. The Father uses Satan as a chastiser of the Chosen, within limits set by the Father and controlled by Jesus. Chastisement by Satan is the Father's means used to test the worthiness of His Chosen.

NOTE: KEEP IN MIND THAT ALL OF SATAN'S ACTIONS ARE APPROVED BY THE FATHER AND CONTROLLED BY JESUS. SATAN'S SURREGATES CONTINUED HIS POLICY OF MASS DECEPTION WHILE HE WAS CONFINED TO THE BOTTOMLESS PIT FOR 1000 YEARS. HE WILL BE RELEASED FOR THE COMING TRIBULATION PERIOD, PRECEEDING THE GREAT AND TERRIBLE DAY OF THE LORD.

We know that the wickedness of man, during the period from Adam to Noah, wroth the anger of God into executing judgment to destroy all mankind with a flood, except for Noah and his family. A major achievement of Satan's counsel was the building of the Tower of Babel. The Tower's building and destruction were in accordance with the Father's

17

will. Both Adam's sin and the Tower of Babel resulted from ego trips counseled by Satan. You can call it Satan's Weapon of Mass Deception. Thankfully, the Father's Will for Noah and his family, was an ark to survive the flood. While this was good, the sin of Adam continued as was required to continue the seed of Adam. Adam's sin, the Tower of Babel, the Flood, Noah carrying the seed of Adam, all fall under the Will of the Father. Under His sovereignty, the Father's Will exercises absolute control over every action in His salvation plan. Being omniscient, He knows everything that has and will happen.

NOAH TO CHRIST

This period is marked by a roller coaster ride under the sovereignty of the Father. While there were many of the Father's Chosen serving Him, Satan was having successes in separating God's Chosen from the Book of Life. Even though the Father provided Moses, the ten commandments, tabernacles, kings, judges, priests, and prophets, man's sin nature remained subject to Satan's counsel. The Father was making it clear that He is in complete control of everyone's destiny.

We can say that the prophecy of the coming messiah was set in motion with the Lord asking for the sacrifice of Abraham's son. It is an example reminiscent of Job. Both were subject to Satan's optimum chastisement permitted by the Father's Will. Both were submissive in total obedience to the Father. We can gain an understanding of the role of obedience plays when we recognize it as the key to giving glory to the Father. The stronger your obedience, the greater the glory to the Father. Obedience to the counsel of the Spirit, during Satanic chastisement, glorifies the Father. Chastisement is an opportunity to demonstrate work's righteousness, as a measure of your worthiness to access the cross and salvation. In this Record, you will find that the Father chastises those whom He loves and warns that IF YOU ARE NOT PARTALKERS OF HIS CHASTISEMENTS, THEN YOU ARE NOT HIS SONS, BUT BASTARDS!

The Father selects Abraham to lead his people into a land of their own. The Father tests Abraham on his total commitment, by asking for the sacrifice of his son. Acknowledging Abraham's commitment, the Father establishes a covenant with Abraham and his seed, calling them His chosen people. The Father worked through the 10 Commandments, kings, judges, priests and prophets, going beyond the pale with these various opportunities, to establish a relationship with His children. The Father knew that man's will and Satan's chastisement would result in turbulent times. Through it all, the Father's chosen have suffered, earned work's righteous points and waited on Jesus to provide the victory on the cross. They are now in paradise awaiting the Great White Throne Judgment. They were prejudged with the victory achieved on the cross, by the shed blood of Jesus. Their names are in the Book of Life.

ADVENT OF JESUS TO TODAY JESUS IS GOD, PERIOD! JESUS WAS TRUE MAN, PERIOD!

BIRTH OF JESUS: Jesus' early life began with a king trying to kill him at birth, exile to Egypt until the king died, returned home after the king died and served his father in the carpenter trade, while growing in the scriptures. Stayed home until John's baptism when the Father announced from heaven that He was well pleased with His son. After the baptism, Jesus was led by the Spirit into the wilderness to be tempted by the Satan.

THE TEMPTATION: After being led into the wilderness, Jesus fasted for forty days and forty nights, followed by Satan's temptation offers to follow him and Jesus' rebuke of his offers. Angels came to minister to Jesus after which he began his service ministry, under the counsel of the Trinity. We, as Chosen, also receive Trinity counsel through the Spirit.

MINISTRY OF JESUS: It was a joint ministry of serving the Trinity and man. The Father chastised His son, to a greater degree than any man, during his ministry. Like man, Jesus was chastised by Satan under the will of the Father, enforced by the DIVINE JESUS OF THE TRINITY. There is one statement the Father made about the crucifixion that clearly establishes the magnitude of His love. "It pleased the Father to sacrifice

His son." The Father sacrificed His son to pay the ransom for our sins. In His eyes, we are special.

The advent of Jesus introduced an era wherein the Father sent His Son as True Man and personal servant demonstrating obedience to his Father, by never compromising truth during his ministry as a servant to the Father and man. The passion of Jesus was inflicted by man and especially the church, who put him on the cross. Have you ever considered the fact that Jesus was the first martyr, dying on our behalf of his followers, followed by many martyrs for Jesus before the first rapture. Needless to say, Jesus was honored by their sacrifices, because only the martyrs were raptured to serve Him during the millennium. Except for John, all of Jesus' disciples were martyrs. These Martyrs gave their lives to start the church. Martyrdom since Christ, has sustained the call to the Chosen in Romans 12:1 "I beseech you therefore, brethren, that you present your bodies a living sacrifice, holy, acceptable to God, which is your reasonable service." Martyrdom of the Chosen has continued from Christ through to today. Many churches shy away of any mention of martyrdom, by focusing on prosperity theology and pre-tribulation rapture. The church is delinquent in preparing Christians for the coming tribulation. THEY DON'T UNDERSTAND, THAT TO BE RAPTURED, YOUR NAME HAS TO BE IN THE JUDGMENT BOOK OF LIFE. TO BE IN THE BOOK, YOU HAVE TO HAVE YOUR SINS CLEANSED ON THE CROSS. TO GET TO THE CROSS, YOU HAVE TO DIE!! I am not suggesting that you have to be a martyr to get to heaven, but what I am saying that your death is controlled by the Father's will, which may lead to martyrdom. The chastisement, that the Father allows Satan to impose, may include Martyrdom. As we go into the coming tribulation, we will experience an ever increasing number of Christian martyrs. If martyrdom is required before the rapture, it follows that the last of the chosen will be martyred before the rapture, on the Great and Terrible Day of the Lord.

I am not here to judge anyone's Chosen status. My Record is to expose biblical truth to quicken the spirits of the Chosen who seek God's Kingdom. I am suggesting that reading this record may provide exposure to the Spirit. If you are one of the Chosen, He will examine your spirit for a desire to seek God's Kingdom. If the desire exists, He will grant access to the narrow gate and begin screening actions to determine worthiness, to access the cross of salvation.

IT'S ALL FOR THE GLORY
OF THE FATHER

THURSDAY, MAY 14, 2015: ULTIMATE REVELATION.

I stopped for a moment, while working on my introduction, when the Spirit quickened my spirit that the Father's salvation plan was designed to bring Him glory. This revelation answered the one question resident in my mind that has lingered since the Father's first visit in 1974 when He called me into ministry by sharing Matthew 6:33 'Seek ye first the kingdom of God ...' and told me I would never worry about my salvation. I just did not understand the Father's great love for David who committed some heinous sins. Now this revelation of glory puts into perspective the Father's will which is exercised to suit His PURPOSE AND BRING HIM GLORY. There is no question that David brought much glory to the Father. It begs the question, what about sin? What I have learned about the Father can give us insight into the Fathers glory:

1. His sovereignty is absolute which means His will allows Him to subject anything or everything to His purpose and glory.
2. His omniscience is absolute. He has complete knowledge of His creation from the garden to the Great White Throne Judgment. Everyone's life is and open book, including our thoughts.
3. He is omnipotent! The is no limit to His power. He uses His power to impact our personal environment from birth to your death. This power is used by Jesus to administer the Father's purpose for your life.

4. He is the potter and we are the clay. Clay does not question the perfect will of sovereignty.

5. The souls were made by the Father to suit His purpose and glory.

6. The Father exercised His sovereignty by selecting a random sample of souls and recorded their names in the Book of Life. This sovereignty issue bothered me and I did not accept it until the Father told me to seek biblical truth. He opened up the Word through the Spirit and thus began my walk as a scribe to the Holy Spirit. I am in the greatest adventure of my life as I continue preparations for serving Jesus in an end times ministry.

7. The souls, whose names are written in the Book of Life, are the prize of the salvation process that began with Adam's sin in the garden. This was the Father's first use of Satan in a screening process to separate the wheat from the chaff. This battle is only for the souls of his chosen, during a salvation walk of faith to the cross. Only the chosen are offered the Grace gift of John 3:16. Those Chosen, who heed the counsel of the Spirit and demonstrate work's righteousness that glorifies the Father, will be provided access to the cross and receive salvation.

The prices you pay during encounters with Satan, while following Spirit counsel as a vessel seeking to bring glory to the Father, will pale into insignificance compared to the treasures you will be laying up in heaven. Such an inheritance bespeaks of your 'your hunger and thirst for righteousness,' during your faith walk of work's righteousness that brought GLORY to the Father.

8. All souls were inanimate but distinguished by whether or not their names were written in the Book of Life.

9. All souls become animate during conception with a free will to control mind and soul.

10. It is God's Sovereignty that cast Satan into the garden to test Adam's will to glorify the Father.

11. Satan counseled Adam during his decision to sin. This sin condemned all of his descendants to hell, including both chosen and unchosen.

THIS SETS THE STAGE FOR THE FATHER'S SALVATION PROGRAM, DESIGNED TO RETRIEVE WORTHY CHOSEN FROM THE SPIRIT DEATH OF SATAN'S LEGACY.

Before describing the salvation's 'glory' program, we need to be reminded that:

1. Sovereignty means absolute and unquestionable power to will accomplishment of His purpose and glory.

2. We have a legacy of clay that started with birth rights of the flesh and the spirit. Without the breath of physical and spiritual life from the Father, Adam would not have existed and there would be no human race. Adam gave up his birth right to his Spirit of Life from the Father when he sinned. Everyone inherited a birth right of both physical and spiritual deaths from Adam whose sin cut us off from the Father's Spirit Life. It is John 3:16 that provides a stay of execution for the chosen. That stay lasts until chosen access to the cross is granted. The chosen granted access will have the ransom for their spirit to Satan paid and maintain their names in the Book of Life. The chosen that were not granted access will lose their spirit to Satan and their names will be removed from the Book of life.

3. Under His sovereignty, the Father exercises absolute control over Satan and his surrogates. Jesus enforces the Father's Will regarding the degree of chastisement that can be administered to the Chosen.

4. The salvation plan is designed to screen Chosen candidates to insure they demonstrate a worthiness to access the cross for cleansing of their sin.

5. The Spirit has the lead Trinity role of the screening process. It includes a narrow gate where the chosen are invited to enter but some refuse, a Counselor teaching of the Word which some will not embrace, baptism of the Spirit with some denied based on zeal of the heart and the faith walk to the cross.

6. The GLORY test examines the Chosen's performance during a Spirit counseled walk of faith to the cross. Here we invoke Ephesians 2:10 "FOR WE ARE CREATED IN CHRIST JESUS

FOR GOOD WORKS, WHICH GOD HAD PREPARED BEFOREHAND THAT WE SHOULD WALK IN THEM. These good works are individual work's righteousness programs prepared by the Father before the foundation of creation. So we have a scenario, in which God sets up the work environment, allows Satan to chastise/harass the Chosen, while Jesus limits how far Satan can go. It is the Chosen's performance during the work's programs, subjected to Satanic chastisement, that will be judged by the Spirit as to whether or not they bring GLORY to the Father. If the Father is pleased, the Spirit will grant access to the cross.

We are aware that the Word has much to say about sin:

+ All have sinned and fall short of the glory of God.
+ There is none righteous, no not one, only the Father in heaven.
+ There is only one unpardonable sin: Blasphemy against the Holy Spirit.
+ Paul calling himself the greatest sinner of all.
+ Etc.

This whole exercise from the soul pool was set up before creation. In His omniscience, the Father established every aspect of the plan in the beginning. But what role does sin play? We need to examine God's purpose described in His Salvation Plan. It was based on:

+ Man's free will.
+ Satan's desire as a Deceiver to chastise any of God's children.
+ Adam's accepting Satan's counsel to sin condemning all of his descendants to hell.
+ The Father setting up screening stations to separate the wheat from the chaff.
+ The Father's John 3:16 offer to provide Spirit counsel along the path to the cross.
+ The Father's allowing His Son to pay our ransom on the cross.
+ Jesus, as controller of Satan's chastisement actions against the Chosen.

+ We need to use the counsel of the Holy Spirit and discernment of His revelations to develop a sense of the Father's underlying truth.

A LAYMAN'S IMPRESSION OF THE FATHER'S SOVEREIGNTY AND GLORY TUESDAY, MAY 19, 2015:

During the day, I was thinking about what I have learned in five plus years as a scribe walking with the Spirit as He shared scriptural revelations. Since Tuesday is one of my sauna nights, the preceding thoughts came back to my mind in the sauna and my spirit sensed that the Spirit wanted me to share how my biblical understandings evolved as Spirit revelations filled my soul. I often thought about the honor the Father has bestowed upon me. I would like to give you the background of a layman that started with little concern over hell.

To begin, I was a farm boy who took a Confirmation class that left lingering impressions that would later reveal some Christian practices that I strongly rejected.

1. Pleading the blood of Jesus for anything but the soul was atrocious.
2. The exegesis of John 3:16's 'world' opening the flood gates of hell with a cheap grace salvation for all who ask. This was Satan's greatest accomplishment which opened up prosperity theology to a church wanting a free ride to seek blessings and not service.
3. The leaders in most churches have lost their moral compass and manhood when taking a stand on social issues. I can remember in the 1950's when Russian leaders called Christianity the opiate of the people. We have hundreds of denominations with hundreds of personalized doctrines. Do you remember Pontius Pilate asking the question of Jesus 'What is truth?' when Jesus said (John 18:37) "To this end I was born, and for this cause came I into the world, that I should bear witness unto the truth. Every one that is of the TRUTH heareth my voice." The disunity of TRUTH in church doctrines begs the question "Which denomination has

the TRUTH?" or "Which one hears the voice of truth through Spiritual revelation? Who has the truth that sets man free?

4. Prior to meeting Joan, my feelings toward Christianity included:

+ I was young and was not worried about hell.
+ I did not feel a love and service relationship with God.
+ I recognized God as a supreme being ruling the universe.
+ I viewed the church as a social club used to gain respectability.
+ The church lacked moral courage to stand for biblical truth.
+ The church witness focused more on Jesus' love at the expense of truth.

RIGHTEOUSNESS

7/22/2014 SAUNA COMMUNION
TIME WITH THE TRINITY

As I entered the sauna, I was thinking about righteousness, work's righteousness and faith regarding their roles in the salvation process. Most, if not all Church doctrine, reflects error in exegesis regarding their link with salvation in Christ. Here are my Spirit led thoughts:

1. In 1974, the Father gave me Matthew 6:33 and told me to seek first His kingdom and His righteousness. Kingdom and Righteousness were bonded together. The present Kingdom includes Paradise and Heaven. The Garden was included until the fall of Adam. The only place you will find righteousness is in the Father's Kingdom. The door to righteousness is the cross and the key to the door is controlled by the Spirit. He is the counselor, teacher and the examiner who decides whether your heart is worthy to access the cross. I want to make it perfectly clear that unrighteous man can't perform righteous works since all righteousness rests with the kingdom of the Trinity. As a chosen, you are only a vessel subject to Spirit counsel. The Spirit judges you on acceptance of Spirit led counsel, during performance of Father ordained work's righteousness projects, based on who receives the glory, you or the Father. Remember, you must be Spirit led to be a child of God. The Spirit examines your heart, to see if the degree of your

acceptance of Spirit counsel reflects a hunger and thirst after righteousness that glorifies the Father.

2. Jesus said there are none righteous, no not one, only the Father in heaven is righteous! Jesus, as true man, did not consider himself righteous! During my tenure as a lay person walking with the Spirit, I marveled at the manipulation of scriptures to provide crass doctrines, that satisfy the intellectual goals of denominations and insure doctrinal controls over seminaries and bible classes. They like to say Jesus was True God and True Man. I AGREE!! As true God, He had to be Divine and Righteous to be part of the unity of the Trinity. Jesus did not consider himself righteous as True Man when he tells us only the Father is righteous. To be True Man, it takes some fancy hermeneutics to justify Jesus as a True Man that is Divine. I deal with this Divinity issue in depth. This is one of the most egregious application of faulty exegesis that I've found in significant denominational doctrines.

3. Abraham's service was counted as righteousness with his salvation linked to our Savior. He, like other old testament chosen servants, would have to go through the same Spirit scrutiny as new testament chosen. ALL CHOSEN MUST ACCESS RIGHTEOUSNESS

THROUGH THE CROSS. There were many servants in the old testament that were identified as "chosen" servants of God. Like Abraham, their works would be counted as work's righteousness, if performed under Spirit counsel standards of righteousness.

NOTE: At this point, I want to establish clarity. The scriptures clearly teach "Many are called and few are chosen and a narrow gate that few enter therein." Since only the chosen of the Father have access to the Spirit under the Father's grace gift, this scripture may suggest only a few of the chosen will complete the faith walk to the cross and salvation. If we assume "the called" applies to the entire soul pool before creation, it would support the John 3:16 position of "world" as all souls from the beginning. My Spirit led examination of the John 3:16 exegesis clearly debunks an all-inclusive exegesis derived from faulty hermeneutics. Why did Jesus tell His Father that he did not pray for the world but only those He had given him (the Father's chosen)?

There is no such thing as cheap grace! The Grace gift of John 3:16 was access to Spirit counsel and teaching awarded solely to the Father's Chosen! James was right about salvation without works being dead! If the works of a Chosen fails a Spirits righteousness test, access to the Cross will be denied. The Chosen granted Spiritual baptism are offered Spirit counsel during their faith walk to the Cross. The faith walk does not guarantee access to the Cross and salvation. Salvation is limited to the Chosen, whose response to Spirit counsel during the walk of faith to the Cross gave glory to the Father. If you do not hunger and thirst after righteousness, you will not survive the rigors and demands of Spirit counsel. Important scriptural truths to keep in mind during the faith walk to the Cross:

+ All of the Father's actions support His PURPOSE and GLORY!
+ You must seek first His Kingdom and Righteousness.
+ If you love self, more than Jesus, you are not worthy of Him.
+ There is no righteousness in man. Including Jesus as True Man!
+ Only the Grace of John 3:16 opens the path to righteousness.
+ The Father is the potter and we are the clay.
+ The Father's sovereignty is absolute.
+ The Chosen were intended to be vessels of the Spirit for works righteousness.

Baptism of the Holy Spirit does not guarantee salvation. It only offers Spirit counseling and teaching during a faith walk to the cross. Scripture states that those led by the Spirit will be known as children of God. Don't let your free will deny the counsel of the Spirit. Such action would qualify as blasphemy of the Holy Spirit, the unpardonable sin.

The failure of the church, to get on board with James and actively promote Spirit led works righteousness, through a chosen vessel as the key to the cross' cleansing action, has caused an inestimable damage on "narrow gate" access. Understanding the role of work's righteousness in the salvation path to the cross, is one of the most significant Spiritual revelations I have received. The vast majority of churches have clothed themselves with dispensational theology, which embraces liberal hermeneutics leading to intellectual exegesis and excludes the Spirit. The effect is for lay persons to be shielded from access to the Father's gift of the counsel and teaching of the Spirit. I will be addressing this issue in my comments on "Satan's weapon of choice to divide the church."

4. Matthew 6:33 "Seek ye first the Kingdom of God, and His RIGHTEOUSNESS ..." Notice the Word "Righteousness!" No chosen of the Father will reach His Kingdom without being righteous. Access to righteousness is the cross.

5. All chosen, old and new testament, saints will face a Spirit examination of their hearts to see if their works reflected kingdom glory to the Trinity. The Trinity reflects the Will of the Father, so when we reference the Trinity, we include each member with the Father as titular head. It is the Father who receives the glory, on behalf of the Trinity, for all work's righteousness. The Trinity will not accept the works of a lukewarm chosen. The Trinity calls us to be a living sacrifice to reflect a commitment that brings Them glory. The history of the church is replete with martyrs who gave their lives as a thank offering to the Father for giving us His Son.

6. The church needs to take a hard look at what happened to the servants who followed Jesus. The church has become weak with bless me theology. It has cowered as Political Correctness (PC) has swept the country, tearing down the church and stripping manhood of any serious effort toward defending God's Word. The church has sat back and watched as political correctness championed the introduction of moral cancer that has spread like wildfire in our country. It is reasonable to assume, that as the Church sits back and watches Rome burn while Cesar plays his fiddle, we are ushering in a heritage of Christian martyrs warning of the Great and Terrible Day of the Lord. We have reaped the winds of moral decay and it's whirlwind is just around the corner. "THE CHOSEN WILL SEE THE SIGNS OF THE TIMES AND KNOW THEIR REDEMPTION DRAWETH NEIGH!

7. One can easily conclude that the organized church has much to answer for regarding the lack of doctrinal unity among the denominations as to the exegesis in the Word. This lack of unity has placed the lay person in a very tenuous position in identifying who has the truth that sets you free. The churches have demonstrated their lack of Spirit led exegesis in their doctrines. THE LAYPERSON NEEDS TO UNDERSTAND AND ACCEPT THAT THERE IS ONLY ONE GUARANTEED BIBLICAL TRUTH TEACHER THAT THE FATHER PROVIDED - THE HOLY SPIRIT WAS SENT TO COUNSEL AND LEAD YOU INTO ALL TRUTH. Let's summarize:

    i.   One needs to be righteous to enter the Kingdom of God.
    ii. Righteousness is achieved only when sins are cleansed by the cross.
    iii. Both new and old testament chosen have to be cleansed by the cross.

My Record will go into detail on these and other issues and justify all of my Spirit led positions. Here are some scriptures to feed on:

1. EPH 2:8 "For by graced you have been saved, through faith; and not of yourself; it is a gift of God." It is the Father's gift of access to Spirit counsel and teaching. It is the Spirit baptism that approves the faith walk. The "through faith" walk begins after the Spirit approves your baptism and allows you to start the walk of faith. Your work's righteousness performance will be monitored throughout the walk concerning acceptance of Spirit counsel and, if inadequate, may be judged a poor heart response to counsel and precipitate removal from the faith walk.
2. EPH 2:9 "Not of works, lest any man should boast." Man can't perform righteous works! The Spirit performs righteous works through you as a vessel when you are yielding to His counsel. This is why scriptures teach that the chosen who are led by the Spirit are children of God. Following the counsel of the Spirit is the only way a chosen can earn works righteousness points to gain access to

the Cross. My 8/2/2014 revelation below should give you a greater understanding of the Salvation process.

3.   EPH 2:10 "For we are His workmanship created in Christ Jesus unto good works which God hath before ordained that we should walk in them." Good = Righteous! This begs the question "Why don't the church's intellectual giants take God's word as written instead of twisting it with their self-serving brand of hermeneutics. They use the same approach in applying their brand of hermeneutics to John 3:16, by saying Jesus is a Divine True Man, Spirit Baptism guarantees salvation, once saved, always saved, etc. This record will examine hermeneutics as Satan's weapon of choice to confuse and divide churches.

8/2/2014: A KEY SAUNA REVELATION ON SALVATION

During my 45-minute drive home from seeing Joan in the nursing home, I was totally preoccupied with what the Spirit had revealed. I knew I was going home to one of my sauna nights with the Spirit. I started to feel a sense of excitement which culminated in one word that provided the common thread to access the Cross for the Old and New Testament (OT&NT) Chosen saints. I would like to lay out my thoughts as revealed by the Spirit during my drive home and the sauna experience.

+   Jesus did many things but His primary mission was to provide an unblemished sacrifice to cover the sins of the Father's Chosen from both testaments. The Jesus of the OT was a gift promised; the Jesus of the NT was a gift received. Both gifts are based on belief in the atonement through Jesus' shed blood on the cross.

+   To think of Jesus as True Man, you have to understand that Jesus' seed did not come from Abraham because of his sin, but from the Father. So Jesus was without sin but was introduced to a real sin opportunity in the wilderness with Satan. Adam too, was without sin until the fall. So our father Adam's sin left us a legacy leading to hell. Jesus did not sin and opened the narrow salvation gate to the Father's chosen who follow the counsel of the Spirit in works of righteousness.

+ What is the Word that links OT and NT Chosen to the salvation victory? We can conclude that their works were prompted by the Spirit. In the OT, we can argue that the leading Spirit was the Father in concert with the Son and Holy Spirit. I am of the persuasion that the Father spoke for the Trinity since the separate functions of Trinity members were not introduced until NT times. The Spirit of the NT was the Holy Spirit. Since God's programs for salvation don't change, it is logical to conclude that the criteria for salvation is constant and applicable to both the OT and the NT. We know there is one fixed requirement for salvation, RIGHTEOUSNESS! The chosen of God are counseled under the new and old covenants by the Spirit. Before access to the Cross, the chosen will be screened by the Spirit when examining their performance on Spirit counseled works projects. If their hunger and thirst for righteousness does not reflect glory to the Father in their response to the Spirit's counsel, they will be denied access to the cross.

The Father's Will insures that everything is accomplished to suit His Purpose and Glory!

The Chosen, under the old and new covenants, deal with the cross and salvation through Jesus. This would suggest that salvation is demonstrated by a Spirit led counsel approval.

Under these guidelines, where do we find God's Chosen? We cannot limit the scope of our outreach because we are tasked by Jesus to go into all the world, preach the good news and let the Spirit quicken the hearts of the chosen. I view 'quicken' as a personal spirit to Spirit experience.

(8/8/14) I would like to share a personal experience and a neat revelation. Faced with knowing Joan had memory problems that lead to dementia, we told the Lord that we understood and accepted that His will and our death dates were set in the beginning. We understood that the Lord's decision for or against healing of dementia for Joan was also set. All we asked for, while waiting on the Lord's will, was that His peace and joy join us in the valley. Satan has been continually attacking Joan's memory and increasing her need for total care. At one point, Joan was sleeping 20 hours a day. In the last few weeks I began to notice she was more alert, speaking more, enjoys being kissed and loves our prayer time. I wanted to share, in particular, an experience that blessed me to no end. I was leaving her room to get her dinner when she stopped me in my tracks with "I want a Hug!" The Father knows that we are content with His will whether He heals her or blesses her with paradise, to await my joining her after completing my commission. As we await Father's will, we do so knowing we will be blessed! Joan has fallen four times resulting in stitches twice for each eye, plus one fall requiring hip replacement. Satin tried, but was not able to penetrate the Father's response to our request for peace and joy. I share this because it demonstrates, for His chosen, that the tribulation path can be a blessing, if we walk with the Trinity! 9/25/15 Note: The Father received Joan by waking her from her sleep to join Him in paradise. When I first viewed her in death, I experienced a joy that far exceeded my sense of loss, knowing where she was and that I would be seeing her soon, so we can begin to enjoy together our Trinity, beholding glory throughout eternity.

Again, my thoughts turned to the righteousness issue. On the one hand, we are told that the prayers of a righteous man availeth much while on the other hand Jesus tells us that no man is righteous, including himself. Sounds like a serious theological issue unless you understand the role of righteousness in the Spirit's domain. We can accept that no man, including the Father's True Man is righteous because of the flesh. Paul gives a good account of the issues with man's control over his flesh. Then what makes man's works righteous? The answer is simple. Man is only a vessel! The works are performed under the counsel of the Spirit. Such works glorify God because they are performed under the full control of a righteous Holy Spirit. So, if we want the prayers of a righteous man, we need to find one of the Father's chosen who is actively engaged in walking under the counsel of the Spirit. Jesus, as true man, is the prime example of walking under the full counsel of the Spirit. The unity of the Trinity is three Spirits with majesty coequal. A Chosen has this Trinity within so the Spirit counsel you receive is of equal value to that Jesus received. Recalling Paul's discussion of sin in Romans Chapter 7, we have to conclude the vessel of a chosen, like all human vessels, is bereft with sin, raising the question of how the works of a chosen vessel qualify as righteous works that meet the standards of the Father's Purpose and Glory. As noted, we are told that the prayers of a righteous man availeth much. Who is this righteous man? He is a chosen vessel, that submits his prayer request to the Spirit to forward to the Trinity. All answered prayer requests submitted by the Spirit are righteous and receive Trinity approval. This means that the Spirit makes a judgment on all chosen requests. If He approves, your request becomes His request. In effect, the righteousness of the request is not the vessel but the Spirit adding His righteousness to the request. Spirit stamped righteous prayer is only available to the chosen embracing the counsel of the Spirit. It can be likened to the condition that the Spirit uses to examine the condition of the heart for Spiritual Baptism that is needed for access to the faith walk to the Cross. That CONDITION is a true Hunger and Thirst for Righteousness. The Father does not want one His Chosen to be guided by their head rather than their heart, when responding to the counsel of the Spirit. Without a hunger and thirst for righteousness, your access to Jesus (life) will be denied.

It was exciting scribing for the Spirit on Righteousness. Now we come the WORD that triggered this revelation. COUNTED or ACCOUNTED! Consider the following scriptures:

1. James 2:17-26: "Even so faith, if it hath not works, is dead, being alone. Yes, a man may say, thou has faith and I have works: show me thy faith without thy works, and I will show thee my faith by my works. Thou believest that there is one God; thou doest well: the devils also believe, and tremble. But wilt thou know, O vain man, that faith without works is dead? Was not Abraham our father justified by works, when he had offered Isaac his son upon the alter? Seest thou how faith wrought with his works, and by works was made perfect? And the scripture was fulfilled which saith, Abraham believed God, and it was imputed (COUNTED) unto him for righteousness: and he was called a friend of God. Ye see then how that by works a man is justified, and not by faith only. Like-wise also, was not Rahab the harlot justified by works,

when she had received the messengers, and had sent them out another way. For as the body without the spirit is dead, so faith without works is dead also."

+ From where I stand, any church or denomination that rejects the works righteousness presented by James above is in danger of a false doctrine that denies access through the narrow gate and high odds of answering to Jesus at the great white throne judgment. They do not understand John 3:16 or the doctrine of grace. Their failure to understand, the "who" of John 3:16's grace role in salvation, is inhibiting access to biblical truth through widespread application and teaching of exegesis based on intellect led hermeneutics. Look at Abraham's works righteousness as a prime example by considering the role of faith, the vessel and the Spirit. The key to understanding the role of righteousness lies in the Father's Spirit that counseled Abraham to sacrifice his son. By faith Abraham accepted the Father's request as a righteous act and served as a vessel through which the Father could satisfy His purpose and Glory. Abraham's willingness to accept the Father's request based on faith was COUNTED as righteousness.

+ I believe that the role of righteousness for the New testament mirror's the Old Testament. However, the role of the players deserves some consideration. Of course the vessel is a designated Chosen. The Holy Spirit is our righteous source in new testament times because He was sent by the Father to be our personal counselor and teacher. Jesus was given all power and authority over creation which includes everything impacting our lives, including our faith walk. From what I have sensed about my Father, I see Him in the personal role of a Father who receives and covets the Chosen who demonstrate a hunger and thirst to be with Him, His Son and the Spirit. So we are a vessel for the righteous works of the Spirit. Your eager acceptance of the Spirit's use of your vessel for righteous works provides an opportunity to have them COUNTED as WORK'S RIGHTOUSNESS. Without work's righteousness, there is no salvation.

ISSUES OF THE MIND, SPIRIT AND HEART

Even considering my marriage, the most significant events of my life were visits by my Father in the Fall of 1974 and December of 2009. In 1974, my Father gave me a scripture (Matthew 6:33) and told me I would never worry about my salvation. This scripture gave me my starting point: seek ye first His Kingdom and Righteousness, which I accepted by entering a nursing home ministry. I did not fully understand His comment on my salvation until after my December 2009 encounter. After providing a replacement for my nursing home ministry, the Father told me that I needed to get into His Word and admonished me with "You can't preach the truth if you don't know the truth. At this point, my church membership spanned over 50 years including a 35 year nursing home ministry. Almost immediately, I found myself studying a bible that had come alive. The Father was right! I didn't know beans about the scriptures.

I decided on the following approach for this record:

> 1st: In my record, I will be speaking in a layman terms using a layman's language that has not been subject to review by anyone but the Spirit. I want to be in a position of full responsibility for the exegesis revealed, subject only to correction by the Holy Spirit. IN EFFECT, THE FATHER CALLED ME AND THE SPIRIT LED ME - I answer only to the Trinity. I believe I am writing this record as a servant of God and willing to submit to His judgment.

2ⁿᵈ: I will include a full testimony that highlights God's interventions during our walk in the Father's Will that shows both blessings and tribulations. The one thing special about our family is that we know we are under God's grace.

3ʳᵈ: I will explore issues of the "Mind, Spirit and Heart" covering six years of walking with the Trinity and considering issues introduced by my spirit and the Holy Spirit. While I believe the Spirit provided guidance to the thoughts going through my mind, this first cut was used to isolate issues for a focused Spirit led exegesis. It was exciting to be able to consider an issue in my mind and have the Spirit "bring into remembrance" scriptures lying dormant from past bible studies. The issues represent many individual sessions with the Spirit, which were initiated by the Spirit and/or my spirit.

4ᵗʰ: I will serve as a scribe vessel of the Spirit, recording what I believe was being quickened to my spirit during Spirit led exegesis."

5ᵗʰ: I will attempt to identify the key doctrines that need to be understood, accepted and applied, to know the truth that sets the captive free, and to exercise his/her right to a Spirit led faith walk to the cross.

6ᵗʰ: Finally, I will summarize the major issues of key doctrines, by showing a suggested progression of episodes identifying (in my case) the full counsel of God, wherein one episode of Spirit led exegesis opens up a second episode, which opens up a third episode etc. In this manner, each exegesis episode provides expanded data bases needed to develop, hopefully, into an expansive understanding of the full counsel of God provided by Spirit led exegesis. It is my prayer the elect reading this record will find this helpful. Once you have done the first few episodes establishing your understanding of the roles of the Father, Son, Holy Spirit, Trinity, Unity of the Trinity and the sovereignty of God, you are in a position to give the reigns of your spirit to the Holy Spirit and experience a ride of joy, as the counsel of the Spirit is revealed to you. If you are like me, you will be experiencing the greatest time of your life.

A WORD OF COUNSEL: You must understand that you are a called servant of the Trinity and, as such, you can only serve man by following the examples of Jesus, John the Baptist, and the disciples who shared counsel of the Spirit that leads to salvation. Please consider:

WHO IS THE GREATEST IN THE KINGDOM OF HEAVEN?

I was driving home from my 79th birthday party when I was led by the Spirit to consider an issue that has been on the back of my mind for some time. How can I counter the skepticism, mostly nonverbal, of being called to serve the Father. The Spirit was asking me to consider the idea of "SERVICE!" I began to think of the Father's great servants:

1. Jesus as TRUE MAN! Jesus said he did not come to be served, but to serve. He provided the greatest service possible - SALVATION FOR THE FATHER'S CHOSEN.
2. Second, I would pick Job! He was the one, whom the Father offered Satan to consider as a faithful servant, to test obedience with only one condition; he couldn't take Job's life. Job is man's gold standard for true commitment to the Father. Take away our missionary folks and the countless martyrs over the years, and there is very little evidence of Jobs in the Christian Church. Most are enamored with the love of a sweet Jesus theology that focuses on being blessed and not being a blessing to the Father.
3. Third would be Abraham's obedience in his willingness to sacrifice his son, which the Father counted as righteousness and put him at the beginning of Jesus' lineage.
4. Fourth would be "John the Baptist" who was under Spirit control to announce the coming savior. Jesus said there is none greater than John. Herein lies an example of a Spirit controlled servant

for us to emulate. I would suspect that John, like Jesus, had the Spirit resident in the Trinity since we are told that the Spirit in man arrived at Pentecost.

These are my personal choices of the Father's greatest servants. Of course, there are many other servants in the Bible, including David who loved the Father but was chastised for sexual misconduct and denied right to build the Temple.

What strikes me:

1. Jesus was special as a True Man, sent by the Trinity to be a living sacrifice that establishes the awesome love of the Father toward His Chosen. Think of the verbal abuse He suffered in sharing truth.

2. The obedience of the old testament servants were based on direct interface with the Trinity that solicited a response of fear and awe. They too, suffered verbal abuse from God's children,

3. Our obedience is measured by our response to Spirit counsel. The degree, to which we satisfy the counsel of the Spirit, measures the magnitude of your servant spirit. Jesus puts it into perspective: "The greatest among you is the servant of the other." The glory of Spirit led action goes to the Trinity and not to the servant being abused while being used as a vessel of the Spirit.

4. THE GREATEST: If you ask Jesus, His answer is found in the first resurrection. He only invited the Martyrs to serve with him during the millennium. Scripture reminds us that we are to present ourselves as a living sacrifice, wholly and acceptable to the Father. The thought just occurred to me, triggered by the martyrs. If Jesus embraced the martyrs who died for Him leading to the first resurrection, it would be rational to assume that all of the Father's martyrs giving their lives for Jesus following the first resurrection, would be among those accessing the narrow gate with immediate access to the cross and salvation. THEY GAVE IT ALL!

WHO HAS THE TRUTH

The record I am sharing is one servant's attempt to be in obedience to and bless the Father. I am sure that there will be many Christian leaders and church members who will decry and challenge my record. There are two counselors contending for control of the mind when considering biblical exegesis. One led by the Deceiver (Devil) and the other by the Spirit. Hundreds of Christian denominations have provided a vast buffet of doctrines and creeds based on individual hermeneutical rules designed to satisfy preconceived theological standards. The only creditable way you can judge who has the Word of the Lord, is to lean on the counsel of the Holy Spirit! It is time for church members to understand that they are responsible for their knowledge of biblical truth and that the only sure source for truth is the Counselor, the Holy Spirit. My record is of my walking with and exploring God's word with the Spirit, while experiencing a strong sense of having been set free to explore God's truths. I believe that my commission goal was to share God's truth in a ELECT layman's guide to salvation victory.

Based on excessive variance in denominational doctrines, the study of God's Word leaves the layman in a quandary, as to where one can find a source of true Spiritual exegesis. Your spiritual life must involve not seeking Church doctrine but the Spirit that Jesus promised that the Father would send providing counseling and Spirit led exegesis. In Joshua 24:15, we are admonished to "… choose for yourselves this day whom you will serve …" Your choice must be based on the biblical exegesis of God's Word that will sharpen your discernment, to recognize biblical truth from any source, up to and including the Pope!

At this point we should study to understand and accept two cardinal biblical facts:

1. ***The power of the word is only available to the Father's Elect! John 3:16's world is the Father's Elect!***
2. The counselor/spirit was not given to the church, who messed up their exegesis, but to the lay persons who walk under the power of

the Spirit. We need to keep in mind that Jesus brought His Word to quicken His Disciples and not the clergy of His day. Don't you think the Father's disciple plan was fixed from the beginning. The first group of disciples were the Father's chosen given to Jesus to teach the Word and establish the church. Subsequent chosen were introduced to life following the Father's random selection of chosen from the soul pool. Recognizing the Father's omniscience and omnipotence, we know that the path of each chosen will be under the Father's will enforced by Jesus. These paths determine the capacity in which each chosen will serve and which chosen will give up their John 3:16 rights. Lay persons are called disciples of Christ for today's ministry? I believe I am one of many lay persons called to share the TRUTH in an end-times ministry; ones committed to being a living sacrifice engaged in Jesus' Great Commission. As lay persons recognizing our sin nature, we know we deserve hell but were randomly selected to receive GRACE!

TRINTY AND UNITY OF THE TRINITY
NEW VS OLD TESTAMENT

We must accept the fact that there is ONE GOD comprised of three persons in perfect unity of Purpose and Glory. While the application of Trinity actions from Old to New Testament varies, the Unity is always maintained. In the OT, the Trinity acted as a Unity Trinity Father in guiding their people. This all changed in the NT with a salvation plan that involved personal involvement with the Father's Chosen. We have a Father who selects His chosen from the soul pool and designed the grace program. We have a Son who agrees to become True Man which required leaving His divinity with the Trinity to maintain unity. YOU CAN NOT BE TRUE MAN AND DIVINE AT THE SAME TIME!! I will provide revealed exegesis to support this truth. So the Spirit instilled a seed without blemish into Mary to complement the soul from the Father's pool. Such souls are not blemished with sin but do possess free will. The question of the seed source, to be holy, had to come from the Father! Since all three members are in total agreement on all actions taken, it follows that the seed

43

reflects a Trinity DNA. The Trinity stood watch over True Man all of the way to the cross, to insure that nothing would diminish the magnitude of the Father's love toward His chosen completing the walk of faith to the cross. Following the crucifixion, Jesus joined His Father to receive His glory and serve as King of Kings over God's Kingdom.

We need to understand the relationship between Trinity and Unity. The Trinity establishes three separate persons while the Unity combines these three persons as one God. We also know that there are separate functional roles for each member. When members are performing in an individual function mode, Unity demands total Trinity agreement on any action taken under the biblical truth that God and Divinity are one. This means that a functional mode of a member serves as the action figure exercising the will of a Trinity, under the constraints of the unity doctrine. Under the unity doctrine, Divinity is confined to the Trinity. You can't understand God is one without accepting a Divinity doctrine confined to the unity of the trinity. This concept confirms that Jesus was true man devoid of the divine nature accepted by many theologians, who argue that He couldn't divorce His divinity when He became true man. Theologians must experience a "Come to Jesus moment," if they do not want to find themselves challenging the mind of God, using their intellect to set up self-defined hermeneutical rules supporting their exegesis of scripture. Considering we have hundreds of Christian denominations separated by doctrines, how can a lay person know which, if any, have Spirit led vs intellect led exegesis? One can conclude that Satan is engaged in the application of 'hermeneutics' during formulation of denominational doctrines. His success is dramatically evidenced by the rampant disunity in church doctrine among hundreds of denominations.

DIVINITY AND TRUE MAN

The concept of Unity requires the presence of all three divine members. To be True Man, Jesus had leave His divinity with the Trinity. If you can accept Jesus as True Man without Divinity, then your exegesis is that of a True Man in every respect, except sin. You are walking on dangerous ground when you use your intellect to challenge the Father on the definition of True Man. It is this kind of arrogance that interprets scripture without the Spirit! To accept Christ as divine, consider:

1. Why did He go to the Father daily for guidance on the next day's activities?
2. The temptation would have pitted Divinity against Satan. No real contest!
3. Can Divinity be crucified?
4. Why did Jesus tell the woman not to touch Him because He had not yet ascended to the Father to receive His glory?
5. If Divinity defines God and God is one, then unity demands a triune Divinity. This is why we are blessed with a Trinity within and a Spirit in functional control.
6. One attribute of a Trinity with unity is all actions come from one God, regardless of the key action figure. This is why Jesus sacrifice is so startling - he had to leave his Divinity with the Trinity to become "True Man!"

During 6 years of Spirit led venture into the WORD, theological discourse expressed by TV evangelists, pulpit preachers and in books, I gathered notes on a large number of biblical issues during my search of scriptures. I found a confusing smorgasbord of conflicting theological discourse. I was amazed that the application of hermeneutics, by so many trained theologians, could arrive at such a wide spectrum of individual truths. The Christian church is hundreds of Christian denominations, separated by individual doctrines and creeds competing for a pool of lay persons. The denominations train their pastors on their doctrines and creeds. These pastors become circus barkers selling the denomination's brand of biblical truth. I once told a Baptist pastor that I doubted that the number of his members acquainted with the doctrines and creeds of his church exceeded 15 percent. He agreed! I wasn't surprised, since my only exposure to doctrine was in confirmation classes. During my varied church experiences, I can't remember attending any church providing a course on comparing their doctrinal positions with other denominations. My sad admission is that I was just another lamb being led by a pastor feeding his sheep with doctrine provided by denomination scholars. The Father's

December 2009 words echoed in my ears: "You can't preach the truth if you don't know the truth!"

THE PROBLEM: How do lay persons know whether or not their pastor is preaching doctrines resulting from Spirit led exegesis?

Because of military transfers to new assignments, I have been a church member of a number of churches associated with differing denominations. Over a period of 50 years, I was exposed to differing doctrines and creeds of unknown veracity. Therefore, I had been teaching and preaching in nursing homes for 35 years, using the questionable source material learned from of differing church doctrines. The December 2009 call was telling me that I needed to search the scriptures myself to know the truth. To me, He was saying that the organized church is providing a myriad of doctrines based on intellectual, and not SPIRITUAL exegesis. As I considered the Father's call, I turned to the scriptures:

> John 14:26 "But the Comforter, which is the Holy Ghost, whom the Father will send in My name, He shall teach you all things, and bring to your remembrance, whatsoever I have said unto you."

> John 16:13 "Howbeit when he, the Spirit of truth, is come, He will guide you into all truth: for He shall not speak of Himself; but whatsoever He shall hear, that shall He speak: and He will show you things to come."

> 1 John 2:27 "But the anointing which ye have received of Him abideth in you, AND YE NEED NOT THAT ANY MAN TEACH YOU: but as the SAME ANOINTING TEACHETH YOU OF ALL THINGS, and is TRUTH, and is no lie, and even as it hath you, ye shall abide in him." This scripture is the elect's KEY to truth! Note that it begins with "anointing" requiring the "born again" experience which is the anointing of the Holy Spirit. The Spirit will lead the Elect/Chosen into all truth.

I had a men's Sunday school class experience that prompted me to share issues that can affect one's understanding and application of biblical truths. A bible class teacher noted that we study the Word to get it into our minds and transfer it to our hearts. I told them that mind (intellectual) focused study efforts to extract biblical truth are futile. One cannot understand the spiritual truths of the Word without becoming a vessel of and led by the Spirit. (Being a vessel involves fostering an in-depth relationship between your spirit and the Holy Spirit that allows the Spirit to supplant the mind to reveal TRUTH through one's spirit.)

Many of today's churches wallow in prosperity theology fed by non-Spirit led pastors. They are feeding sweet Jesus gospel rather than the 'hard sayings' of Jesus. Consider John 6:60 & 66. "Many therefore of his disciples, when they heard this, said, this is a hard saying; who can hear it?" and "From that time many of his disciples went back, and walked no more with him." This is the malady that faces today's churches. They are afraid of what happened to Jesus when He preached truth and lost many of His disciples, would happen to them.

By teaching prosperity theology, the church is offering salvation for the asking and without cost. They love to sing "Jesus paid it all!" This self-righteousness supports the proposition that, for the most part, many of today's churches have been de-fanged and neutered. A full gospel church is hard to find. God's sovereignty is widely sugar coated, ignored or challenged. Members focus on self-gratification vs serving God. Churches focus on internal ministry while providing a token effort on external ministry to satisfy the great commission command. Jesus' decree to offer one's self as a living sacrifice, wholly and acceptable to God is recited with little or no application. The chutzpah of the church has morphed into a meek, non-offensive, weak kneed attitude entity that manifests a religiosity feeding on prosperity theology. Ask yourself if you are a living sacrifice that is holy and acceptable to God. If you are not led by the Spirit, you are not a disciple of Christ and there is no way you can please God. If you are an Elect/Chosen of God and fail to present yourself as a living sacrifice to the Holy Spirit, you will find that resting on "once saved always saved" is a ticket to hell! You must understand that the "narrow gate" is one of several screening actions that the Father uses to separate the Wheat (Chosen) from the Chaff (unchosen). Not all chosen will gain access to the cross. Scripture warns us that few will enter the narrow gate. Don't squander God's grace that gave you the opportunity to walk with the Spirit.

Don't seek to serve self over seeking the Kingdom of God and His righteousness; don't allow yourself be controlled by your mind to the detriment of being a vessel of the Spirit; don't refuse to present yourself as a living sacrifice, holy and acceptable to God; and understand that messing with biblical truth and the sovereignty of God can place you before the Great White Throne Judgment. There is no excuse for the elect not knowing Truth since they were chosen under Grace and provided access to the Spirit, who leads you into all truth. The key to knowing truth is to understand the magnitude of God's sovereignty. God does everything for HIS PURPOSE AND GLORY! Begin your understanding by knowing that Jesus has complete control over every activity anyone experiences whether good or bad. The rain falls on the just and unjust, because of the sin in the garden. God's grace to the elect does not preclude trials and tribulations. Just accept that no one is in a position to question God's right to do anything He wants. Remember what happened to your ancestors during creation! They were created from dirt (TOTAL DEPRAVITY). This is the starting point for us to begin to embrace the awesome majesty of a Holy Father! The issue of God's sovereignty can become a major stumbling block to exegesis, as demonstrated by the abundance of available doctrines and creeds, across a myriad of denominations and their churches.

I can recall in the mid 80's of listening to male church members singing on stage on mother's day. The thought occurred to me that I would not feel comfortable going through tribulation with anyone in the group. They were not preparing for tribulation because of their acceptance of the pre-tribulation rapture doctrine. Their approach to personal witness is to be careful to not offend. Let me cut to the quick up front! Withholding the truth during witnessing so as not to offend is an affront to Jesus. Jesus did not pick disciples based on refined speech and education. He saw their hearts knowing they would be willing to die for HIM. They spoke a layman's language with a courage that can best be understood by today's elect men as chutzpah! They understood speaking Jesus (truth) was laying their lives on the line. Looking back, they knew that, when Jesus said "pick up your cross and follow me," failure to speak truth (JESUS) was not an option! Excluding God's missionaries who understand Jesus' call and are willing to lay their lives on the line, courage displayed in today's church is going forward for an alter call. Many times, repeated urgings of the Pastor were needed to get a respectable count for his performance report. Serving a sovereign God is not a parlor game. It requires immersing your spirit with the Spirit, in search for the truth to serve and bring glory to God.

When witnessing, there is no room for a "look at me" display a self-righteousness or false humility. Churches that cower under the "We shouldn't offend non-believers with truth" is an egregious sin against Jesus leading to spirit life consequences. If you are or were a recipient of election resulting from Grace and don't understand failure to witness truth is a failure to witness Jesus, you are endangering your Spirit led faith walk to the cross and salvation. While God's grace provides the elect access through the Narrow Gate (what I like to call the Spirit Gate), access does not guarantee immunity to erasure from the book of life. Also, if an elect does not aggressively adopt the guidance of MAT 6:33 "Seek ye first the Kingdom of God and His righteousness ...," and actively hunger and thirst after His righteousness, he or she is a candidate for erasure from the Book of Life and facing a Great White Throne Judgment. Jesus has sacrificed his life for sinners and now sits on the throne with great glory and power. We can celebrate a personal victory in Christ, if and only if, we complete the Spirit led faith walk to the cross. The cross is not a fantasy journey provided for pre-tribulation rapture and prosperity theology advocates. Jesus said "I did not come to bring peace but a sword!" Why do you think you deserve a pre-tribulation rapture ahead of the end of the age, while our Lord is continually being honored by incoming streams of martyrs?

When are Christians going to stop using their pious judgment based on questionable doctrine spewed from the pulpits or in a bible classes? When are Christians going to assume personal responsibility for knowing the "truth" that leads to salvation, instead of trusting a pastor, priest or pope's declaration of "truth" as they know it. Most Christians are not in a spiritual position to question false teachings in their churches. Don't they realize that the Spirit judges the contents of one's heart. Those who are led by the Spirit shall be called children of God. Our access to truth is provided solely by the Spirit. Only the Spirit can open up the Word of truth.

Lip-service Christians remind me of the serious issue raised in Isaiah 29:13 "Wherefore the Lord said, forasmuch as this people draw near to me with their mouth, and with their lips do honor me, but they have removed their HEART far from me, AND THEIR FEAR TOWARD ME IS TAUGHT BY THE PRECEPT OF MAN." This scripture highlights the cause of division between churches and denominations is competing doctrinal truths. Many congregational pulpits are filled with seminary trained pastors toeing the party line, on doctrinal truths that may have little or no Spirit led exegesis of the scriptures. This puts congregations in the position of being forced to feed on doctrine of unknown veracity. I hope to show the Father's elect how to understand and avoid the pitfalls of false doctrine, on the faith walk to the cross. There are scriptures that show all of the ELECT have been blessed with GRACE but not all ELECT will attain SALVATION - that "once saved - always saved" is false doctrine. It is the personal walk with the Spirit that leads to the Spiritual exegesis that sets the captives free. As one grows in the Spirit taught exegesis of the bible, the Spirit will gain an ever increasing control of your spirit and you will bask in the truth that sets you free. Jesus told His disciples that it was important He go to be with the Father who would send the comforter, the Holy Spirit who would LEAD THEM INTO ALL TRUTH!

"AND THEIR FEAR TOWARD ME IS TAUGHT BY THE PRECEPTS OF MAN." This type e of activity goes back to the early Catholic Church when bibles were withheld from the people in the church. The history of Christianity is marked by a martyrdom of believers giving their lives to save and share truth. Today, we have dispensationalism and prosperity theology, that twists scriptures to provide doctrines that give one a warm fuzzy feeling with the Spiritually dead teachings of men, while straying away from Spiritual exegesis. The condition of many of the churches today, based on man's intellect derived doctrine, demands that every elect member understand that grace was not a guarantee of salvation, but an opportunity to be counseled and taught biblical exegesis by the Spirit. The elect must know, accept and conform to the counsel and teachings of the Spirit. Accepting and adopting false doctrine from church pulpits, evangelists, bible teachers and up to and including the Pope is tantamount to pushing the Spirit aside - smells like blasphemy! - the UNPARDONABLE SIN. If our church leaders are not led by the Spirit, they are in no position to teach truth. The Spirit was sent to the disciples upon Jesus' glorification. We are called to be disciples of Christ and tasked with the Great Commission. As disciples, being Spirit led is the key to growing in Grace and Truth. If you have not been counseled on how to access the Spirit, I pray this witness will bless you.

11/4/15: Counsel from the Spirit for those betting their salvation on escaping the tribulation. Consider these truths and recommendation:

+ We are called to ENDURE to the end.
+ You must die to access the cross for salvation.
+ You are called to be a living sacrifice.
+ Only martyrs who had their heads cut off joined Jesus in the first resurrection. The remaining Chosen in the Book of Life, will be taken up in the second resurrection.
+ Through Church history, there have been countless martyrs who have given their lives in witness to Jesus. Martyrdom's witness toll continues today with increasing frequency, suggesting that tribulation is approaching and our redemption draws neigh.
+ Adam's sin condemned ALL descendant's physical bodies to the first death. Jesus ransom was paid for the spirit and soul of the Chosen named in the Book of Life. The soul and spirit of the unchosen were cast into the Lake of Fire.
+ Is pre-tribulation rapture counsel sanctioned by Satan or the Spirit? Is this an eternal life and death issue? Consider the following guidance.
+ Let this record reveal a course of action that will provide an introduction to the Spirit. If you are among the chosen in good standing, the Spirit will examine the desires of your heart to

determine whether you are worthy of His counsel. If you are not among the chosen, you will not be approached by the Spirit.

I am concerned over the number of denominations that are exposed to hand me down doctrine based on intellectual exegesis. Are the students entering seminaries being exposed to false denominational doctrines to the point of indoctrination, that inhibits the Spiritual exegesis needed to promote the development of a "Workman approved of God!" 2 TIM 2:15 "Be diligent to present yourself approved to God, a worker who does not need to be ashamed, rightly dividing the word of truth." To wit, after 35 years of nursing home ministry, the Father admonished me with: "You can't preach the truth if you do not know the truth!" He was telling me to get into the word under the counsel of the Spirit.

Are elect seminary students Spiritually equipped with the courage to question false teaching by seminary professors? Have they embraced their own relationship with the Spirit, that allows them to embrace the truth of God in power? Do they reject false teachings found in most churches to assure a Spirit led victory stroll to the cross? False doctrine is not amusing because we are talking life and death for some of God's chosen. False doctrine mocks the sovereignty of the Trinity, through a blasphemy that draws God's elect away from the counsel of the Spirit (Blasphemy against the Holy Spirit). I can't help but think of the adverse impact of false doctrine by pastors and teachers. They are subject to God's judgment based on failure to know the truth that sets the captive free. Many are purveyors of intellectual vs Spiritual doctrine.

The elect layperson needs to understand that he or she is responsible for being responsive to the lead of the Holy Spirit in their walk to the cross. This means, that if you reject the leading and the counsel of the Spirit, your name is subject to removal from the Book of Life. This is one of those issues, where the church needs to reconsider Jesus words about leading His children astray. They need to understand that only the elect, through Grace, were given the opportunity to embrace the Spirit to serve the Lord in Spirit and Truth. The application of doctrine based on man's intellect vs Spirit led exegesis, can offer God's elect a sweet Jesus prosperity theology vs a pick up your cross, living sacrifice theology that offers the choice of serving. Did you not notice in the scriptures that Jesus and his disciples were suffering servants? For the Father's sake, preach the full Gospel so that your elect members can chose between man's intellect derived exegesis and the Spirit's exegesis. If one does not live a life that hungers and thirsts after righteousness, you have little or no understanding of the meaning of Grace and the magnitude of the Trinity's love, in agreeing to provide the only acceptable sacrifice for sin. Do you really understand that sacrifice, involves worship of Jesus and the Father through the Spirit? No one comes to the Father but by Jesus, that the path to Jesus is controlled by the Spirit" and it all starts with an elect aggressively seeking first the Kingdom of God and His Righteousness. By now you have concluded that I won't play games with true exegesis, which comes by Spirit revelation to the Father's elect. The Father has called me to learn the truth and preach the truth. I am fully engaged in trying to understand the Sovereignty of God and adopting it as the absolute standard needed to reveal His truths. I fully embrace the Grace of God and understand the severity of the Son's suffering on the cross, as revealed to my spirit by the Holy Spirit. What the Trinity has given me and other elect, demands full engagement in studying and applying truth. My application of truth will not apply the current "sensitive sweet Jesus" approach that is conditioned on deceit, based on a non-offensive coward's approach to witnessing sponsored by many churches. I cringe every time I hear a church member say we have to be sensitive to someone's feelings, when sharing God's truths. What do they think sets the captive free.? They need to rethink what Jesus means when He says in Mark 8:38 "For whoever is ashamed of me and my words in this adulterous and sinful generation, of him the Son of Man also will be ashamed when He comes in the glory of His Father with the holy angels." Those churches using a sensitive witness (SW) approach to an "adulterous and sinful generation" are comparable to the politically correct (PC) supporters whose approach is to destroy this nation. Both approaches lead to the Great White Throne Judgment. One can argue that the SW has been PC anesthetized into washing down the great commission by withholding the truth that sets the captive free. I believe a SW, who was selected as one of the elect under Grace, can face White Throne Judgment under Mark 8:38, for being ashamed of Jesus when being exposed to and embracing the false doctrines offered in many churches. Once again, as an elect, you are responsible for accepting and following the lead of the Spirit. IF YOU ARE NOT IN THE SPIRIT, you can't worship the Father in Spirit and Truth and you can't be part of those blessed with salvation. ENTER: The Great White Throne Judgment!

It appears that Pastor's lack courage in telling his congregation that John 3:16's 'world' only includes the elect. The congregations want their chance at salvation but don't want to hear that God had chosen an elect before the foundations of the world. Satan has used dispensationalism as his greatest weapon against the organized church. Last I heard, 80% of our Christian churches have adopted it. Satan must have a legion of his troops picketing the narrow gate to stop the chosen from entering. He must be doing well because scripture tells us few will enter therein.

If pastors are culpable for teaching false doctrine, how far up the ecclesiastical church ladder can we go to find the origin of false doctrine? I would suspect that the head of most Christian denominations, including the Catholic church, are derelict in their protection of the sanctity of the WORD. Jesus took the clerical elite of his day to the wood shed for their doctrine and told his disciples to wait until receiving power from on high. The disciples embraced the Spirit power of Pentecost. They spoke truth with boldness and conviction under the counsel of the Spirit. Jesus has centuries of martyrs asking how long before He returns. The organized church, beginning with the apostles, has dealt harshly against those questioning their theological positions. This country is rapidly moving toward experiencing a second Sodom and Gomorrah as evidenced by the majority of our churches that have been neutered into accepting compliance with main stream thought, even in the case of abortion, without an effective cry.

It is time for the elect to join the ranks of the apostles to do, what the neutered church refuse to do, speak God's truth under the power of the Spirit with strength and conviction. If you don't know if you are among the elect, this record will introduce the Trinity and it's Unity, the sovereignty of God, grace and the elect, the path to salvation and the road blocks you will experience during that walk. You will need to understand that many of your predecessors were martyrs who presented themselves as living sacrifices honoring the Father's gift of His Son. All martyrs are preordained by the Father for martyrdom. Preordained martyrs are special to the Father and Jesus. The Father said He was pleased to offer his son as our martyr and Jesus invited martyrs to join Him in His first resurrection and rule with Him for a 1,000 years. MARTYRDOM IN THEIR HONOR PROVIDES THE OPTIMUM GLORY THE FATHER CAN RECEIVE!

Churches members need ask their Pastor, if there are any Chosen /Elect staff and church members in oversight positions, controlling the application of hermeneutics to insure Spirit led exegesis. If you can't verify the efficacy of your doctrine, then the church must alert the congregation that it is their responsibility for the truth their spirit accepts. Given the large number of denominations separated by doctrinal truths, the layperson should be advised to seek the gift of the Holy Spirit sent by the Father. Obviously, this is not being promoted with conviction, by the vast majority of churches.

DECEMBER 9, 2013 - A SAUNA EPISODE. I was watching a local church pastor on TV when he referenced "No one knows the mind of God!" I have heard this expression from the pulpit many times over the span of 55years of church involvement and, like most Christians, attributed it to an awesome God. Recently I began to consider/question the role my Father's mind in our relationship. Based on my walk with the Spirit, following are a collection of thoughts that the Spirit revealed to me:

+ The bible reflects a history of His mind from creation through today and will continue to be revealed by and through His Chosen until the Great White Throne Judgment.
+ The mind of God can only be opened by the Spiritual exegesis of the Word.
+ Only God's chosen have access to the counsel of the Spirit, who the Father sent to lead them into all truth. "Those who are led by the Spirit shall be known as children of God."

+ I strongly believe the God's mind is only opened to His chosen who conform to the counsel of the Spirit. Non-conformance to the Spirit's counsel can be blasphemous-the unpardonable sin. One needs to rethink "once saved, always saved" and the narrow gate. The chosen must be cognizant of the fact that a free will rejection of the Spirit's counsel can cause his name to be erased from the Book of Life. Your walk along the salvation path must be one of a hunger and thirst for righteousness found only in the Spirit. Your free spirit must be ever diligent to discern the exegesis of scriptures, coming from the pulpit or a bible class teacher. Biblical discernment is a gift of the Spirit. Therefore, it is imperative for any chosen offspring of grace to walk with the Spirit, to develop and strengthen his gift of discernment. You don't want to find yourself defending your failure to follow the counsel of the Spirit. The fact is that you may appear before judge Jesus, to account for your sins under the judgment of Matthew 25:41 "Then He shall also say unto them on the left hand, depart from me ye cursed, into the everlasting fire prepared for the devil and his angels. These words come from Jesus as He sits upon His throne of glory separating the sheep from the goats. Matthew 25:34 "Then shall the King say to them on His right hand, come ye blessed of my Father, Inherit the Kingdom prepared for you from the foundation of the world."

NOTE: : THERE IS NO SUCH THING AS CHEAP GRACE! Especially for God's chosen! If you seek a life of God's blessings and not serving Him, you need a serious attitude adjustment, because you are among those on the left. Over years of following the counsel of the Spirit, I have stopped many times to marvel at the significance of the Scripture the Father shared with me, when He called me into service in the fall of 1974: Matthew 6:33 "Seek ye first the Kingdom of God, and His righteousness; AND ALL OF THESE THINGS SHALL BE ADDED UNTO YOU." You serve the Father and His blessings will more than compensate your needs.

+ EPH 2:8-9 "For by grace you have been saved through faith; and that not of yourselves: it is the gift of God not by works, lest any man should boast. For we are His workmanship, created in Christ Jesus unto good works, which GOD HATH BEFORE ORDAINED THAT WE SHOULD WALK IN THEM." When I read these verses, I see God's mind regarding His plan for salvation. I don't believe the Father's mind is fully understood and embraced in most of our churches. Here is how I understand God's Mind on these scriptures:

1. John 3-16"'s God did not give His Son to the entire world. Jesus' sacrifice was for the Father's world of the chosen.

2. The Father's soul bank contained souls of both the chosen and unchosen. All souls were inanimate.

3. The Father used faith as a qualification test to screen out chosen candidates whose free will violated or rejected the counsel of the Counselor. In effect, the Counselor judges your heart as to your suitability for the Fathers family. The Father didn't envision a cake walk for his chosen, as attested to by Jesus' martyrs through the centuries.

4. "Not by works? Created in Christ Jesus unto good works?" Read James Chapter 2 to understand that faith without works is dead. If the counsel of the Spirit doesn't result in good works, blasphemy occurs and erasure from the Book of Life follows.

5. The Father's mind regarding His creation was locked in from the beginning! The bible declares total sovereignty with absolute controls that enforce His will. To understand God's sovereignty, you must recognize that it is used to insure that all of His actions are designed to suit His Purpose and Glory.

UNDERSTAND THIS: The Father's mind focuses on nurturing chosen souls found worthy to achieve righteousness, through ransom of shed blood paid by an unblemished sacrifice. His salvation mind is found reflected in the bible for His chosen. His goal was to test His chosen willingness to reject Satan's promoting the desire of the flesh in favor of Spirit counsel yielding to the Father's will. The Father cleansed his Kingdom by getting rid of Satan. The will of heaven is the will of the

Father. This is why the Spirit decision for chosen access to the cross is based on work's righteousness trials. Your work's righteousness must clearly demonstrate a will in full submission to the Father will, to convert your work's righteousness to righteousness gaining access to the Father's Kingdom.

TUESDAY, 12/16/13 My sauna thoughts returned to the Trinity to compare parallel functions of man's trinity.

+ Jesus was begotten of His Father while man was born of parents.
+ The spirits of Jesus and man were introduced by the Father during conception.
+ Now the soul is interesting when linking Jesus' soul and man's soul. Here, I share my thoughts of how my Father could arrange the link. To me it makes sense to go back to the soul pool and link the soul and spirit to conception. When the seed was introduced, Jesus received seed from the Father and man from Adam. Jesus' soul was free from sin while Adam's soul was bound with sin that contaminated the seed of all of his descendants.

MORAL VALUES

One can easily conclude, from the malaise in the Spiritual fortitude of most church leaders, that they hold responsibility for the Spiritual and moral decay in the church and country. If you feel Jesus will not hold the church responsible for the attacks on a myriad of anti-Christian values, you need to understand that once Jesus paid our ransom on the cross, he returned to the Father to receive his glory and His commission as King of Kings and Lord of Lords. You are going to find yourself facing the "Righteous Jesus" that you have been trying to milk with your prayers for a blessing, without having "studied to prove yourself worthy!" Don't you understand that you are letting political correctness subdue your witness to the Father's greatest creation achievement - the soul of man. You can rationalize all you want, but you don't want to find yourself in opposition to a Sovereign Father, who does everything for His purpose and Glory. You have got to understand, if you are among the elect as a servant of God, you are responsible for your knowledge of God's truth. You will stand alone before the Great White Throne Judgment (GWTJ), if your works do not glorify the Father. No evangelist, pastor, bible teacher, or even pope will be available to blame. They are likely going to face the GWTJ for false teaching. The church better wake up to the real Jesus of the Trinity! You may need to be reminded, that following the cross, He was glorified and seated at the right hand of the Father:

+ He is on the throne as King of Kings and Lord of Lords.
+ He was given all power over creation!
+ He said he did not come to bring Peace but the Sword!
+ He came to divide the family.
+ He said that if you loved self, more than Him, you are not worthy of Him.
+ He asked that we pick up our cross and follow Him.
+ BEST ADVICE: Mat 6:33 "Seek ye first the kingdom of God and His righteousness."

This is the scripture the Father gave me during His first call and added that "I would never worry about my salvation." This scripture was my starting point for a Spirit walk to the cross and salvation. The only way to the cross is to seek righteousness by seeking Jesus under the counsel of the Spirit. If the counsel of the Spirit is not heeded and embraced, your access to the cross and salvation in Jesus will be denied.

+ Jesus is waiting on His Father's command to go and get His bride.
+ His return will be preceded by a half hour of silence to reflect on the beginning of the Great and Terrible Day of the Lord.
+ He will be accompanied by the hosts of Heaven as He dons His two edged sword as the Father's commander.
+ He will execute judgment from the Great White Throne on those whose names are not written in the Book of Life.

What the church needs now is more 'John the Baptists' to Prepare the Way of the Lord!" The more I get into the scriptures, the words "few will enter therein," talking about the narrow gate to salvation increasingly looms as a warning to the elect, that the faith walk to salvation is not a cake walk. Christian elect lay persons need to take their walk with the Spirit seriously. If you say you are a Christian and don't take the price paid for salvation seriously, don't feel a hunger and thirst for the righteousness, just play church without actively engaging the Spirit, then you are a prime candidate for erasure from the Book of Life.

Since my Fathers second call in November 2009, my concept of the Once Saved - Always Saved" doctrine reflects it to be a gift for the gullible from our enemy! Playing games with the scriptures, by cherry-picking those that give you a nice warm fuzzy feeling and setting aside those that require a living sacrifice, bespeaks of biblical illiteracy. In some cases, we find application of scripture in music, evangelism and bible studies to be offensive and self-serving. Sadly, we find our churches appear to be engaged in the feel good liberal and prosperity theology that tries to make the Trinity more acceptable to man. My biggest concern is that most churches in this country have given up the search for challenging TRUTH in favor of embracing doctrines of entitlement conjured up by man's intellect vs Spirit derived exegesis of scripture. I sometimes wonder about the number of FULL GOSPEL churches we have in this country. Most churches have turned inward to bless themselves while shying away from picking up the cross and following Jesus. Should you be concerned about the manhood of your Church? Are the elders happy with the status quo and languishing in the ignorance of their church's doctrines and creeds? If you are one of the Grace blessed elect, you are responsible for seeking God's kingdom and righteousness or face the erasure of your name from the Book of Life. Your salvation depends on being elected by the Father (GRACE), being born of the Spirit and maintaining the Spiritual condition of your heart during your faith walk to the cross. THE BIGGEST THREAT TO THE ELECT'S SALVATION WALK OF FAITH IS IGNORANCE OF GOD'S SPIRITUAL TRUTH. JOHN 8:32 "AND YOU SHALL KNOW THE TRUTH, AND THE TRUTH SHALL MAKE YOU FREE." If you accept unsound doctrines from your pastor or bible teacher, you are embracing an IGNORANCE OF GOD'S SPIRITUAL TRUTH that may result in erasure from the Book of Life. Remember, a faith walk yielding to the leadership of the Spirit is essential to gain cleansing from the shed blood of Jesus. Do you understand what election means? As an elect, you have been chosen of the Father and given the gift of Grace. When I consider the "narrow gate" and realize how unworthy I am as one of the Fathers elect, I feel a strong desire to seek and serve Him. There is nothing I can do to repay my Father for the gift of His Son but I can commit to honoring the Trinity in worship and deed. If an elect does not get engaged in MAT 6:33, "Seek ye first the Kingdom of God and His righteousness ...," they are mocking the Trinity's Spiritual walk of faith requirement for salvation, which can qualify as blasphemy - the sin that erases names from the Book of Life. Am I taking a harsh understanding of the Trinity? I think not! We need to get a whole lot of 'Lot' in us to understand the SOVEREIGNTY of the TRINITY! It is not a SUGAR DADDY OR A SWEET JESUS that just wants to be on our beck and call to cuddle us. Keep in mind that we are standing under the scrutiny and in the presence of THE POWER, GLORY AND MAJESTY OF SOVEREIGNTY. Maybe we need to remind ourselves that, as an elect, the Trinity resides within us and is well aware of our actions and thoughts. Who are we when we try to exercise our self-righteous indignation when questioning any action of a sovereign God? The answer is simple, God's truth is not in you and you live in a perceived environment of self- worth, demonstrating a lack of discernment resulting in a total loss of Spiritual acumen. If you are/were among the elect, you are now following a new spirit and coming out from under God's grace, by losing the counsel of the Spirit.

How does one know if he or she is among the elect! I shared my experience earlier when a pastor raised the question. I would like to share some other ideas with you. The first thought that comes to mind is James and his ideas on works righteousness. Up to my Father's December 2009 call, I believed the mantra that works are divorced from Grace. Earlier I introduced a new concept of Grace, wherein Grace is described as a special opportunity for God's elect to have access to the Spirit Counselor to be led into TRUTH; this is The Gift of Grace. At this point, we need to understand that the elect has not been denied free will. If free will is involved, then it becomes an issue of the submission of the will to the Spirit. The first test of the will occurs when the elect is offered an opportunity, to be a student of the Spirit by accessing the Spirit Gate. If this offer is refused, the Spirit is grieved and erases his name from the Book of Life. If the offer is accepted, then the elect is led by the Spirit into biblical Truth. Upon completion of his training, the Spirit examines the condition of the elect's heart and, if it has a hunger and thirst for righteousness, he or she will experience the new birth and given the OK to start his/her walk of Faith to the cross led by the Counselor. If the condition of the elect's heart fails the Spirit's examination, erasure from the Book of Life will terminate his or her walk with the Spirit.

You concur the elect are not any different than the non-elect in that both are given free will, experience comparable adversities in life; "it rains on the just and the unjust," but you as an elect "are in the world but no longer of the world." Here is where James' introduces the importance of works in your walk of faith. Consider:

+ EPH 2:8 "For by grace you have been saved through FAITH, and that not of yourselves: it is the gift of God."
+ JAS 2:20 "But do you want to know, O foolish man, that FAITH without works is dead.
+ JAS 2:26 "For as the body without the spirit is dead, so FAITH without works is dead also.
+ EPH 2:10 "For we are His workmanship, created in Christ Jesus unto good works, which God had before ordained that we should walk in them."
+ COL 1:10 "That we might walk worthy of the Lord unto all pleasing, being fruitful in every good work, and increasing in the knowledge of God."

So let's link GRACE, SPIRIT, FAITH and WORK to the ELECT's walk to the cross. A POINT OF CLARIFICATION: THERE TWO KINDS OF FAITH WE ARE DEALING WITH, THAT SEPARATES FAITH IN SELF AND FAITH IN GOD: John 3:16's Faith is added upon Spirit baptism, to provide Spirit counsel during the Father's prepared chastisement, to test your worthiness.

GRACE provides the elect with access to the SPIRIT. The SPIRIT provides counseling and instruction on biblical truth, followed by examining the condition of the elect's heart for the NEW BIRTH, which opens the door to FAITH. At this point, the student has graduated to a faith walk with the Spirit. Failure to get the new birth results in erasure from the Book of Life. But the New Birth does not guarantee completing the salvation journey. You are still in the world and exposed, not only to the world's trials and tribulations, but also to false doctrines espoused by pastors and teachers in many churches. You must understand that you are responsible for your faith walk to salvation. I would strongly recommend a counselor for your faith walk who was recommended by Jesus, who told His disciples, "It is important that I go to be with the Father, so that He would send the Comforter, the Holy Spirit WHO WOULD LEAD YOU INTO ALL TRUTH!" BEING A VESSEL OF THE HOLY SPIRIT IS THE KEY TO COMPLETING YOUR FAITH WALK TO THE CROSS. If you yield to a false exegesis promoted by a pastor, teacher, up to including the pope, you are removing yourself as a vessel of the Spirit, which blasphemes the Spirit (the un-pardonable sin) - leading to erasure form the Book of Life.

I am sure that many will raise the issue of "everyone is given a measure of faith." The question then becomes "Who is everyone and what kind of faith?" Starting with JOHN 3:16, I could never accept the premise that "World" meant "EVERONE," even before I experienced the new birth. This was confirmed after my encounter with the Father in December 2009, when He told me to get into the Word because I couldn't preach the Truth if I didn't know the Truth. Subsequently, the Word came alive and showed me that the "world" of JOHN 3:16 is the "elect." The question then becomes who among the elect is given "a measure of faith?" It is my judgment that a chosen's faith enters with the "new birth." This would place all of the elect accessing the Spirit Gate on equal footing during Spirit training on biblical truth, leading to the conditioning of the heart based on exposure to truth. The Spirit then examines the condition of each student's heart to select those that qualify for the new birth and the Spirit led walk to the cross. Since these new born-again elect continue to retain free will, their victory in Christ still requires a FAITH WALK LED BY AND UNDER THE COUNSEL OF THE SPIRIT.

Now let's consider the role of works! James tell us faith without works is dead. Ephesians tells us that we are created in Christ Jesus unto good works, which God had before ordained that we should walk in them. Colossians tells us that we might walk worthy of the Lord unto all pleasing, being fruitful in every good work and increasing in the knowledge of God. Faith and Works walk hand in hand along the path from the New Birth to the cross. It is important to understand that only works performed under the counsel of the Spirit can demonstrate faith that pleases the Father.

How does one know if they are among the elect? In 1974, the Father gave me Mat 6:33, Seek ye first the Kingdom of God and His righteousness ..., and told me I would never worry about my salvation. For 35 years of nursing home weekly ministry, "election" was not in my spiritual lexicon. Then in 2009, the Father told me I needed to get in the bible, while admonishing me with "You can't preach truth if you do not know the truth." All of a sudden, the bible came alive and as I studied the Word, I came to realize the significance of the role of the Holy Spirit as the source for Spiritual exegesis to open up truth of God's Word. UNDERSTAND, IT IS THE ROLE OF THE HOLY SPIRIT TO CONTROL YOUR WALK FROM THE GATE TO THE CROSS. GAINING ACCESS TO AND INSURING YOUR FAITH WALK IS CONDITIONED ON YOUR SUBMISSION AS A VESSEL OF THE HOLY SPIRIT. If an elect withdraws from the counsel of the Spirit, it is an affront (blasphemy) that results in removal from the Book of Life. Do your pastor and church officers promote a spiritual growth atmosphere that stimulates a growth of hunger and thirst for righteousness and service? Do you know or understand the doctrines of your church? Is your salvation based on prosperity or service theology? Can you discern spiritual truth coming from the pulpit, teachers, Christian publications or friends? The quandary facing church members, regardless of denomination, requires Christian discernment. Your church, denomination, pastor and teacher need to be challenged on truth! You need to be in a position of having developed as a "vessel" relationship with the Holy Spirit to gain Spiritual discernment.

In this book, I will be sharing my effort to do what my Father admonished me to do: "Study to know the truth!"

A DISCUSSION WITH A PASTOR.

It was a blessing to talk to a pastor who is hung up on Jesus with an attitude of blessing and serving. I told him of my background and that I believed the Father had called me to search the scriptures to know the TRUTH and to share the truths the Spirit reveals. I expressed my positions on several issues:

1. Isaiah 53: I expressed the opinion that "Pleading the blood of Jesus" should be limited to prayers for the soul and salvation. While he didn't argue against my position, he didn't express verbal support!

2. John 3:16: I told the pastor that I believed this verse was reserved for God's elect. He responded with the common verses used to support "everyone" and asked the question "How do you determine who is among the ELECT? I told him the Father told me in 1974 I would never worry about my salvation. It was 35 years later, when introduced to the ELECT of the scriptures, that I made the connection to the Father's 1974 words on salvation. I suggested that if lay persons were introduced to election as a personal issue to examine, only those LED BY THE SPIRIT would be motivated to seek "God's Kingdom and Righteousness" and desire to activate the gift of Grace that was theirs from the beginning.

3. A discussion ensued on the role of Jesus and the Spirit during new testament times. It was my position that it was the Spirit that controlled the elect's faith walk to the cross. The discussion was interesting and informative with the Pastor providing many supporting scriptures (as he understood them) and, as I was driving home recalling the Pastors arguments, I began to feel the pastor's arguments sounded good. However, after some thought, I concluded, he was selling the idea that it is Jesus telling the Spirit what to do, that I was not supporting the Spirit during the salvation process and that I was an ambassador of Christ. Considering his

church motto "Not I, But Christ," I can understand his focus on Christ! I woke up at 3:00 AM the following morning thinking about this issue. I asked the Spirit, if I was out in left field with my understanding of the role of the Spirit. I was pointed to the word TRUTH and it's meaning in scripture. JESUS, WORD and TRUTH are synonymous. A quick scriptural survey revealed the following scriptures providing food for thought on the role of the Holy Spirit:

1. ROM 8:14 "For as many as are led by the Spirit of God these are the sons of God."
2. GAL 5:18 "But if you are led by the spirit, you are not under the law."
3. JOHN 4:23 "But the hour is coming, and now is, when the true worshipers will worship the Father in Spirit and truth."
4. JOHN 4:24 God is SPIRIT, and those who worship HIM, must worship in spirit and truth.
5. JOHN 6:63 "It is the SPIRIT who gives life; the flesh profits nothing."
6. Romans 8:11 "But if the SPIRIT of HIM who raised JESUS from the dead dwells in you, HE who raised CHRIST from the dead will also give life to your mortal bodies through HIS SPIRIT who dwells in you."
7. JOHN 14:17 "even the SPIRIT of TRUTH, whom the world cannot receive, because it seeth Him not: neither knoweth Him; but ye know Him; for He dwelleth with you, and shall be in you."
8. JOHN 15:26 "But when the helper comes, whom I shall send to you from the Father, the Spirit of TRUTH who proceeds from the Father. He will testify of me."
9. JOHN 16:13 "However, when He, the Spirit of TRUTH has come, He will guide you into all TRUTH."
10. 1 COR 2:10 "For the SPIRIT searches all things, yes, the deep things of God."

I would like to step back and start with the Trinity's "In the beginning" and share my thoughts. I concur that the Trinity contains three separate persons with "Majesty Coequal." I believe that the Trinity has the Spiritual unity of a Perfect Glorified God Family. As a family, the bible provides three distinct persons with clear responsibilities for projects. However, I "feel" that creation was a unity of Spirit project - a Trinity effort defined as the Father, Savior and Counselor functions. Considering the salvation Project, it appears that the Father selected candidates for His Grace program; Jesus provided the sin sacrifice and ruled the world following His resurrection; and the Holy Spirit nurtured the elect from the gate to the cross. They all agreed that the perfect sacrifice would have to be without blemish and that narrowed the search to the Trinity. The Father must have been blessed by Abraham's willingness to sacrifice his son as a sin offering testament to the Father's sovereignty. I believe one can speculate that one man's total submission to the Father, blessed the Trinity's selection of another Son as the only acceptable sin offering, to set the stage for GRACE. We need to keep in mind the distinction between Abraham's offering and the Trinity's offering; one was blemished with sin and one was without blemish. Abraham's obedience in offering his son as a sacrifice set the gold standard for serving and blessing the sovereignty of the Trinity. The crucifixion was the greatest gift the Trinity could offer man. It was then agreed, that upon Jesus return to Glory after the Cross, the Holy Spirit would be sent as a Comforter and truth teacher to manage the Father's Grace program for the elect's trip from access through the "Narrow Gate," to the cross and salvation. However, we must keep in mind that Jesus was given all power and authority over creation after being seated at the right hand of the Father. He is the one who prepares the environment for the minds and spirits of the elect and non-elect passing by the narrow gate. Those, of the elect, who are drawn by the Holy Spirit, will pass through the gate and be counseled and led into the truth of God's Word as a gift of GRACE from the Father. Considering the price paid, I don't believe "Once saved, always saved," can be called a rational or legitimate option, for guaranteeing completion of the faith walk to the cross. The elect were given free will, causing some to fall by the wayside and be erased from the Book of Life. Maybe we need to look at GRACE as a gift of a Spirit walk to the cross, based on one's responsiveness to the Spirit! It is the very special

Grace gift of John 3:16 that provides the Spirit as your counselor and the purveyor of truth that leads to life. Refusing the counsel of the Spirit allows false doctrine to engage your spirit, and disengages the Spirit needed to assist and insure your completion of the faith walk. Grace's victories are measured by the number of elect members joining the family of believers, who are higher than the Angel family but lower than the Trinity family.

I believe this simplistic division of salvation responsibilities was set up in the beginning by a unity of majesty coequal, which means all three maintain their unity as each member performs individual responsibilities. Except for Jesus' role as savior, this unity is fully engaged as a family unit while performing separate leadership or support responsibilities. The unity of the Trinity is also found in the elect.

This brings us to the issue as to whether Jesus was divine while on earth. Believing the Trinity lives within the hearts of the elect, one can argue that the Trinity should reside in Jesus as True Man, as it would reside in the elect after Jesus' glorification. How do we define "True Man?" Can we conclude that a man, like Jesus, is divine because the Trinity lives within us? NO!! Can Jesus be divine as true man apart from the trinity within? NO! Can we say a "divine" Jesus could not sin? YES! If so, can we say that there is no equitable comparison between a "Divine True Man" and a "True Man?" YES! One can argue that the unity of the Divine Trinity must be maintained. But Jesus would have to divest Himself of His divinity to assume the role as True Man like the true man of the elect.

Scripture suggests that the playing field between Jesus, as True Man, and man is much harsher toward Jesus. It appears that Jesus' lineage is what separates us from Him. Abraham provided the seed for the mother of Jesus, while the Father provided the seed for Jesus to usher in the perfect sacrificial lamb. Dictionary definitions of divine include: relating to or proceeding directly from God, a god, supremely good, clergymen and theologian. This an exciting issue for further study. As a man, who has been developing a servant relationship with my Father, I don't believe He plays games with his Word as many dispensationalists do. When Jesus is described as True Man, He was subject to the will of the Father like any man: "Let thy will and not my will be done." While He entered man's world without sin, He was subject to all of the strife and temptations of man! When He performed miracles, He spoke what was revealed by the Father. In effect, Jesus shed His divinity, walked as a man along a path more challenging than any man had walked, to show you the price the Trinity was willing to pay for a sacrifice WE DO NOT DESERVE. HE SUFFERED AND DIED FOR OUR SINS! To suggest in any way that Jesus had a "divine crutch" on His walk to the cross is ludicrous! It degrades the act of GRACE by a sovereign God, who provided a suffering servant to cover the sins of the elect, that they could become children of God. The Father could not even look at His Son on the cross. Also, if one considers the unity of the Trinity, one can conjecture that what Jesus experienced on the cross was felt by each member of the Trinity. THE TRINITY DOES NOT PLAY GAMES!! If you mess around by denigrating the sovereignty of the Trinity you will be, putting it in the vernacular, stepping in enough "dung" to guarantee erasure from the Book of Life!" One final thought, when Jesus walked among us, He said there is none righteous, no, not one, ONLY the Father in heaven. He was including Himself, which begs the question: "Can one be unrighteous and divine at the same time?" I think not!

The question is "Did He divest Himself of His divinity" when He became True Man? I believe Jesus forsook His divinity and came to earth as one without sin, performing as a suffering servant obedient to the Father. I believe the divinity of Jesus remained with the Trinity, while he provided an avenue to salvation as True Man. The pastor and I did not agree on the issue of Jesus' divinity as True Man.

A LATER INSERT: I was musing over the divinity issue when several thoughts came to my spirit that favor True Man over a Divine True Man. Consider:

1. Can divinity be crucified?
2. What was special about Jesus? We say He was without sin! But there was another True Man that was without sin in the beginning. He was called Adam! Jesus is referred to as the second Adam. But the first Adam sinned and the second Adam did not!

3. The final issue that came to mind was the soul. Was Jesus provided a soul from the Father's inventory? Does Divinity have a soul? What is the purpose/function of a soul! I will share some thoughts now but it is an issue for serious consideration, if we are to round out our understanding of "True Man."

It is interesting to NOTE the significant activities of the Spirit: Mary's conception, Jesus resurrection, narrow gate keeper identifying and granting entrance to the Father's Grace program, counseling and teaching the grace candidates on biblical truth, examination of their hearts to determine qualification for the new birth and providing guidance and counseling during the FAITH walk to the cross.

Consider ROM 8:11 "But if the Spirit of Him who raised Jesus from the dead dwells in you, He who raised Christ from the dead will also give life to your mortal bodies through His Spirit who dwells in you. Now let's examine the word 'Life.' In my NOTE on significant activities of the Spirit, I am saying the Spirit is your grace life line to the cross. I am firmly convinced that 'free will' is the greatest enemy to your 'Life Walk' to the cross. When I cited activities that could result in erasure from the Book of Life, they were actions you took to draw away from the leading and counsel of the Spirit, which resulted in the Spirit cutting your 'Lifeline.' John 4:23: 'But the hour is coming, and now is when the true worshipers will worship the Father in Spirit and truth." Without the Spirit, your worship of the Father is to no avail since we must worship in Spirit and truth. In fact, you can only serve God while a vessel controlled by the Spirit! KEEP IN MIND THAT YOUR SPIRIT IS BEING COUNSELED BY TWO COMPETING SPIRITS, ONE IS SATANIC AND OTHER IS HOLY.

Being of Finnish heritage, I built a sauna in my home, which I frequent several times a week. It provides me a special place to share my thoughts and receive feedback from the Spirit. Recently, I was talking about His role in the exegesis process. I was thinking about the role of hermeneutics in proper exegesis.

John14:6 "Jesus said to him. 'I am the way, the truth, and the life.'"

John 1:17 "For the law was given through Moses but grace and truth came through Jesus Christ."

John 8:32 "And you shall know the truth, and the truth shall make you free."

Truth is inexorably linked to Life and Jesus, which clearly establishes that knowledge of biblical truth is the search cornerstone for salvation. The church has to understand that preaching and teaching false doctrines is an affront to the Spirit and threatens the salvation of members. Salvation is not the piece of cake offered by a church misunderstanding of "world" in John 3:16. This misunderstanding was promulgated by a sweet Jesus, prosperity theology which was supported and introduced into the USA, as Dispensational Theology (Darby's New Wine) in circa 1830. It was a theology that embraced a future pre-tribulation rapture of the church and premillennialism. In my opinion, this theology appears to define their name by application of dispensations to twist the exegesis of scripture to fit their intellectual (not Spirit led) hermeneutics. From what I also understand, some 80 % of our Christian churches embrace most or all of this doctrine. I understand there is currently a shift away from dispensationalism as a viable doctrine. I go back to the bottom line, you are responsible for your salvation. In any case, there is no access to truth other than through the Spirit and you can't separate Jesus from truth.

How can I have such a caustic view of the church? My theological exposure up until the Father's call in the Fall of 1974 was one of going with the flow of normal church membership; going to church and Sunday school; serving on church councils and teaching Sunday school classes; neighborhood witness activities; and last but not least, pot lucks and fellowship. I experienced a lot of Sweet Jesus, Praise the Lord and hallelujah shouts to conjure up an intervention of the Holy Spirit, that focuses on receiving a perceived "rightful blessing" and putting aside serving God.

I attended a men's breakfast meeting that included a presentation by a Gideon member. He talked about their efforts to get the scriptures to multiple tribes all over the world, who never heard of Jesus or saw a bible. I recalled the end time condition that ushers in Jesus' return, the need for the Word to be available to the entire world. Then I was convicted with the significance of getting the Word out to the world in all of the differing languages. The role of the missionary is to get the Word to the world whether written or spoken. What really excites me is linking a native with a bible in his language being led by the teacher God sent, the Spirit. He will be exposed to only one version of the truth provided by God Himself. He won't be presented with a Heinz 57 variety of doctrines and truths from which we can select a path to salvation. He would be locked into truth (exegesis) by the SPIRIT, without distractions.

8-19-2012: I was blessed by this morning's Sunday school class which discussed the book of Ruth. It is exciting how the Spirit can add new insight to issues for which you are seeking resolutions. Since I believe only the elect are under God's grace, I have been having problems dealing with how grace and elect are handled in the Old Testament. The Holy Spirit focused my attention on Ruth and the Spirit began introducing thoughts that were revealed in Ruth:

1. On the surface, not being of Abraham's seed, Ruth was not covered by the Abrahamic covenant.
2. She was a pillar of humility, obedience and love.
3. She was exposed to and likely receptive of the Jewish God and willing to accept Him as her God.
4. From Ruth's portrayal in the scriptures, the condition of her heart was one to emulate.

I believe that Abraham, Isaac, and Jacob were chosen of God (elect) and Ruth was granted a special dispensation by the Trinity that suggests being chosen as one of God's (elect). She was special because of her servant attitude, love and courage qualities that suggest a strong Spirit relationship. It is worth one's time and effort to fully understand the qualities of a servant of God. As an elect believer, the question is raised as to who is and is not eligible for God's GRACE consideration. I have no problem with God cherry picking grace candidates on a random basis. Bottom line: Since we don't know the location of all elect, we can't exclude anyone from the Great Commission consideration.

You don't hear much about a personal Holy Spirit in the Old Testament while the New Testament requires a Spiritual rebirth as the starting point of a faith walk to the cross. The Spirit examines the Heart of a rebirth candidate before granting the faith needed to walk with the Spirit to the cross. It is easy to accept, given the condition of Ruth's heart, that she was an exemplary candidate for Grace's Spirit journey, resulting in being counted worthy to share in the salvation provided by a promised Savior.

The thought of Old Testament "rebirth" is a new idea for me. I like to think that my friend, the Spirit, grabbed my attention by suggesting I consider Ruth as one favored of God and how she fits into the Father's grace program. As I established above, the Father randomly selected His "elect" candidates. There are no soul qualifications! Following this line of thought means, we can postulate all will enter life at conception, unworthy under the sins of Adam; all will be given free will, but only the elect will be given a measure of Grace (A Grace Card) that opens the gate to the Holy Spirit. The Grace Card is not a "once saved, always saved" guarantee. Man's free will can be an anathema for attaining salvation, by failing to gain access to the narrow gate (the Spirit Gate); failing the screening of the heart; and proving one's self unworthy during the faith walk to the cross. I believe the Spirit walk of the elect is fully applicable to old and new testaments.

At this time, I am reconsidering my assertions of the Father's random selection of the elect. I will address this issue in depth later.

Contrast this with my earlier comments on the impact of the Gideon's worldwide missionary effort to provide bibles in native tongues. I can still remember the excitement I felt when I fully realized it's impact on the great commission. I was particularly excited about the special opportunity presented to the Spirit, to be the only teacher available to many tribes.

Since the Guideons provide the Word only, tribes were blessed to be counseled and led into all truth by the trinity's divine counselor - the Holy Spirit. While I feel a slight touch of envy of the tribes, I am excited at the total control God has over His creation even to the point of providing a Spirit counselor to bible-only tribes all over the world. Think of it, the Trinity provided the Spirit as a substitute for the shortage of missionary teachers. This action by the Trinity briefly engenders a fleeting thought of jealousy over a special group having THE TEACHER opening up the Jesus of the bible, followed by feeling of the awesomeness of our Trinity. However, the thought comes to mind of the need for our seminaries to be filled with Spirit controlled faculty, teaching Spirit led exegesis rather than exegesis generated by the intellect of one's mind. We need to keep in mind that the only access to Jesus and salvation is through the Spirit. It takes time and effort to fully learn, understand and embrace the qualities of a true servant of God. THE KEY is the Holy Spirit.

As I was finishing the last paragraph, the Spirit reminded me that as a chosen, my truth comes from Him directly. I, too, receive my counsel/ teaching directly from the Spirit. FLASH: THE FATHER SENT HIS COUNSELOR TO HIS CHOSEN ON A PERSONAL SPIRIT TO SPIRIT BASIS. IT HAS TO BE A PART OF HIS SALVATION PLAN TO LIMIT SPIRIT COUNSEL ACCESS TO HIS CHOSEN. It suggests the following Father actions:

+ He sends Satan to chastise the church by offering counsel to control intellect application of hermeneutics generating false exegesis for their doctrines. This intellect led exegesis supports prosperity theology based on dispensationalism which feeds the desires of the flesh to increase membership, fill the coffers, while withholding truth that may be denying some members the truth that reveals their chosen status. TALK ABOUT UNPARDENABLE SINS!

+ He uses the false teachings of Satan as a screening test of the chosen's response to Satanic counsel feeding the flesh while being under Spirit counsel during Father ordained works when being chastised by Satan. IT IS A BATTLE OF THE FLESH

AGAINST THE SPIRIT. Satan seems to being well but we know his success is within the will of the Father's Plan.

+ The last screening of His chosen will likely occur late in the tribulation period, when the last chosen will qualify to access the cross. I believe the Father is preparing a later day John the Baptist's legion of the Father's chosen, to replicate John's effort to 'prepare ye the way of the Lord' for the second coming. It is going to be something to behold multitudes of Spirit trained chosen, putting on the full armor of God, to announce the return of the King of Kings and Lord of Lords. Think of it! Multitudes of John the Baptists, in full spiritual armor; shouting out the approaching of Jesus' victorious second coming. I also believe the Father has selected a large number, similar to the number in the tribulation period of the first return, of martyrs to glorify the Father and the Son. Most people don't realize that church martyrdom has continued through church history to today. While all chosen are called to present ourselves as living sacrifices, the Father has preselected the chosen for martyrdom. The Father has preordained who among the chosen will be honored with martyrdom.

An elect lay person MUST UNDERSTAND that their pursuit of salvation MUST begin with the SPIRIT! You can study the bible, listen to sermons, attend bible classes, tithe, pray daily, join a congregation and praise God all day, to no avail. You MUST UNDERSTAND that any "Christian" action you undertake, any exposure you have to the scriptures, any praises to the Trinity you offer, any tithe you give and prayer you offer is unacceptable to the God unless you comply with Romans 12:1 "I beseech you therefore, brethren, by the mercies of God, THAT YOU PRESENT YOUR BODIES A LIVING SACRIFICE, HOLY, ACCEPTABLE TO GOD, WHICH IS YOUR REASONABLE SERVICE." This scripture should take your breath away, if it is understood completely and correctly! How does a layperson fulfill this directive? The only option is through offering our bodies as a living sacrifice, under spiritual counsel and control of the Holy Spirit. Your spirit has to be under the control of the Spirit for any action you initiate to be HOLY and ACCEPTABLE to GOD. Now recognize that this is "YOUR REASONABLE SERVICE!" Unless you, as a layperson and one of the elect, offer him/her-self as a living sacrifice under control of the Spirit, you are denying yourself access to the Counselor and the Spirit of truth. Denying truth is denying Jesus and salvation. Keep in mind that even an "elect" has a free will exposed to false teaching on TV, from the pulpit, bible studies and church members. The "TRUTH" provided by the Spirit allows you to discern the veracity of exegesis coming from evangelists, pastors, bible teachers up to and including the pope. Let's recall Isaiah 29:13 again:

"Wherefore the Lord said, Forasmuch as their people draw near to me with their mouth, and with their lips do honor me, but have removed their heart far from me, and their fear toward me is taught by the precept of men."

The Father is not interested in lip service but desires a living sacrifice of service that blesses His purpose and glory. The Father honored the sacrifices of His martyrs with the sacrifice of His Son. We have no justification for not complying with Romans 12:1 requiring a living sacrifice as a reasonable service. Jesus' disciples set the sacrifice example for modern day disciples to emulate but, except for most missionaries and their converts, they shutter at the idea of any suffering for Christ. I am greatly concerned that the church in America is on life support because it has ignored the counsel of Romans 12:1 on living sacrifice! The Christian church's greatest need is for a unified doctrine of truth based on Spirit led exegesis. To achieve this goal, the church would need to identify true compliers to Romans 12:1, regardless of educational training. Only Spirit led exegesis provides truth. It is my considered opinion that the greatest obstacle to Spirit led exegesis of scripture is the bloated ego of the flesh led intellect assigned to develop church doctrine and creeds. I believe it is common practice for the intellect's performance of hermeneutics to lack engagement of the Spirit, resulting in the intellect paying lip service to the Spirit. My belief is strongly evident in the myriad of church doctrines. We need students submissive to the Spirit to attain sound doctrine. The layperson needs to understand they are personally responsible for knowing the truth of scripture to gain salvation. Sweet Jesus and prosperity theology is a cancer to salvation by promoting false church doctrines riddled with false exegesis. Jesus is not a sweet sugar daddy but a King of Kings who exhorts us in

Matthew 16:24 "Then Jesus said to His disciples 'If any one desires to come after Me, let him deny himself, and take up his cross, and follow me.'" The church has to understand that to be a Christian is to be a disciple in a soul seeking search to share the Way, Truth, and Life known as JESUS!

I did not accept the idea of "ELECT" until my Father's visit in November 2009. While I consider the concept of the elect is crucial to a walk with the Spirit, it also requires total acceptance of the Father's sovereignty. I firmly believe that Spirit led exegesis of the new testament is impossible without embracing the special gift of Grace provided by the Father. The New Testament was the Trinity sharing the Father, Jesus, Spirit and Salvation to the church. Consider John 6: 64 - 6-66. (6:64) "But there are some of you that believe not. For Jesus knew FROM THE BEGINNING who they were that believe not, and who should betray Him." (6:65) "And He said. 'Therefore said I unto you, that no man can come unto me, except it was GIVEN UNTO HIM OF MY FATHER.'" (6:66) "From that time many of His disciples went back, and walked no more with Him." Consider:

1. Jesus knew from the "beginning" who were unbelievers! UNELECT
2. Jesus said only those given to Him by the Father could come to Him! ELECT
3. Even some of His disciples left Him. UNELECT
4. John 6:66 is interesting because it marks disengagement of the UNELECT.

What we have here is a clear example of the Father giving the elect/chosen to Jesus. John 6:66 divides the church on the basis of Jesus' teachings and leaves Him with 12 disciples.

Let's take a look at ELECT AND CHOSEN:

1. Mat 20:16 "So the last shall be first, and the first last: for many be called, but few are chosen."
2. Mat 24:22 "And except those days should be shortened, there should no flesh be saved: but for the elect's sake those days shall be shortened."

3. Col 3:12 "Put on therefore, as the ELECT OF GOD, holy and beloved, put on tender mercies, kindness, humbleness of mind, meekness."

Never underestimate the role of truth in your life. If you don't embrace the truth in God's Word, you have no part in Him; and, if you were an elect under grace, your name would be removed from the Book of Life. Truth was challenged by a "new wine" from England that introduced dispensational theology in the early 1600s embraced by some 80% of our churches.

The "world" of John 3:16 is limited to the elect/chosen of God. When Jesus was praying to His Father in the garden, He told the Father that He did not pray for the WORLD but only for those the Father had given Him. How about the "Narrow Gate" and the "Flood?" As a layman, I can only conclude that the exegesis of dispensational theology includes a caveat in established hermeneutics, that allows application of "dispensations," to change the exegesis of scripture, while pulling the teeth of biblical truth. Consider my assertion that the triad of Truth, Life, and Jesus are the cornerstone to salvation. It also has a major impact on the number completing the Spirit led walk from the Gate to the Cross and victory. Every church member should demand that their church doctrine be clearly explained, including any dispensational hermeneutics used to compare with main line conservative church doctrines, including this Record. Such a demand will not be well received and strongly resisted, but must be demanded!

I once told a Baptist preacher that I didn't think 15% of his membership knew the doctrine of his church and he agreed. It then becomes a personal issue, in which you accept the status quo or embrace Matthew 6:33 in actively seeking first God's kingdom and righteousness. It begins with truth! After 35 years of nursing home ministry, the Father told me to get into the Word and find the Truth. I believed the Father was charging me to search scriptures with the Spirit, wherein I would serve as a scribe recording what the Spirit reveals. This record/book was commissioned by my Father to provide a vehicle of truth for His chosen elect. This record provides a layman's walk with the Trinity, with emphasis on service as a scribe to record the Spirit Led exegesis/truth of biblical scriptures.

Up to this point in my ministry, I did not consider myself a spiritual Christian from the Fathers 1974 visit to His second visit in 2009. My desire to serve was based on realizing the awesomeness of a Father who expressed His love by allowing His Son to become a sacrificial lamb. I knew, based on righteousness, I deserved hell. I can remember many times, during this period, thinking that I could not fault the Father if He decided to withhold His grace, even though I was serving Him out of respect for His love expressed by the cross. The Father opened my eyes in 2009 when the Word came alive. I knew I was among God's elect and I understood my Father's 1974 words "You will never worry about your salvation!" I never did worry about my salvation because I focused on "unworthy" and was willing to wait on the Father's decision on grace. I guess I was caught up with the idea that there is nothing you can do for your salvation, that was being promoted by most churches. I now realize that as an elect of the Father, only praise, works and worship performed in concert with the Spirit, is acceptable to the Father. "We must worship in Spirit and Truth!" There is no doubt in my mind that the Trinity is real to me. I am fully engaged with the Father, the Son and the Spirit.

Note: Joan and I were sharing some scriptures when "righteousness" came up. We noted that Jesus said that there is none righteous, no, not one, only the Father in heaven and that we won't get to heaven, if our righteousness does not exceed the righteousness of the scribes and Pharisees and others. We are to hunger and thirst after righteousness! Elect sinners are not righteous, which leaves us with the Spirit within, that is holy. So we can come to the conclusion that He who is within us is holy/righteous and as we walk as a vessel under the control of the Spirit, our actions reflect a Spirit led righteousness. At this point, it is appropriate to consider three scriptures that clarify our "righteousness."

1. Matthew 6:33 "Seek ye first the kingdom of God and His RIGHTEOUSNESS …"

2. Romans 12:1 "I beseech you therefore, brethren, by the mercies of God, that you present your bodies a living sacrifice, holy, acceptable to God, which is your reasonable service."
3. Romans 3:10 "As it is written: There is none righteous, no, not one.'

We begin, by seeking God's righteousness and are told to present ourselves as a living sacrifice, holy and acceptable to God which is our REASONABLE SERVICE. Then the apostle Paul tells us that we are not righteous! When seeking God's righteousness, only one righteous option is accessible to us and that is Holy Spirit. So we are to seek the Holy Spirit. Since we are told that we are not righteous, we must back off and note that we are to SEEK righteousness. Now we can take the next step: we "seek" by becoming a "living sacrifice" that is acceptable to God. It becomes reasonable to conclude that it is the Spirit who needs to find us acceptable. All that remains to be tied down is the "living sacrifice and reasonable service."

THIS IS WHERE THE RUBBER MEETS THE ROAD. FAILURE TO HONOR THIS TRINITY REQUEST IS TO SAY 'NO' TO THE SPIRIT. DENYING THE SPIRIT IS TO DENY THE TRINITY. THIS REQUEST IS CONSIDERED TO BE "OUR REASONABLE SERVICE."

The "living sacrifice" is a "vessel" controlled by the Spirit, wherein we offer total commitment to service controlled by the Spirit. Keep in mind that the only way the Father will receive your efforts to serve is through Spirit concurrence. If your efforts do not glorify the Father, it means you refused or failed Spirit counsel by not laying up treasures in heaven that glorify the Father.

"REASONBLE SERVICE": As I begin to consider the issue of "reasonable," I am struck with the magnitude and complexity of this issue. It impacts one of the greatest, if not the greatest, concern among Christians. Through 35 years of ministry with old folks in nursing homes, I have witnessed very little excitement of Jesus or confidence in individual salvation. Through the years, my view of the organized church worsened as I became more disenchanted with the quality of messages and the focus on prosperity theology. I recalled my Father's December 2009 words which were etched in my spirit, after He provided a replacement for my nursing home ministry saying, "You can't preach the truth if you do not know the truth!" After exposure to 50 years of church membership, including 35 years of nursing home ministry, my Father tells me I don't know beans! Thanks to my exposure to a myriad of false doctrine containing false exegesis, my Father intervenes by telling me I need to study the "truth," with the implicit implication that I needed the counselor/Holy Spirit to get into the truth of scripture. When I say "implicit," I am acknowledging the existence of pseudo purveyors of confusing exegesis coming from pastors, bible teachers, and evangelists up the Pope, that narrows my truth purveyor options to the Holy Spirit. In any case, I immediately understood that I was to search the scriptures as a vessel scribe of the Spirit.

The dilemma that faces the church today is ignorance of the individual roles of each member of the Trinity. Shortly after my December 2009 encounter, I sought the Father on His role as member of the Trinity and what my spirit sensed was the idea of "FAMILY." I was left with the idea that my Father WANTS a family!!! What the church wants to accept is a "sugar daddy," demonstrated in a "name and claim" prosperity, which reduces the Father to a servant of man, who just can't wait to bless anyone who asks for a blessing "In Jesus name." Yes, the Father wants a family to share His creation but His Word clearly shows that man embraced sin from the beginning in the garden. We need to recognize that the seed of Adam provided a legacy of sin that condemns mankind to separation from God. This kind of separation continues today. The Father knew from the beginning that free will would condemn man to sin. I marvel at the ease with which Satan tempted man's ego by simply suggesting that he could be like God. The fall of man was permitted under the Father's Will.

However, God's LOVE accepts only children, chosen under His grace, that fully accept His sovereignty and the full counsel of His Word. If you, as a grace member of the elect exercise your free will without constraint, you have not presented yourself as a "living sacrifice" under the counsel of the Spirit, i.e., you are not a qualified grace candidate for salvation and a future child of the Father.

Members are comfortably sitting in their churches having little or no understanding of the doctrinal truth being taught. Recall my earlier comment wherein a pastor agreed with me, when I said that I doubted that more than15 percent of his members were familiar with his church doctrine.

Pastors and all Christian teachers are charged to be truth leaders. They are responsible for preaching "truth," but most church members are ill-equipped in spiritual discernment to ascertain the exegesis of preached/taught scriptures. Add to this the fact that there are hundreds of denominations in this country with differing doctrines. As I suggested earlier, doctrines for the most part, are based on "intellect led" exegesis and not Spirit led exegesis. I believe the church's obvious abuse of exegesis is the reason I and other chosen are/will be commissioned for end times service under Jesus' Great commission.

The current organized church is not the church "Victorious" but sorely needs life support in Gods "ICU UNIT." It needs a good dose of God's truth to set the captive free.

Recently I listened to a sermon on 1 JOHN 4:1- 6 and as I listened my spirit was quickened to take a different approach that focused on the need to recognize we are dealing with competing spirits that can be "a clear and present danger" to our Spiritual health. I hasten to add, that the sermon was excellent, focusing a real and manifest desire to serve and please God. What quickened my spirit is the battle between the Holy Spirit and the spirit of the Antichrist. So I want to focus on the first two verses.

John opens Chapter 4:1 with "Beloved, believe not every spirit, but try the spirits whether they are of God: because many false prophets are gone out into the world." Then John provides a way to test the spirit in verse 2 "Hereby know ye the Spirit of God; Every spirit that confesseth that Jesus Christ is come in the flesh is of God." While John is warning us about false prophets, we must understand that being fore warned does not guarantee being fore armed. YOU CAN'T BE FORE ARMED, IF GOD'S TRUTH IS NOT IN YOU. Many self-proclaimed false prophets, evangelists and pastors are preaching a sweet, feel good prosperity theology in concert with the false doctrines, generated by intellectual exegesis. Since scripture states that it is truth that sets the captive free, an elect should understand that discernment of truth requires knowledge of truth. It would be easy to argue that many, if not most church members have only the most rudimentary acquaintance with Spiritual Exegesis, which requires being led by the Spirit into biblical truth. To many church members rest their salvation hopes on "Come to Jesus" invitations from the pulpit or through evangelistic invitations. This salvation approach completely ignores or puts down the functional role of the Spirit, who shares majesty coequal with the Father and the Son. YOUR ONLY ACCESS TO SALVATION IS THROUGH THE HOLY SPIRIT. Remember what Jesus told His disciples:

> John 15:26 "But the comforter, which is the Holy Ghost, whom the Father will send in my name, He shall teach you all things, and bring all things to your remembrance, whatsoever I have said to you."

> John 16:7 "Nevertheless I tell you the truth; It is expedient for you that I go away: for if I do not go away, the Comforter will not come unto you; but if I depart, I will send Him unto you."

> John 17:13 "Howbeit when He, the Spirit of TRUTH, is come, He will guide you into all TRUTH: for He shall not speak of Himself; but whatsoever He shall hear, that He will speak: and he will show you things to come."

The Spirit counsels the elect from the narrow gate with Spirit counsel, Spirit Baptism, the walk with the Spirit to the cross and for sin cleansing by Jesus. The Spirit was provided to guide and counsel the elect's walk, burdened with "free will," through a minefield of false teachings of doctrines alien to the bible. Consider John 8:32 "And you shall know the truth and the truth shall set you free." and John 14:6 "Jesus said to him, I am the way the TRUTH and the life. No one comes to the Father except through me."

We can now conclude that the WORD = JESUS = TRUTH and we are led into TRUTH by the SPIRIT. Now, if we are to test the spirits encountered in our lives as to whether they confess "Jesus Christ is come in the flesh is of God," testing can only be accomplished through the Spiritual gift of DISCERNMENT, wherein your spirit testing is done through your interaction with the Holy Spirit. We are dealing in the spiritual realm wherein the Spirit reveals the spirits of the Antichrist. It is only the elect; who can offer themselves as a living sacrifice, to appropriate Spiritual powers to identify and defeat the Antichrist's revelations that abound.

Consider John 4:2 "Hereby know ye the Spirit of God; That every spirit that confesseth Jesus Christ is come in the flesh is of God." and I COR 12:3 "Wherefore I give you to understand, that no man speaking by the Spirit of God calleth Jesus accursed; and that no man can say the Jesus is the Lord, but by the Holy Ghost." As I was looking at these two scriptures, my spirit was quickened to understanding by the Spirit that the speaker/confessor was either the Holy Spirit or the spirit of the Antichrist. Then the question becomes "Can a spirit by itself, or led by the spirit of the Antichrist confess Jesus is Lord?" We need to understand to whom these scriptures are addressed and who can apply the guidance contained therein. Here we need to step back and note the role of the Holy Spirit in these scriptures. Discernment is a Holy Spirit gift available only to the Spirit led elect. So when an elect appropriates the gift of Spiritual Discernment, to examine another's spirit guidance, as to whether it is coming from the Holy Spirit or the spirit of the Antichrist, he can apply the tests of JN 4:2 and I COR 12:3. If the spirit is not the Holy Spirit but the spirit of the Antichrist, he will not acknowledge Jesus is Lord or that He came in the flesh and is of God.

In a call from a church bible class member, I was told that several members of the class asked, based on my comments in class, if I believed Jesus was divine while on earth. I responded that I didn't believe Jesus could be true man and divine at the same time because a true man would not be on equal footing with a divine Christ. It raises the question of Jesus' ability to sin. Could a divine Jesus sin? If not, then Jesus' being tempted in the wilderness provides a scenario wherein satin was dealing with divinity.

Accepting Jesus' divinity puts a sin wall between Jesus and sin while true man is not protected from sin. If we accept this sin wall exists, then we are saying that Jesus' sacrifice needed a crutch to overcome sin and the wilderness experience with Satan. Can anyone see even a hint of divinity in ISA 53's description of Jesus.

> ISA 53:2 "For he shall grow up before him as a tender plant, and as a root out of dry ground: he had no form or comeliness; and when we shall see him, there is no beauty that we should desire him."

> ISA 53:3 "He is despised and rejected of men; a man of sorrows, acquainted with grief: and we hid as it were our faces from him; he was despised, and we esteemed him not."

> ISA 53:4 "Surely he hath borne our griefs, and carried our sorrows: yet we did esteem him stricken, smitten of God, and afflicted."

> ISA 53:5 "But he was wounded for our transgressions, he was bruised for our iniquities: the chastisement of our peace was upon him; and with his stripes we are healed."

> ISA 53:10 "YET IT PLEASED THE LORD TO BRUISE HIM; he hath put him to grief: when thou shalt make his soul an offering for sin, he shall see his seed, he shall prolong his days, and the pleasure of the Lord shall prosper in his hand."

> ISA 53:11 "He shall see the travail of his soul, and shall be satisfied: by his knowledge shall my righteous servant justify MANY; for he shall bear their iniquities."

> ISA 53:12 "Therefore will I divide him a portion with the great, and he shall divide the spoil WITH THE STRONG; because he hath poured out his soul unto death: AND HE WAS NUMBERED WITH THE TRANSGRESSORS;

AND HE BARE THE SIN OF MANY, AND MADE
INTERCESSION FOR THE TRANSGRESSORS."

ISA 53 provides the most graphic description of the depth of the Father's love, in allowing Satan to buffet Jesus during his ministry all the way to a horrible death on the cross. How can one degrade the Father's greatest act of love, by saying Jesus was a true man who couldn't sin because of his divine nature. If we define "true man" as having the same attributes as Jesus, we must conclude we would possess the attribute of divinity, which of course is incredulous. So it is reasonable to accept Jesus as true man who did not possess the added attribute of divinity. If we consider the sinful seed of Abraham, we know it was passed on to the mother of Jesus. To preclude Abraham's sinful seed being passed on through Mary, the Father sent the Spirit to Provide a sinless seed. The focus of the Father's action was to provide a sinless sacrifice. I have not found any scripture that supports the Father allowing Jesus to retain divinity, to insure a sinless walk to the cross. Jesus could not fully experience the trials and tribulations of true man, while being blessed with divinity.

If we compare the Father's servant Job with His servant Jesus, we can see some interesting insights into the Father's dealing with Satan. In so doing, we must understand that everything the Father's does is for His purpose and glory. In Job's case, Satan's access was limited by Job's life. In Jesus' case, the limit of life was removed. This act of the Father clearly establishes the depth of His love, as unfathomable, when one fully recognizes the depth of Jesus' suffering on the cross. Though Job was highly favored of the Father, He let Job experience the wrath of Satan on his possessions and health excluding his life. Like Job, I believe Satan was loosed to interfere with Jesus' ministry, including bribery in the wilderness and death on the cross. The Father honored Job's service with an outpouring of blessings that far exceeded what he had ever possessed. Jesus received his gift after the cross when his glory was restored. I BELIEVE THAT DIVINITY ACCOMPANYING JESUS THROUGH HIS TRIALS AND TRIBULATIONS DENIGRATES THE MAGNITUDE OF THE FATHER'S MOST PRECIOUS GIFT OF LOVE TO MAN.

If Jesus, in the flesh, possessed the divine nature of God:

+ He couldn't sin.
+ He couldn't be a true man.
+ He couldn't bear any one's sin.
+ He couldn't be crucified on a cross to provide a sin covering.
+ He wouldn't have to have His glory restored.
+ Satan's enticements in the wilderness to chastise him would be farcical.

There is nothing in ISA 53 to suggest divinity was crucified, died and was buried. To accept the divinity of Christ as TRUE MAN is to greatly diminish the magnitude the Trinity's sacrificial gift to man. Consider: 1) Spirit power was needed for the conception and the resurrection; 2) the unity of the Trinity is present at all times, whether functioning as one or individually and 3) while True Man, Jesus' did not host the Trinity or Divinity. NOTE: Man was introduced and began hosting the Trinity at Pentecost. So we can conclude by definition of true man, Jesus was not divine.

When the Word says Jesus is divine, it is an attribute that each TRINITY member shares as MAJESTY COEQUAL, within the constraints of UNITY. When then Word says Jesus was divine, such divinity can only be exercised with within the confines of the Trinity. To accept Jesus as a divine True Man, is to challenge the magnitude of the Father's love by questioning the veracity of His 'True Man." It denigrates the attribute of divinity by bringing it down to man's level and suggesting that Jesus needed a crutch during his suffering. THIS IS AN EXTREME EXAMPLE OF ACCEPTING SATANIC COUNSEL IN THE EXEGESIS OF THE DIVINITY DOCTRINE. It takes two separate scriptures, 1. Jesus is True God. and 2. Jesus is True Man.

IT IS A VIVID EXAMPLE OF CANCER FOUND IN CHURCHES THAT ARE LED BY THE FLESH AND NOT BY HE SPIRIT. They don't accept the Omniscience, Omnipotence and the Will of the Father. They don't want to admit that the Father's Will controls the thoughts, words, and deeds of anyone and everyone. The Father's salvation plan provides satanic counsel to be used in development of church doctrine within His Will under Jesus' control.

NOTE: Lacking Spirit Led exegesis, most churches are defined by the scripture "No one knows the mind of God!" They don't know that the Father is in complete control of His churches. The Father is using the Churches as a gathering place for Chosen and unchosen. The churches represent a major activity of His Salvation plan wherein Satin is used to chastise the chosen in congregations, as a screening tool to separate the Wheat from to Chaff, in a refining process to identify Chosen for access to the cross. The church's congregations also serve the Great Commission by attracting chosen and unchosen members to allow the Holy Spirit the opportunity to speak to the spirits of Chosen, both members and staff.

In fact, today's churches do not seriously embrace the Jesus of ISA 53, because they don't feel comfortable with a living sacrifice!" We don't feel comfortable with, nor understand and fully accept, a Jesus that tells us that if we love self, brother, sister, etc., more than Him, we are not worthy of him. Sharing of TRUTH is rejected in favor of presenting a sensitive sweet Jesus that would not offend anyone. Biblical truth has been seriously eroded in many churches promoting prosperity theology. It begs the question "Are we allowing Jesus to retain his divinity through false exegesis, so as to provide a Jesus who doesn't fully experience our trials and tribulations, thereby giving us a divinity argument for the sin of our lives."

Can you imagine the Father's disgust with fallen man's treatment of His son, as depicted in ISAIAH: 53. The Trinity recognized that the blood sacrifice sin offerings of the Old Testament (OT) needed a more permanent solution. Herein, we see the love of the trinity made manifest in the price of a sin offering by the Son of God who, divested himself of his divinity, became true man, suffered throughout his ministry without sinning, rejected by man during his trials and crucified on a cross as a sin offering. I can remember in the mid-80s turning back to the cross to rejuvenate/rededicate my walk with the Lord. As I marveled at God's love, in allowing His son to die for me, I felt an inadequacy in my service with a sense that His return will be in my life time and that I may not be ready. Since then, I have often asked the Father for a new ministry, and He responded by providing a replacement for my 35 year nursing home ministry, and told me I needed to get into the word admonishing me with "You can't preach the truth, if you don't know the truth." The December 2009 contact was exciting to me in understanding the Father's personal involvement with His elect:

A servant operates under His time table. It was 35 years from the Father's first contact in 1974 to His second contact in 2009. During the 35-year period, I felt somewhat guilty, at times, when experiencing the Father's joy and blessing. In the mid 90's, I began to feel I would be called to serve in an end time ministry. Following the 2009 contact, I understood that I was charged with getting to know the truth. After 50 years of church exposure, including a 35-year ministry, I realized I needed a new teacher and knew the only way to get exposure to God's truth is to be led by the Holy Spirit.

NOTE: When we talk about biblical truth, we have to understand that the truths in churches are based on myriad of denominational doctrines. Many church members, if not most, are not familiar with their church doctrines. There is a real danger here when congregations do not challenge the veracity of its doctrinal truth. If it is truth that sets the captive free, is there any chance of getting theologians from mainline denominations, to humble themselves and recognize they need to divest themselves of their parochial chains, when it comes to true exegesis of scripture? They don't understand that Satan is one smart dude, who is a lot smarter than they are and strongly supports the intellectual pursuit of biblical exegesis. We see Satan dividing the church, by appealing to the intellect of church leaders to overrule the counsel of the Holy Spirit. How much damage has been done over the years through false teaching? I would suspect that the church has been blinded by the euphoria of prosperity theology with little or no preaching on repentance, contrition, living sacrifice, and cross bearing.

So, from the garden, we can now embrace our heritage as coming from dirt, have been born in sin, will die, and return to dirt. While disgusted with Eve's response to the snake, the Trinity was still willing to provide a family plan for salvation. At this point, we need to understand that every action, regardless of how it affects your sense of good and bad, is always accomplished for the Father's purpose and glory. While we are in the garden, we need to understand "Depravity" in our relationship with the Trinity. Depravity simply describes our relation with the Father as one between potter and clay. When you fully embrace your role as clay, you realize that you have no say on any decision or action of any member of the Trinity. Your acceptance, as a member of the elect, allows you to walk in fellowship with the Triune God, that will never leave you and will bless you through all adversities, while following the counsel of the Spirit. Keep in mind that any act of your free will that breaks the counsel of the Spirit, can separate you from the walk to the cross and salvation.

The second time around, the Lord allowed Noah's family to survive the flood as a new opportunity for man. This time a new leader (Abraham), a chosen people and covenant was provided. In fact, the Lord set in motion for the seed of Abraham to be transmitted to Mary's father, to provide a mother for Jesus. From the garden to today, man has lived in sin and destined to go to hell, save for God's chosen who survive their free will walk to the cross. We can separate a salvation grace from other forms of perceived grace attributed to God. It would help to understand that most references to grace in daily life would fall under the purview of Jesus' role, when exercising His full power and authority over creation, given by the Father upon His return to glory. I view salvation as a special dispensation of the Trinity since the functions of the Father, Son and Spirit have separate and distinct roles in the salvation process as I have noted previously. Since God is omniscient, omnipotent and omnipresent, He was fully aware of and in control of the past, present and future. The Trinity knew that man, allowed free will, would be incapable of righteousness and a holy God could not accept an unholy man. Biblical history shows the Father's great desire for a family was introduced by identifying Abraham as the source for Mary's father's seed. While Jesus would provide atonement for sin, the Father would need to exercise a special grace opportunity for a select number of elect candidates for the faith walk to the cross. Considering the free will of the elect, the Father would need to account for attrition in determining the number of grace candidates achieving salvation. Would that number be hard and fixed? NO! Free will is free will! From what my spirit senses when talking to the Father, there is a cost to the salvation walk which will cause some to fail the walk and never reach the cross. We are to seek first the kingdom of God and its righteousness; present ourselves as living sacrifices wholly acceptable to God; hunger and thirst after righteousness; love Jesus more than self, brother, father, etc. As an elect, when you pick up your cross to follow Jesus and consider the walk of the trials and tribulations of Jesus and His disciples, you had better understand that the walk of a disciple of Christ is not a cake walk. The elect's faith walk experience to the cross will be under the scrutiny of the Trinity. Don't be misled by the prosperity theology of John 3:16. For Spiritual health, never forget there is a "Narrow Gate and Few Will Enter therein in." Consider Jesus' words in Matthew 15: 8,9 "These people draweth nigh unto me with their mouth, and honoureth me with their lips: but their heart is far from me. But in vain do they worship me, teaching for doctrines the commandments of men."

Why is it that we seldom, if ever, hear the wrath of God being preached? The barkers on most TV evangelism shows operate under the influence of the great deceiver offering carte blanche credit cards for unlimited access to God's blessings of salvation to pizza. OF COURSE THEY REAP THEIR REWARDS BY BEGGING SUPPORT OF THEIR MINISTRIES. MANY REAP THEIR PROFITS BY PREACHING PROSPERITY THEOLOGY, A FORM OF SELLING EARLY CHURCH INDULGENCES TO ENSURE SALVATION. It is not the fault of God's word, but rather the self-righteous, egotistical, and intellectual individuals controlling Christian doctrines in many seminaries and churches. These doctrines pervert God's truth to anesthetize the layperson into accepting a benevolent charlatan, representing a god of their perceived values, that require little or no commitment to the cross. Without sound doctrine, the church becomes a social club with feel good theology providing a breeding ground for Satin's recruiters. Consider Jesus' words in John 6:63 "It is the spirit that quickeneth ; the flesh profiteth nothing : the words that I speak unto you they are spirit, and they are life." (Note: "spirit" here is Jesus speaking as true man under the power of the resident Spirit within the Trinity.) Continuing in 6:64 "But there were some of you that believe not. Jesus knew from the beginning who they were that believed not and who should betray him." They were not of the chosen/elect, except for Judas, the son of perdition! And another chosen/elect reference in 6:65 "And he said, Therefore, said I unto you, that no man can come unto me, except it were given unto him of my Father." AND THE KICKER IN JOHN 6:66 "FROM THAT TIME MANY OF HIS DISCIPLES WENT BACK, AND WALKED NO MORE WITH HIM." I find this one of the most intriguing verses in the scriptures. The number 666 is intriguing in and of itself. In verse 6:26 "Jesus answered them and said, Verily, verily, I say unto to you, Ye seek me, not because ye saw the miracles, but because ye did eat of the loaves, and were filled." It is after Jesus explained who He was and His link to the Father, that the 6:66 separation took place. In this country, in the early 1600s, prosperity theology was introduced and, from my perspective, bastardized biblical truth with intellectual replacing Spiritual exegesis, coupled with an insatiable thirst for applying unholy dispensations to their exegesis of scripture. This unholy theology continues today, beckoning the Father, to sound the trumpet. Considering the moral and spiritual decay in this country and the cowardice of church leadership being a major contributor, this country is due a recompense, of the magnitude described in Isaiah 13:9 "Behold, the day of the Lord comes, cruel, with both wrath and fierce anger, to lay the land desolate; and He shall destroy the sinners thereof out of it." Has your church compared your Prince of Peace with the Lord's return day? I would like to share some thoughts on the Chosen/Elect issue. This issue is evidenced by adverse impact on pastors being unwilling to take a strong position on the Father's sovereignty, as it would require teaching/preaching a doctrine on this issue that is a 'Hard Saying' poorly received.

I often think of the great men of the church that have formulated Christian doctrine with both good and bad exegesis of the scriptures. There are intellectual giants on both sides of doctrinal truth that begs the question of my qualifications to judge doctrinal truths. This epistle is directed at God's ELECT describing a layman's walk as a scribe to the Spirit, in obedience to a request of the Father. It is a road map that describes the obstacles facing a "free will" elect, of the Father's GRACE. It begins with Grace's Chosen entering through the narrow gate, Spirit screening for Spirit baptism, and finally a walk of faith with the counselor/Spirit to the cross. I am adamant, in warning that completion of the faith walk without the Spirit is a death trap. Jesus was adamant, telling his disciples he had to return to His Father before the Father would send the counselor/Spirit to lead them into all truth (Jesus). This walk, of necessity, must be preceded by an intimate understanding and relationship with the Trinity and functional relationships; followed by in depth appreciation and acceptance of the Father's sovereignty! One of the most crucial doctrines on biblical truth is the Father's right to choose His elect. It is the cornerstone on which the new testament exegesis is built and a stumbling block that even the elect can't ignore. WHO DO I THINK I AM? In and of myself, NOTHING! I totally accept the doctrine of DEPRAVITY! My desire is to honor and bless the Trinity with all I have, including my life. From where I stand, I feel an opportunity for bearing witness to Jesus as a martyr is possible in my life time. I have made it clear to the Trinity, that if this epistle does not bless them, I would not want it published. At this point, after repeated regurgitation, I have not discerned any displeasure from the Trinity. To the contrary, I sense that what I have written acknowledges concurrence of the Spirit. To any of those who question my epistle, you are not questioning me, but the right of a layman, whose biggest attribute is his personal love and relationship with all members of the Trinity, with a desire to say "thank you!" with all he has, including martyrdom.

31. 1-13-13 Sunday School Bible Class. We were discussing the prophet Amos' warning the people of the consequences of their sin. As I was listening, I was reminded of the role of Grace and John 3:16 in the salvation process which I shared with the class. I pointed out that while God so loved the world, He limited those who would qualify for grace to receive a chance at the salvation process. That scripture teaches we are saved by grace through faith which is the gift of God. (Ephesians 2:8). In John 3:3 Jesus answered and said unto Nicodemus, "Verily, verily I say unto thee, except a man be born again, he cannot see the kingdom of God." Therefore, we can conclude that only those who are born again can participate in a salvation walk to the cross. If we agree that the Father chose us from the beginning, we must conclude that only the elect will be offered the Spiritual Baptism

(Born Again) opportunity which, as I discussed earlier, is not a guarantee for salvation because of "Free Will.

When we talk about the love of John 3:16's world, one can argue that there is one form of love wherein there is equity for both the just and unjust, i.e., "rain falls and the just and unjust," and

"you are not of the world, but you are in the world." There is no difference in the state of the just and unjust at birth. Both fall under the sin of Adam and exercise free will. The only difference is the Father has chosen some of the sinners for a grace opportunity, to prove themselves worthy for Spiritual baptism and a faith walk to the cross. As I have explained earlier, there are several barriers along the salvation path to hinder achievement of the salvation goal.

The elect's path to salvation is not, by any stretch of the imagination, a cake walk. Consider:

1. Seek ye first the Kingdom of God and His righteousness - Failure to focus on the Kingdom can result in the loss of your Spiritual birthright. Matthew 6:33
2. Present your bodies yourself a living sacrifice, holy, acceptable to God, which is your reasonable service. Romans 12:1
3. He who does not take up his cross and follow me is not worthy of me. Matthew 10:38.
4. For many are called, but few are chosen. Matthew 22:14
5. Because narrow is the gate and difficult is the way that leads to life, and there are few who find it. Matthew 7:14

From my walk with the Spirit, I am grieved with the proliferation of false exegesis spread over almost the entire spectrum of the "Christian Church!" This is the most visible evidence of a dying church.

A Few Thoughts:

1-6-2013: I was taking a break from income tax preparation by trimming plants in the back yard when my thoughts turned to the Trinity. I have never run across a man of the cloth nor a Bible teacher who had a clear and comfortable understanding of the Trinity. I admit I haven't had a great deal of exposure to the subject. And as I write this, the thought came to me that this was an area the Spirit wanted to open up to me. In over three years since the Father told me to get into the Word and chastising me with: "You can't preach the TRUTH if you don't know the TRUTH," the door was opened to a walk with the Trinity. So after 35 years of nursing home ministry, my Father honored my old and continuing request for a new ministry. He provided a retired Baptist minister and his family who "Just wanted to bless people." A servant response that I am sure blessed the Trinity!

It didn't take long to find that biblical truth in most of today's churches is left to the intellectual hierarchy that focuses hermeneutics on the power of the intellect with little or no input from the Spirit. Christian doctrine has been subjected to providing a feel good adventure with Jesus! I have heard there are over 100s of significant denominations with their own individual brand of biblical truth. I was one of a multitude of biblical lay persons, living in ignorance of rightly dividing God's Word as presented by a pastor or teacher, because we were spoon fed doctrine of unknown veracity. The Father's intervention made it clear to me that I was responsible for the biblical truth I received and accepted. Jesus gave us the key to truth which is either misunderstood or ignored:

> John 16:13 "Howbeit when He, the Spirit, is come, He will guide you into all truth: for He shall not speak of himself; but whatsoever He shall hear, that shall He speak: and He will show you things to come."

NOTE: It occurred to me that what is shared here is an understanding of the Trinity that was new to me. Feeling my spirit quickened, I sensed the presence of the Spirit. I have been actively engaged in a strong desire to know the Trinity, believing as I do, that one's ability to rightly divide the Word of God rests solely on one's relationship with each member of the Trinity. If one can't gain an understanding of the functional role of each member, he/she his hard pressed to understand the Trinity and the unity of the Trinity. Consider John 16:13 above! The role of the Spirit is clearly defined: "He will guide you into ALL truth!" Where did He get His truth? From Jesus who walked as true man and shared truth with His disciples. Where did Jesus, as true man, get His truth? From His Father through the Spirit. True man's spirit receives TRUTH through the Spirit. One can easily argue that as True Man, Jesus would have received the truth in like manner. One can conclude that Jesus' divinity remained in the Trinity to maintain the Unity of the Trinity. Some will argue that Jesus was divine as "true man" and so can reveal truth on His own. This is to say God walked in the form of Jesus as "True Man." Linking divinity to Jesus' suffering and death is ludicrous and an affront to the Father and the Trinity. DIVINITY DOES NOT DIE ON A CROSS! A SACRIFICE WITHOUT BLEMISH DOES! The Trinity does not play games with exegesis, as do the intellectuals parsing scriptures in their hermeneutical efforts, to provide exegesis for a vast array of biblical doctrine. The Father, with the assistance of the Spirit, supported Jesus' service as True Man. The Father's interface with His Son, absent His divinity while as true man, was clearly one of support. The Spirit's role is also one of major support when one considers he brought Jesus into the womb of Mary, returned Him to His Father in the resurrection, and was actively involved in the miracles Jesus performed. Finally, the current role of Jesus is the King of Kings and Lord of Lords. He is responsible for all activities that affects our lives. He controls the path of believers and non-believers. I am convinced that the Trinity, in Unity, is never separated in any actions regardless of their separate functional roles. Of course, there was a unique intervention when Jesus served the Trinity as true man. In this case, Jesus enjoyed the presence of the Trinity through prayer as a True Man, like His fellow believers, while maintaining His unity role with the Trinity. Why does man seek to be more relevant by trying to bring down divinity? The Trinity would not provide an acceptable sacrifice without blemish, by providing a crutch of divinity which would demean the most precious gift given man!

Now if you will look at the rest of John 16:13, you can see a perfect example of Trinity and Unity in action. The Spirit functions as the Trinity's truth guide, while being fully engaged with all of the UNITY decisions proceeding from the Trinity. The concept of Unity within the Trinity suggests that there is absolute concurrence in thought, word and deed, whether in a triune mode or a functional mode. In effect, operating in an individual functional mode enjoys full Trinity concurrence. REMEMBER GOD IS ONE! To become True Man required Jesus' divorcing Himself from His divinity, so that denying it's knowledge and power placed Him on equal footing with true man. This is why Jesus said he only did what he saw the Father do. By example, Jesus was showing His disciples that access to God's kingdom and power was available to all believers, adding that they could do even greater things than He had done. So anything that happens in your life is approved by the Trinity. That is why the Father chose the souls to be His elect, the Spirit was sent to be our counselor who would lead us into all truth and Jesus was sent to be our sacrifice plus rule as King of Kings over our lives upon His return to Glory.

In the fall of 1974, the Father gave a verse of scripture that has become one of the most meaningful scriptures in my walk with the Trinity. Matthew 6:33 'Seek ye first the kingdom of God and His righteousness ...,' is a must first step. You will not embrace the fruits of this scripture, if there is no hunger or thirst for righteousness. This hunger and thirst must start with knowing the Trinity!

2-15-2013 Joan and were talking about the impact of unclean spirits on people with Alzheimer's disease. One has to conclude that the progression of ALZ reduces the ability of the mind to withstand the attacks of unclean spirits to gain control of your soul. We agreed that we would walk in the Will of the Father and petition Him to provide peace and joy while traversing the valley of ALZ. During these special times, it had become a habit to share the issue on my mind and then to reflect back over the four plus years of my scriptural walk with the Spirit. I would then share with the Spirit the scriptures I believed dealt with my issue and my conclusions. It is as this time when I feel the Comforter's presence as He adds other scriptures and tweaks my spiritual understanding and acceptance of a Holy experience. I would hasten to add that, with each member of the Trinity, I feel both humble and excited about being in the presence of God. Joan enjoyed my sharing Spirit revelations with her!

So let's take a look at this issue. First, I always feel it is important to identify the key players:

1. The mind, spirit and soul of the person with ALZ.
2. The unclean spirit of Satan.
3. The Holy Spirit of God.
4. Jesus' oversight control.

The stage is a walk to the cross being buffeted by Satan's unclean spirits weighed against acceptance of God's grace in the form of His Counselor and Spirit. If we keep our eyes upon Jesus, He will never leave us or forsake us. Whenever we walk into a battle with Satan's forces, we keep in mind as Christians that we need to claim victory in Jesus' name. The prize is the soul of a believer. The role of the Spirit is prime minister over the Father's family.

MY STAND AS A SERVANT OF THE FATHER:

1. I WRITE AS A LAYMAN WHO WRITES IN LAYMAN'S TERMS.
2. I LAY NO CLAIMS TO LITERARY SKILLS.
3. I WILL NOT BE BEHOLDING TO ANY THEOLOGINS.
4. MY WALK IS WITH THE SPIRIT OF TRUTH INTO THE WORD OF TRUTH.
5. MY FOCUS IS TO BLESS MY FATHER, WHO CALLED ME.
6. I BELIEVE THAT MY FATHER COMMISSIONED ME TO OPEN HIS TRUTH TO HIS ELECT.
7. I PRAY THAT MY EFFORTS TO FOLLOW THE LEAD OF THE SPIRIT WILL BLESS THE TRINITY.
8. THIS IS A "LAYMAN TO LAYMAN EFFORT" TO SHARE ONE LAYMAN'S DESIRE TO HONOR THE FATHER'S CALL TO KNOW HIS TRUTH AND TO SHARE IT, WITH HIS FELLOW ELECT.

9. It IS INTENDED TO PROVIDE AN OPTION TO AN "ELECT" LAY PERSON, TO CONSIDER TAKING PERSONAL CONTROL OF HIS SPIRIT WALK TO THE CROSS AND SALVATION, THAT CAN ONLY BE ASSURED BY A PERSONAL WALK WITH THE SPIRIT OF TRUTH!

FATHER'S FAMILY PLAN – THE PATH TO SLVATION

The Father's plan provides a bible that clearly shows "No one knows the mind of God!" There are hundreds of denominations with distinctive doctrines that set them apart from each other. Most lay persons would be in a quandary trying to select a church denomination from a smorgasbord of prepackaged doctrines. Realty is a lack of member exposure to their own church doctrines. Most members have little or no idea of what their church doctrines are. I have been a member of many different denominational churches. I based my theology on what I heard from the pulpit or in bible classes. In many cases, what I heard I could not agree with the exegesis presented. After my first real confrontation with the Gospel, through confirmation as a eleven year old, I drifted away from the church. Then I met my wife, who told me she would only marry a Missouri Synod Church member. I did not view that as an obstacle and for the first 16 years of marriage, I was a very active member without fully accepting the Gospel I heard from the pulpit and in Sunday school. For example, I have never believed that the Jesus of the bible died for the whole world nor could I accept pleading the blood of Jesus for anything but salvation. In 1974, the Father gave my spirit Matthew 6:33 and told me I would never worry about my salvation. I came to accept Matthew 6:33 as a key cornerstone doctrine of biblical exegesis. I didn't understand why the Father gave a worry free salvation, until December 2009, when the Father told me to get into the Word admonishing me with "You can't preach the truth, if you don't know the truth." I knew, if I was to know the truth, I had to engage the Holy Spirit. Almost immediately the bible came alive; I knew I was one of the elect based on the Fathers telling me in 1974 that I would never worry about my salvation; that the Election doctrine was the key to understanding John 3:16; and that work's righteousness is required to access the cross and salvation.

I believe that the Father entered our names, Joan and Doug, in the Book of Life and that we were programmed to walk in His Will before creation. I have been walking with the Trinity for almost six years now, excited over the opportunity of being commissioned to serve as a scribe to the Spirit, as He arms me with a Record of Spirit revelations, to share worldwide. The focus of the Record is to get it into the hands of the Father's Chosen/Elect worldwide. The Father told me I would never worry about my salvation in 1974 and it took me 35 years for me to understand I was among the Chosen. Considering the plethora of false doctrines in our churches, it is easy to conclude there are millions of living Chosen in the world who are not aware of their blessing under John 3:16.

As I was writing this part of my Record, I recalled listening, as a child, to a radio show called "The Shadow." Each show began with "Who Knows what evil lurks in the hearts of men - the Shadow knows," followed by a sinister laugh. The Shadow claimed to have the power to cloud men's minds so they could not see him. It seems the Spirit reminded me of the radio show to draw a comparison with Satan's weapon of mass confusion. So, if we replace "shadow with "Satan" and our spirit with "Spirit," we can conclude that the control battle for the mind is a Good versus Evil battle for the soul.

The Father only allows His Chosen access to biblical truth revealed by the Spirit. False doctrine is offered by Satan or one of his unclean spirits. The Father, through Jesus, controls all satanic action allowing Satan to separate the wheat from the chaff in Christian churches. Remember that God chastises those whom He loves. The Father planned, from the beginning, to use Satan's deceiver talents to screen out those among the Chosen who yielded to Satan's seduction and they were removed from the Book of Life. More on this later! I was reminded of the Father's agreement to allow Satan to chastise Job. Everything the Father does is for His purpose and glory. Again, we can think of Jesus and all of the martyrs chastised to bring glory to God. All Chosen will be chastised to determine their work's righteousness in following the counsel of the Spirit. Your work's righteousness record is a record of treasures that brings glory to the Father. Of course, the stronger the record, the greater the treasure received in heaven.

Most churches select their pastors on basis of a charismatic persuasion and/or their social programs. I base this on my personal observation during some 50 years of attending, teaching and preaching in Christian venues. WHERE DOES ONE GO FOR BIBLICAL TRUTH? WHAT IS CAUSING THIS MALIGNANT ATTACK ON THE TRUTH OF GOD'S WORD? I will give you the short answer now! SATAN IS USING HIS WEAPON OF MASS DIFFUSION WHICH IS SIMILAR TO WHAT HE DID TO ADAM; ATTACK ONE'S INTELLECT AND EGO! SELF ESTEEM AND SELF RIGHTEOUSNESS PROVIDE A FERTILE TARGET FOR SATANIC PURSUASION. Satan first applied his favorite deception tactic on Adam in the garden and discovered his favorite weapon against Spirit led exegesis. He didn't have much luck with the second Adam who he only wanted to glorify and serve his Father. No on can argue against the success of Satan's weapon of mass diffusion in church doctrines, since denominations define their uniqueness by their exegesis of biblical truths.

Christian leaders and lay persons don't seem to understand that the Word was written for lay persons, it's exegesis was to be revealed by the Spirit and not conjured up by man's intellect. Access to Spirit led biblical exegesis is only available to His Chosen. They include those, who accept the Word, who receive work righteousness approval by the Spirit, and who are baptized in the Spirit to begin their walk of faith to the cross. So the purpose of the Father's plan is to populate Heaven with RIGHTEOUS children. It develops a screening plan with obstacles to separate the wheat from the chaff. For those who expect a cake walk, consider Matthew 10:22 "An ye shall be hated of all men for my name's sake: BUT HE THAT ENDURETH TO THE END SHALL BE SAVED." Our future is not a primrose path but an endurance path with many valleys. Don't you believe the Father chastises those whom he loves? Consider the chastisement of Jesus as True Man. The martyrs were chastised right up to being received in paradise. Chastisement is a redemptive act of love by the Father. The history of the chastisement of the Chosen is evidenced by peak martyrdom periods marking the advent of Christ. We all need to be vigilant and prepare for a possible advent martyrdom experience in the near future.

11-4-14: As I was driving home from voting, I was thinking about all of the Christians who were voting for candidates of a party platform that supports violating many of the "thou shalt nots" of the bible. Political correctness is an anathema to Christianity. You reap what you sow! In addition, the Spirit reminded me of God's greatest creation and Jesus being the author and finisher of our Faith. When I got home, I turned to the Word to examine the Spirit revelations I had received. Hebrews 12:1- 8 paints a stark picture of the chastisement of Jesus as an endurance example for the Father's Chosen:

> Hebrews 12:1-8 (1) "Wherefore seeing we also are compassed about with so great a cloud of witnesses, let us lay aside every weight, and the sin which doth so easily beset us and let us run with patience the race that is set before us, (2) Looking unto JESUS, THE AUTHOR AND FINNISHER OF OUR FAITH; who for the joy set before him ENDURED the CROSS, despising the shame, and is set down at the right hand of the throne of God. (3) For consider him that endured such contradiction of sinners against himself, lest you be wearied and faint in your minds. (4) Ye have not yet resisted unto blood, striving against sin. (5) And ye have forgotten the exhortation which speaketh unto to as unto children, my son, despise not thou the chastening of the Lord, nor faint when thou are rebuked of him; (6) For whom the Lord loveth, he chasteneth, and scourgeth every son whom he receiveth. (7) If ye endure chastening, God dealeth with you as with sons; for what son is he whom the Lord chasteneth not? (8) BUT IF YE BE WITHOUT CHASETISMENT, WHEREOF ALL

ARE PARTAKERS, THEN ARE YE ARE BASTARDS,
AND NOT SONS.

Jesus, as author and finisher of our faith, describes the walk of faith for
a chosen as a vivid example of endurance in withstanding the attacks of
Satan and/or his surrogates. The faith walk of a Chosen begins after Spirit
baptism establishes a Spirit led walk of faith toward the cross. The Spirit
led walks provide counsel for chastisement attempts of satanic origin
under control of Jesus. If you resist the counsel of the Spirit in favor of
satanic deception, you are sinning. In regard to verse 8 above, if there is
chastisement of a group of Chosen and you are not chastised, you are not
one of His Chosen sons!

I just can't help but observe, that anyone who believes in the Pre Tribulation
rapture, is accepting a theology provided by the Deceiver. Go back and
read Hebrews 12 again. You are risking your life for a feel good theology
that is twisting truth that serves Satan.

Regarding God's greatest creation; it has to be HUMAN LIFE! God just
spoke and the universe was formed out of nothing. When God created man,
it was personal because He was creating a future family. We were made
in His image, formed with clay and given a soul, spirit, seed, free will and
His breath to start life. A LIVING GIFT WITH THE OPPORTUNITY
OF ETERNAL LIFE.

I feel a need to share a truth that is essential to my understanding of the
FATHER:

+   Everyone's entire life span has been set by the Father since the
    beginning of time.
+   Everyone's life is under the control of the Father's will.
+   Only those names listed in the Book of Life, before the beginning
    of time, will be given an opportunity for Spirit counsel in a faith
    walk to the cross. The walk will include chastisement to determine
    your worthiness for redemption and heaven.

All meetings with a Trinity member is a spirit to Spirit exchange. My first discussion was a very pleasant spirit to Spirit fellowship. What was received by my spirit, was the Father's strong desire for a family that would be chosen and screened for righteousness. In His Plan, the Father used the Garden event to demonstrate that man's free will exercised under Satan's deception, would lead to sin and separation from God. This first screening condemned all mankind to hell. After Satan's God approved counsel, Adam sinned. Satan's services would continue under the control of Jesus on an as needed basis. Under the Father's plan, Satan would be used to cull the Father's chosen by separating the wheat from the chaff. Earlier, the Father had randomly selected Chosen souls from the soul bank and entered their names in the Book of Life. The soul bank was set up before creation and is the first body part made for man. We can argue about when man's free will was introduced and we can agree that we have three options; the soul bank, Adam's lifeless body or God breathed. I began by considering the soul because it was the object of Jesus' True Man's salvation efforts and Satan's recruiting efforts.

Following is a litany of my understandings of basic truths that are needed to rightly divide the Word of God. They served as my benchmark in understanding the counsel received from the Spirit. It began with my commitment to my Father in December 2009. It reflects my desire, in layman terms, to show how serious my Father is about sharing His creation with a righteous family of His own. Since my first call to a nursing home ministry, by the Father in 1974, He has known my heart's commitment to serve Him in a manner that brings Him glory. I am convinced, after years of fellowship with the Trinity, that their concurrence is a given, based on my walk with the Spirit. The basic truths that strengthen my fellowship include:

+ God is Omniscient. God knows everything, even my thoughts.
+ God is Omnipotent. God has the power to do whatever He wills with my life.
+ God is Omnipresent. He never leaves me. God is present in all places at all times. For God's chosen, it includes a Trinity support role to my spirit. They provide the means by which truth is revealed to my Spirit.

+ God is Immutable. God's attributes do not change. The God of the past, present and future is the same. Church bible studies focus on obedience in the Old Testament and the promises of blessings in the New Testament. Many Church members exhibit heartburn over the Father's sovereignty and will as demonstrated in their oft expressed question "How can a loving God allow this to happen?" I can't recall ever hearing a sermon on the Father's purpose and glory being preached. God's attributes are in full compliance with His Purpose and glory. They have not changed! Today's social gospel has removed the image of a sovereign and awesome God.

+ God is Holy. An attribute to help me understand His position on sin.

+ God is Righteous. An attribute that expresses God's holiness in a God - man Relationship. I need attributable work's righteousness to access the cross. No person is righteous until he/she demonstrates work's righteousness that brings glory to the Father.

+ God's Sovereignty: God's right to do whatever He wants with my life. In my December 2009 commission, the Father told me to get into the Word saying I couldn't preach the Word if I didn't know the Word. This opened the door to the Trinity and sovereignty. Now, in November 2014, looking back at the role of sovereignty in my life, I recognize it as the door to my spirit's salvation and the stumbling block to the unchosen and chosen who had their names removed from the book of Life. Acknowledging the Father's total sovereignty is condition for attaining salvation. You are given a measure of faith with your Spirit baptism. If, at the end of the salvation path, your spirit has not accepted the total sovereignty of the Father, you will be denied access to the cross and have your name removed from the Book of Life.

10/06/2914: During my round trip to the nursing home, I discussed free will with the Spirit and received the following revelations:

+ Free will did not exist in either the soul of Adam or Jesus before the Father breathed life into their souls at conception. There is no free will without life. In the new testament, we are told that

Jesus is the Way, the Truth and the LIFE. Life is controlled by and proceeds from the Trinity.

+ The Father's plan, needed to define True Man, required that Adam and Jesus start life with no record of sin. Therefore, Adam's and Jesus' seed had to be provided by the Father and had to be resident in their bodies at conception. Therefore, at birth, Adam possessed unblemished seed to support his role as True Man comparable to Jesus as True Man. Neither Adam nor Jesus acquired free will until conception was activated by the Father's breath of life. All life is God breathed, including Adam's and Jesus! Adam, like Jesus, was holy until contaminated by exercising his free will to sin. Adam's sin was a death knell to all of his descendants.

The Fathers Family Plan was formulated before the foundation of the world. Being omniscient, the Father knew that Adam, exercising his free will, would sin and condemn all of his descendants to eternal spiritual death. The plan allowed and controlled a role for Satan to be an adversary for all of the chosen. Jesus would always control Satan's actions to conform to the Father's will and purpose. If you are one of the Chosen walking under the counsel of the Spirit, your life is under control of the Trinity. The Trinity has a vested interest in you, in a fellowship manner, that blesses you and the Trinity. The stronger your fellowship with the Trinity, the stronger you will sense their presence and the greater you will feel their peace and joy. Joan and I did not face the future with fear but with Joy knowing we were in the will of the Father.

If you have love for Jesus and have a hunger for the Word, you need to confirm you are a member of the Chosen with your name in the Book of Life. To be included in the Father's family and desire to be led by the Spirit, you MUST seek the Kingdom of God and His Righteousness. The intent of this Record is to open the eyes of the Father's Chosen, who have not been exposed to Spirit revealed Chosen doctrine or imputed work's righteousness.

Without Grace provided Spirit counsel, you would face Satan's deception with a faith hampered by free will. You are no match for Satan's power to deceive, without the power of the Counselor. A number of Chosen with weak faith, will reject Spirit counsel and yield to Satan's deception. The failure of these Chosen to complete the faith walk can be laid at the door of church doctrine. Consider the following:

+ John 1:17 "For the law was given through Moses but grace and truth came through Jesus Christ." This verse tells us that Grace and truth are the keys to access the cross and salvation.
+ Ephesians 2:5 "For by grace ye have been saved through faith; and that not of yourselves; it is a gift of God." This verse tells us that faith is the gift vehicle used during your walk to the cross.
+ John 8:32 "An you shall know the truth, and the truth shall make you free." Truth is the most critical factor in the Father's Family Plan. This verse tells us there is no freedom to access the cross without a truth basis.

Jesus Stated 'I am the Way, the Truth, and the Life; no one comes to the Father but by Me.' So we can conclude that the Father's Way is led by the Spirit of TRUTH who offers counsel to the Chosen, on their Faith walk to the cross and Salvation. The significance of truth is evident. A walk to the cross without the Spirit lacks truth and is a nonevent. Without Spirit counselling, your access to the cross will be denied and your name removed from the Book of Life.

God is truth, the Word is truth, Righteousness and Holiness are truth. Creation is built on a truth foundation. This is why the Father selected souls for His Book of Life. This is why the Father used Satan as an adversary to deceive His Chosen. Satan's contribution to the Father's plan was to separate the Chosen from the unchosen on the basis of knowing and accepting the truth.

The organized church has also been exposed to the Father's truth screening agent. Satan's performance in confusing the Church intellects, who establish church doctrines, shows widespread divergence of hermeneutical and exegetical results among hundreds of denominations divided by doctrinal differences. The results strongly suggest absence of Spirit led exegesis. How many chosen fed false biblical truth were denied the faith walk with the Spirit counselor.

Faulty exegesis of Ephesians 2:8-10 ignores being created in Christ Jesus for good works, that the Father had before ordained that we should walk in them. To mess with the Father's ordained work requirement for salvation is to mess with His Will and Sovereignty, triggering a subpoena to appear before the Great White Throne Judgment. Considering the widespread proliferation of contending doctrines, it is reasonable to assume that the reigning fallacy of many church doctrines could be holding members captive to bad doctrine. Any purveyor of false doctrine is especially repugnant to the Trinity. They are jeopardizing the salvation of those who receive and accept such doctrine.

The Father's Will introduces times of tribulation for His Chosen to satisfy the Father's purpose of separating the wheat from the chaff. Keep in mind that all of Satan's actions are controlled by the Divine Jesus of the Trinity. The Chosen's reactions, to Satan's efforts to torpedo Spirit counsel works performed by a Chosen, are judged by whether or not the Chosen's works bring glory to the Father. Works that bring glory to the Father are imputed to the Chosen's Work's Righteousness Account. This Account will serve as the basis for the Spirit's evaluation, as to an acceptable standard of righteousness required to access the cross and receive redemption. This "imputed work's righteousness" process was used to identify old testament saints, such as Abraham, who qualified for Jesus' redemptive act. Abraham looked forward to the cross while we look backward. The big difference between a pre-cross Abraham and a post-cross Christian, is that we were blessed by Grace to receive personal Spirit Counsel for our faith walk to the cross. Most churches echo with a loud, self-righteous shout regarding salvation: "It is by GRACE, through faith, as a free gift, and not by works less we should boast." Their misunderstanding of grace is demonstrated in their application of Satan's counsel over Spirit counsel in performing exegesis of scriptural truth. Satan's favorite Weapon is Mass Confusion counsel used to pit the desires of the flesh to deflect the Spirit led counsel for man's spirit life.

Satan's success is evidenced by the smorgasbord of doctrines denigrating unity of biblical truth. The conclusion that can be drawn is that the organized church is in no position the say "Thus sayeth the Lord!" What the church doesn't understand that the Father's Plan provides many temporary victories for Satan while the Father enjoys eternal victories by screening His chosen to attain access the cross. The harder Satan's counsel efforts to acquire the Father's chosen, the higher the work's righteousness quality of the chosen accessing the cross. While it appears to be a win-win for Satan and the Father, you have to look to the future for the real winner. Satan's side goes to the Lake of Fire while the chosen enter an eternal kingdom as the Father's children. If there is one thought that often frequents my soul, is the joy of knowing I have a Divine Father.

Distortion of truth is Satan's weapon of choice to divide the church, as evidenced by the hundreds of denominations and their seminaries offering a smorgasbord of doctrines providing an abundant opportunity to find one satisfying social needs.

The Father's grace as expressed in John 3:16 is limited to His Chosen, who are identified in the Book of Life before the foundation of the world. The grace of John 3:16 is a salvation opportunity, given as a gift to the Chosen to walk the salvation path to the cross, under the counsel of the Spirit. Now consider the issue of works and salvation in light of the following scriptures:

+ Ephesians 2:8-10 "For by Grace ye have been saved through Faith; and that not of yourselves; it is the gift of God. Not of works, lest any man should boast. For we are his workmanship, created in Christ Jesus unto good works, which God had before ordained that we should walk in them." The church's elite intellectuals responsible for doctrines are derelict in their application of biblical exegesis, when they buy verses 8 & 9 while ignoring verse 10. Their application of exegesis in applying a Sweet Jesus and Santa God theology, may promote their happy church goal, but leaves members biblically ignorant and putting their salvation in jeopardy! Don't put the social needs of members ahead of the spiritual needs of the soul. When denomination pastors and bible teachers mess with the exegesis of scripture, they are messing with Jesus who will ask them to explain their doctrines when He convenes the Great White Thorne Judgment.

The Grace gift, open to the Father's Chosen only, provides free access to Spirit counsel during a walk of faith. Under the Father's plan, you will be tested on your desire to bless the Father, with services that impute works righteousness credit. The faith walk was part of His plan to screen candidates to separate the wheat from the chaff, before granting access to the cross. Basically, the Spirit is examining you free will in terms of willingness to totally accept the Will and Sovereignty of the Trinity. Based on man's free will record, I would anticipate a high rejection rate from these screenings. The first screening occurs when a number of Chosen will ignore the Spirit's invitation to enter the Narrow Gate; the second screening occurs when a number of the Chosen fail the Spirit's Word study course required to receive Spirit Baptism; the last screening occurs upon completion of the faith walk, when the Spirit examines the zeal in the heart to bless the Father with imputed work's righteousness account points. This final screening is critical to insuring that the condition of heart displays a fervor to please God, as demonstrated by total acceptance of the Counsel of the Spirit. It is designed to show total acceptance of the Father's Sovereignty and Will. There is no place for ego in the Father's Kingdom. Satan tried it and failed; resulting in being kicked out of heaven with a third of the angels that supported him. Currently bound in a bottomless pit, Satan will be released for a second tribulation screening effort, defeated by the King of Kings, and cast into the lake of fire, with all of his angels and convicted sinners.

HOW CAN A RATIONAL MAN QUESTION THE SOVEREIGNTY AND WILL OF A GOD, WHO SAID IT PLEASED HIM TO SEND HIS SON TO SUFFER AND BE CRUCIFIED FOR THE SINS OF A CHOSEN FAMILY HE SO DEARLY LOVED. THERE IS NO GREATER LOVE THAN A GOD GIVING A GOD SON TO BE SACRIFICED FOR THE REDEMPTION OF SINNERS. THESE ARE THE LOVE CONDITIONS OF YOUR HEART THAT THE

FATHER YEARNS FOR IN THE CHILDREN WHO WILL BE SHARING HIS CREATION. IT TOOK LONG SUFFERING AND THE SACRIFICE OF HIS SON TO PAY FOR OUR SALVATION. This is the Bible's gift of love that few Christians understand and apply. Only the Chosen, who survive the screening, will be able to embrace an adventure grounded in God's love.

+ John 14:12 "Verily, verily, I say unto you, He that believeth on me, the works that I do shall he do also, and greater works than these shall he do ; because I go unto my Father." Sounds like a pep talk at a Great Commission Rally. I wonder if it would have affected the couch potato who loves to quote Salvation by "Christ alone!"

+ THE FATHER'S FAMILY PLAN REFLECTS THE FATHER'S WILL AND ALWAYS SUITS HIS PURPOSE AND GLORY.

+ THE FATHER'S SOVEREIGNTY DEMANDS EVERYONE TO HONOR AND RESPECT HIS WILL, REGARDING MANAGEMENT OF HIS CREATION.

+ These last two issues of will and sovereignty cause the greatest heartburn and lowest acceptance in the churches and bible classes. Prior to the Father's visit in 2009, I was among those asking the question "How could a loving God allow such a thing to happen." Then, as I considered the Doctrine of Total Depravity in terms of the Potter and Clay example, I fully recognized that I came from dirt in the Garden of Eden and I will return to the dirt in Chattanooga's Military Cemetery. The battle between Satan and Jesus is not for your body but your soul. It is the condition of your heart based on the condition of your soul, that determines whether you rest in heaven or are tormented in hell. When the Father says He chastises those whom he loves, he is watching for your response as to whether your witness brings Him glory.

All of the trials and tribulations in history were carried out in accordance with His will; even Jesus' ministry leading to the cross. When we recite the Lord's prayer, We are asking that His will be done on earth as it is in heaven. From what I understand, there are no complaints in heaven. For those who are waiting for the pre-tribulation rapture of church, please read and understand the following Revelation scriptures:

+ Revelation 20:2: Satan bound for a 1000 years.

+ Revelation 20:3: Satan cast into a bottomless pit and must be released after the 1000 years. for a little season (7 years?). Released for the coming tribulation.

+ Revelation 20:4: "And I saw the thrones, and they that sat upon them, and judgment was given unto them: and I saw the souls of them that were beheaded for the witness of Jesus, and for the word of God, and which had not worshiped the beast, neither his image, neither had received his mark upon their foreheads, or in their hands; and they lived and reigned with Christ a 1000 years."

+ Revelation 20-5: "But the dead lived not again until the 1000 years were finished."

+ Revelation 20-6 Those in the 1st resurrection will reign with Jesus for 1000 years.

+ Revelation 20-7 Satan loosed from prison after 1000 years expired.

+ Revelation 20-8 Satan will deceive the nations of the world, Gog and Ma-Gog, to gather them together to do battle.

+ Revelation 20-9 Satan compassed the saints and fire came down from God in heaven and devoured Satan's troops!

+ Revelation 20-10 "And the devil that deceived them was cast into the lake of fire and brimstone, where the beast and the false prophet are, and shall be tormented day and night for ever and ever."

+ Revelation 20-11 "And I saw a great white throne and Him that sat on it, from whose face the earth and the heaven fled away; and there was found no place for them."

+ Revelation 20-12 "And I saw the dead, small and great, stand before God; and the books were opened: and another book was opened, which is the book of life: and the dead were judged out of those things which were written in the books, according to their Works.

+ Revelation 20-13 "And the sea gave up the dead which were in it; and death and hell delivered up the dead which were in them: and they were judged every man according to their Works.

+ Revelation 20-14 "And death and hell were cast into the lake of fire. THIS IS THE SECOND DEATH." Death of the unchosen spirits.

+ Revelation 20-15 "AND WHOSOEVER WAS NOT FOUND WRITTEN IN THE BOOK OF LIFE WAS CAST INTO THE LAKE OF FIRE.

IMPORTANT NOTE: THE CHOSEN, WHO SURVIVED SATAN'S SCREENING ON WORK'S RIGHTEOUSNESS AND RECEIVED REDEMPTION AT THE CROSS, WERE GRANTED THE CONTINUED RIGHT TO HAVING THEIR NAMES REMAIN IN THE BOOK OF LIFE. IT WAS THE HOLY SPIRIT THAT REVIEWED THEIR WORK'S RIGHTEOUSNESS RECORD AT THE CROSS, BEFORE THE GREAT WHITE THRONE JUDGMENT COURT CONVENED.

While no one knows the mind of God, I would like to share some comments regarding my Father:

NOTE: YOUR RIGHT TO ACCESS THE CROSS SEALS A YES VOTE IN THE BOOK OF LIFE. IN EFFECT, YOUR SALVATION WAS ESTABLISHED BEFORE THE GREAT WHITE THRONE JUDGMENT CONVENED.

+ God's Love. This is one of the most attractive, misunderstood and abused attributes of God, because of man's preference for being served over serving. It promotes a farcical brand of theology that seeks God's blessings on the basis of tainted man centered vs Spirit centered hermeneutics, which dictates exegesis.

+ God's Mercy. God's provision for mercy is misunderstood in terms of scope. The Father's mercy is a gift, not a right. How can we, who are unrighteous, demand anything from a sovereign righteous

God. His blessings are based on Righteousness achieved by His Purpose and will.

+ The Trinity is a Unity of Majesty Coequal. The Members attributes are the same.

+ The Father's Will always supports His Purpose and Glory

+ Jesus guarantees attainment of the Father's Purpose and Glory, through absolute control over all actions required to enforce the Father's will.

+ The Father has a total aversion to sin.

+ Adam's sin denied him access the Tree of Life in the center of the garden.

+ Satan was active in the garden, through the first tribulation to the first rapture, bound in a bottomless pit for 1000 years, released for the 2nd tribulation period preceding the 2nd coming and ending with his defeat during the Great and Terrible Day of the Lord. There will be a rapture just prior to release of Jesus wrath on the Great and Terrible Day of the Lord, to remove His children from danger. During 1000-year absence of Satan, his surrogates will continue Satan's chastisement contract with the Father.

+ The Father set up a soul bank, before the foundation of the world, to provide sufficient souls to cover conceptions beginning with Adam and Eve up to the Great White Throne Judgment.

+ The Father randomly chose souls, from the entire soul bank, and entered their names in the Book of Life. Those names included Adam and Jesus. Jesus' name in the book supports his True Man and second Adam status.

+ Salvation provides righteousness and holiness but not Divinity. Our status is like but higher than the angels.

This record is a good faith effort to take guidance from the Spirit, who uses scriptures in my memory bank, to bring into remembrance what I had studied in the bible. Also, it may be just a random word or thought that my spirit receives that triggers my search of the scriptures under Spirit counsel. Of course, any Trinity member can use verbal communications as documented many times in the scriptures. The most famous example is Jesus' baptism recorded in Matthew 3:17 "And lo a voice came from heaven saying 'This is my beloved son, in whom I am well pleased." The longer I walk with the Spirit, the more frequent the thoughts received. They are especially active when I am working on this Record.

I would like to share how this effort began. The Father paid His first visit in the Fall of 1974, with a Spirit quickening of my spirit to Matthew 6:33 "Seek ye first the Kingdom of God and His righteousness and all these things shall be added unto you." and told me I would never worry about my salvation.

Almost immediately I found myself conducting bible classes in a nursing home in Montgomery, Alabama. In 1978, the Air Force moved me to Scott AFB, Illinois where I conducted nursing home bible studies. In 1980 I retired from the Air Force and moved to Chattanooga, Tennessee where I began to preach in a nursing home. In the mid 80's, I started again asking the Father for an end times ministry for several reasons:

1. The moral and Spiritual decay experienced worldwide has spawned a breeding ground that has eclipsed Sodom and Gomorrah by, at least, an order of magnitude. It is getting close to the bottom of the mire, where it's degradation would trigger the Father's decision, to release His Son to execute judgment, by initiating the events leading to the Great and Terrible Day of the Lord!
2. The lack of significant church wide acceptance and understanding of "The Book of Life" and the "Chosen's" role regarding John 3:16's salvation gift.
3. The apparent large number of God's Chosen walking in ignorance of their names being in the Book of Life.
4. The flagrant widespread damage to biblical truth based on intellect led vs Spirit led exegesis. There are 100s of denominations and seminaries selling their brands of biblical truth.
5. To thank my Father for the gift of His Son

THE PLAN

THE CAST:

- + FATHER-SON-HOLY SPIRIT-ANGELS-CHOSEN-TRINITY
- + SATAN - FALLEN ANGELS
- + ADAM - EVE - CHILDREN

CONSIDERATIONS:

- + TRINITY IS A UNITY OF THREE IN ONE AND MAGESTY COEQUAL
- + THE UNITY OF THE TRINITY IS ALWAYS MAINTAINED.
- + DIVINITY RESTS SOLELY WITH THE TRINITY.
- + RIGHTEOUSNESS AND HOLINESS ARE REQUIRED TO JOIN GOD'S FAMILY.
- • FREE WILL IS GUARANTEED UNTIL SALVATION WHEN OUR WILL IS TO DO THE FATHER'S WILL.
- + ALL ACTIONS MUST SATISFY THE FATHER'S PURPOSE AND GLORY.
- + THE FATHER'S SOVERIGNTY MUST BE HONORED.
- + THE TRINITY IS OMNICIENT - KNOWS PAST, PRESENT AND FUTURE.
- + THE TRINITY IS OMNIPOTENT - CONTROLS ALL, INCLUDING SATAN.
- + TRUE MAN IS TRUE IN EVERY SENSE.

GUIDING PRINCIPLES:

- + SATAN WILL BE PERMITTED ACCESS TO GOD'S CHILDREN UNDER THE CONTROL OF JESUS. SATAN'S SURROGATES WOULD CONTINUE CHASTISEMENT ACTIONS WHILE HE IS BOUND FOR A THOUSAND YEARS.
- + IN EFFECT, SATAN WILL BE USED AS A SCREEN TO CULL OUT WEAK SPIRITED CHOSEN CANDIDATES.

+ THE SPIRITUAL WALK OF FAITH MUST INCLUDE WORKS RIGHTEOUSNESS TO ACCESS THE CROSS FOR REDEMPTION.
+ ONLY THOSE WHOSE NAMES REMAIN IN THE BOOK OF LIFE DURING THE GREAT WHITE JUDGMENT OF LIFE QUALIFY FOR SALVATION.
+ ONLY THOSE WHO ACCESS THE NARROW GATE QUALIFY FOR BIBLE TEACHING UNDER SPIRIT COUNSEL.
+ ONLY THOSE WHO QUALIFY FOR SPIRIT BAPTISM WILL RECEIVE FAITH AND SPIRIT COUNSEL FOR THEIR WALK TO THE CROSS.
+ THE SPIRIT WILL JUDGE THE CONDITION OF THE HEART TOWARD THE FATHER ON THE BASIS OF THE ATTRIBUTABLE WORK'S RIGHTEOUSNESS ACCOUNT ACTS.
+ THE SPIRIT JUDGMENT IS THE FINAL SCREENING FOR THE CHOSEN'S ACCESS TO THE CROSS AND RIGHTEOUSNESS.

Ephesians 1:4 "According as He hath Chosen us in Him BEFORE the foundation of the world, that we should be holy and without blame before him in love.

I admit there is no way that I can scope the activities in God's mind when grappling with all of the issues regarding His Family Plan, but I can express the feelings of unbelievable awe that grew in the last SIX years of our relationship. I can remember a few years back considering the Doctrine of Total Depravity and realizing that all of humanity has the same legacy problem of going back to Eden's garden dirt.

When the Father commissioned me to get into the Word and learn the truth, He also provided a Trinity fellowship, that included the Holy Spirit who is the counselor and teacher charged to open up biblical truth to the Father's chosen. As a scribe to the Spirit, the bible came alive as I quickly received the counsel of the Spirit. As truth upon truth embraced my spirit, a real hunger and thirst for righteousness kicked in. As biblical truths linked together, they began to weave a mosaic of the Father's Family Plan. Excitement grew as the mosaic gelled and revealed more and more understanding.

While I don't know everything in the Father's mind, fellowship with the Trinity has renewed my spirit with the total assurance, that the Trinity within me is the greatest treasure I possess. In our relationships, I think in terms of My Father, My Savior and My Spirit Counselor and Teacher. It is a personal relationship with each of them. We need to understand that our spirits are directly linked to the Three Spirits of the Trinity. Our work's righteous efforts are subject to our free will, which is subject to Satan's efforts of deceit. If the actions of your will favors Satan, you are out of God's will. The Spirit will be judging you on your will at the end of your faith walk, to see if it brings glory to the Father. If not, you will just be like another Adam descendant after your name is removed from the Book of Life.

Regarding my layman's understanding of the Father's Family Plan, I want to say that the revelations I received came with peace and excitement of the Spirit's presence. I have no doubts about what I am sharing, came from counseling and teaching received from The Holy Spirit. This Spirit counsel and teaching has been detailed in depth above. Since I have been commissioned twice by Father; once in 1974 for a 35 year nursing home ministry, and again 2009 to search and find the truths in His Word, followed by a ministry announcing Jesus' second coming, I have never worried about my salvation. However, I did experience an ever increasing desire to serve my Father, as a thank you gift for His Grace and Mercy. It is the greatest gift of love I have ever known, where God the Father sacrificed His Son to cover my sins, so I could be a part of the family he waited on since the beginning of time. For the Father, it was a time of long suffering that started in the garden and continues today. If you measure the decadence in today's world as a harbinger of the Jesus' second coming, and if you are quiet, you may hear the voices of the martyrs, crying out from under the alter "How long O Lord, How long!"

119

LOVE - BOOK OF LIFE - JUDGMENT

OCTOBER 16, 2014: After the evening meal, Joan and I talked about the love we had for each other agreeing that the foundation of our love was our Father's love. We have experienced an abundance of joy and peace as we remember many blessings of a loving Father. I would like to share the background of this special evening to show that the ALZ valley can be a very special blessing of the Father. The Father does not leave nor forsake His children. Actively seek Him and you will find Him, if you are among His Chosen.

When Joan was diagnosed with ALZ, we discussed it with the Father. When I say Father, I know I am talking to the Father member of the Trinity. I say Father often because He commissioned me twice; once in 1974 and again in 2009. When you address one member of the Trinity, you are really speaking to all members of the Trinity. Since the Counselor is charged to open up the Word to the Chosen, almost all of my contact with the Trinity for this Record, comes from the Spirit. The Father has become a very special father figure and friend. I like the sound of "Father" and may say Father when receiving revelations from the Spirit. I don't think the Trinity has any heartburn over my use of Father because of their Unity, Love and Majesty Coequal. Getting to experience the fellowship of the Trinity inspires a strong desire to serve Them now and join their holy family later. I often think about Job's relationship with the Father and I share his sense of TOTAL DEPRAVITY when comparing myself with God. When I obeyed the Father's directive to get into the Word and began my walk with the Spirit 2009, the Bible came alive. One of the most important doctrines, revealed by the Spirit, was TOTAL DEPRAVITY. I recognized and confessed my understanding of my role in the Trinity's economy that my legacy began in the garden with sin providing a destiny of hell. That I was one of countless identical lifeless souls, without any human value and destined for hell from conception. The only avenue to the Spirit filled life and salvation was the Father's Grace Option. This option began with the random selection of His Chosen for the Book of Life. It was clear that I was not involved in or deserved having my name in the Book of Life. My future depends totally on GRACE. I am in no position to question any aspect of the Father's sovereignty and Will, while recognizing everything He does is for His PURPOSE AND GLORY.

We are in no position to question the Father, but we are provided the opportunity to demonstrate work's righteousness that glorifies Him and qualifies us for access to the cross and salvation.

Joan and I acknowledge the following facts regarding our situation:

1. Our souls were chosen by Him before the foundation of the world.
2. Our names are in His Book of Life.
3. He knows our lives from beginning in the soul pool to eternity in His Kingdom.
4. His Will for our lives, including dates of birth and death, were established while we were still in the soul pool.
5. We accept His Will, regarding healing Joan's ALZ/Dementia.
6. In accordance with the scriptures, we continued to raise our prayers to His throne of grace for healing while reaffirming our complete support for His Will.

Based on His omniscience, we knew He coveted our prayers when He selected our souls for the Book of Life and that they were considered in His Will decisions. Our youngest son died of cancer after many years of prayers. When the doctor asked Wayne if he wanted medical intervention to prolong his life, his answer was "Why! I can't lose, the Lord will either heal me or take me home." Wayne's last sentence, when he suddenly awoke from a disturbed sleep was "Satan, you are defeated!" and returned to a quiet sleep. A couple of hours later, without awakening, he repeated multiple Hallelujahs and left to meet his Father. Joan and I have discussed her going home to paradise and waiting for me to join her. We have complete joy and peace over placing our future in the hands of a Father, who is second to none, when it comes to blessing those who love and serve Him.

The understanding and acceptance of God's will and love is based on a God breathed exegesis (TRUTH) which is opened up and revealed to the Chosen by the Spirit. The screening of the chosen begins with Adam who started a legacy of death for all of his descendants. The Father knew all of His children would be locked into Spiritual death because of Adams sin. This is the beginning, when the Father set in motion his plan for salvation of His Chosen. Prior to creation, His plan called for pre-screening the souls in the soul pool, on the basis of the chosen and unchosen. Therefore, all of Adam's descendants, not listed in the Book of life, remained under the curse of Spiritual death because of Adam's sin. To continue His plan for the chosen, the Father set up a series of screens to weed out the chaff from the wheat. The bible tells us that "few will enter the narrow gate." This gate is the second screening station weeding out chosen from the Book of life. We don't know how many there are in the "few" who entered the narrow gate. The Spirit is the gate keeper who invites only the chosen to enter. I believe a large number of the Chosen will have their names removed from the Book of Life, by four screening stations set up to separate the wheat from the chaff. All children, chosen and unchosen, have free will. The unchosen were screened out in the Father's random selection of those whose names would be entered in the Book of Life. The Chosen screening stations were set up to challenge the heart condition on their willingness for giving unconditional love toward the Father in recognition of the love gift given by the sacrifice of His son. You must come to the Father allowing your will to become part of His Will by joining the combined will of the Trinity. THIS IS OUR SALVATION VICTORY IN CHRIST. A LOVE VICTORY ONLY EXPERIENCED IN THE FAMILY OF GOD.

Like the expression "You have come a long way baby" that was used to describe great improvement toward a goal, we can understand the Father's character trait of "Long Suffering" by the following path:

1. The Father used dirt in the Garden to create a son in His own image and providing him a help mate. Adam and Eve were both holy until Adam sinned. Jesus has been referred to as the second Adam. Both Adams were alike in every respect as true man until Adam sinned. They received seed from the same Father, came from the same soul pool, given a free will spirit and tempted by Satan. The first Adam stained us with his sin while the second Adam provided the sacrifice without blemish that was the only acceptable anecdote for the stain of sin. After the fall, the first Adam was divorced from the Spirit and the Tree of Life. The second Adam's legacy began with the Book of Life and entered life with the seed of the Father, bypassing the sin of Adam communicated by his seed to his descendants. The seed of Jesus is designed by the Father to initiate His salvation plan providing an escape from Adam's second death communicated to All of his descendants. To escape the second triggered death by Adam's sin, a sacrifice without blemish was needed. The only possible source for such a sacrifice was the Trinity. At this point, we can ask the question, why does a divine sovereign God, who rules with His will to serve his purpose and glory, allow His son to become True man by divorcing His divinity to suffer and die for sinners? We can ask what the Father received for His grace, mercy and blessings. The only thing that comes to mind is His desire to share a new heaven and earth with a family worthy enough to be called the bride of Jesus, our savior.

SINCE GOD'S SOVEREIGNTY, WILL, OMNIPOTENCE, AND OMNISCIENCE ARE ALWAYS ACTIVE, WE KNOW SATAN IS UNDER THE CONTROL OF THE TRINITY. IT APPEARS THAT THE FATHER'S PURPOSE IS TO USE SATAN'S POWERS OF DECEPTION TO SEPARATE THE WHEAT FROM THE CHAFF AMONG THE CHOSEN. AS I RECALL, SATAN AND A THIRD OF THE ANGELS WERE KICKED OUT OF HEAVEN BY THE

FATHER. IT APPEARS THAT SATAN AND A THIRD OF THE
ANGELS EXCERCISED THEIR FREE WILL AND THE FATHER
RESPONDED APPROPRIATELY BY EXERCISING HIS WILL IN
JUDGMENT.

WARNING!!! IF THE FRUITS OF YOUR FREE WILL LACK WORK'S
RIGHTEOUSNESS TO GLORIFY THE FATHER, YOU ARE NOT
ONE OF HIS CHOSEN OR YOU ARE A CHOSEN THAT WILL BE
SCREENED OUT OF THE BOOK OF LIFE, FOR YIELDING TO
SATAN'S DECEPTIONS. THE FATHER WANTS A FAMILY BUT
WILL NOT ACCEPT A FREE WILL OR HEART THAT IS NOT IN
HARMONY WITH THE TRINITY. KEEP IN MIND THAT THE
FATHER IS OMNISCIENT, KNOWING US BETTER THAN WE
KNOW OURSELVES.

2. The continued degradation, of spiritual and moral values
    demonstrated by Satan's impact on the free will of man, called for
    stage two of the Father's plan: wipe out civilization with a flood
    and start anew with Noah's family in an ark. While the sin issue
    continued after the flood, two important plan issues surfaced
    regarding Jesus' lineage from Abraham and the introduction
    of the 10 commandments. The significance of Abraham is his
    demonstration of work's righteousness, by his willingness to obey
    the Father's request to sacrifice his son, thereby identifying him
    as one of the Father's Chosen. There are many Old Testament
    Chosen, like Abraham, who earned work's righteousness credit
    to access salvation through Jesus, the promised Messiah. This
    established Jesus as a descendant of one of the Father's Chosen,
    who was willing to give up his son upon the Father's request. What
    the Father asked of Abraham, as a test of his obedience, was a
    precursor to asking His son to be sacrificed for our sin. There is
    no greater act of love than our Father sacrificing His son to cleanse
    us of our sins. It provides insight into the depth of His desire to
    have a family, who desires Trinity acceptance and become one with
    each member of the Trinity. The only way we can thank our triune

God is to give Him glory for the grace we received and continue to honor Him throughout eternity.

There is a need to know biblical truth before sharing your understanding of truth in witnessing God's love. It is scary to think about the spiritual damage caused by a large number of contending denominational doctrines, selling their brand of God's love that promises a primrose path to salvation. If your understanding of John 3:16 is a free gift of salvation available to anyone who asks, you are living in a dream world of false biblical doctrine. Have you ever had the following biblical truths explained to you?

1. Before the foundation of the world, the Father randomly selected a number of souls and placed their names in the Book of Life.
2. The names in the Book of Life are called God's CHOSEN or ELECT.
3. Only the Chosen are invited to join the Holy Spirit in a faith walk to the cross.
4. The free will of a Chosen exercised in disobedience to the Spirit can result in his/her name being removed from the Book of Life.
5. The Great White Throne Judgment clearly identifies the recipients of the Father's love as those whose names still remained in His Book of life on judgment day.
6. There is no access to the cross and redemption without work's righteousness
7. There is no salvation without work's righteousness.
8. There is no glory given to the Father without work's righteousness.

God used Satan to deceive Adam and Eve into sinning. God is using Satan to deceive you in a work's righteousness test of your will to follow the flesh rather than the Spirit. Your spirit yielding to Satan's deceit puts you outside of the Father's Will and your name will be removed from the Book of Life.

The lip services of baptism and alter calls will not gain access to a righteous kingdom, currently inhabited by the Trinity, angels and martyrs of the first resurrection, who were invited by Jesus to rule with Him for a 1000 years.

THE FIRST COMING - CIRCA AD 70

Consider the scenario of the first resurrection found in Revelation 20:1-6

> Verse 1: An angel comes down from heaven with the key to the bottomless pit and a great chain in his hand.

> Verse 2: Angel binds Satan for a thousand years.

> Verse 3: Angel Casts Satan into the bottomless pit, puts a seal on him so he could not deceive the nations for a thousand years after which he will be released for a little season.

> Verse 4: John sees the thrones and those sitting on them who were to give judgment; and he saw the souls who were beheaded for witness of Jesus, the Word of God, had not worshiped the beast or his image, had not received his mark on their foreheads or hands: They lived and reigned with Christ a thousand years.

> Verse 5: The rest of the dead did not live again until the thousand years were finished.

THIS IS THE FIRST RESURRECTION!

> Verse 6: Blessed and holy are those in the first resurrection; the second death has no power over them; they shall be priests of God and Christ and reign with them a thousand years.

Did you notice who Jesus selected for His thousand-year reign? The martyrs who gave their lives as a thank offering to the Father, for the gift of redemption in Jesus' sacrifice! The remaining dead members in the Book of Life would be taken up in the second resurrection. We are called to lay up treasures in heaven. When you consider Abraham's and the Father's righteous gifts of their sons, it is clear that life is the gift of greatest value to you and the greatest treasure you can lay up in heaven. The Father's first gift to man in His creation was the gift of life breathed into Adam. THE GREATEST GIFT YOU CAN GIVE THE TRINITY IS THE LIFE THEY GAVE YOU. We were born with two lives - the physical and the spiritual. One way we can separate the chosen from the unchosen is in the number of times you die. The Unchosen are born once and die twice, having died a physical death followed a spiritual death at the Great White Throne Judgment (GWTJ). The chosen die the physical death but their spiritual death is held in abeyance, pending the results of screening actions deciding access to the cross. Those denied access to the cross will join the unchosen and their names will be erased from the Book of Life. Those who gain access to the cross, will be cleansed by Jesus' blood that pays the ransom for their spirits. The battle for the soul is a spiritual battle between Satan or Satan's unclean spirits and the Holy Spirit. Satan knows he had the unchosen in his camp since Adam's sin. We need to understand, that as God's chosen, we carry the burden of sin as Christians until cleansed by the cross.

> Paul:12-1 "I beseech you therefore, by the mercies of God that you present your bodies a living sacrifice, holy, acceptable unto God, which is your REASONABLE SERVICE."

YOUR RELATIONSHIP WITH GOD IS PERSONAL AND HE WILL HOLD YOU PERSONALLY RESPONSIBLE FOR THE TRUTH YOU ACCEPT AS GOSPEL.

There are those who do not accept the fact that the first resurrection described above happened in AD 70. They also believe in the rapture of the church before tribulation saying God wouldn't allow His children to suffer! The truth you embrace leads to the Lake of Fire or the Father's new creation prepared for His children.

THE SECOND COMING OF THE
LORD - THE FINAL VICTORY.

I believe that the first coming, described using Revelation 20:1-6 above, occurred in AD-70. The chosen will share in the Second Coming. Revelation 20:7-15:

> Verse 7: And when the thousand years are expired, Satan shall be loosed out of his prison.

> Verse 8: Satan will deceive nations all over the world, including Gog and Magog and gather them together to battle. Their number is like the number of the sand of the sea.

> Verse 9: They encircled the camp of the saints and the beloved city: Fire came down from heaven and devoured them.

> Verse 10: The devil was cast into the lake of fire and brimstone to join the beast and false prophet where they will be tormented day and night for ever and ever.

> Verse 11: And I saw a Great White Throne, and Him that sat on it from whose face the earth and heaven fled away.

> Verse 12: I saw the dead, small and great, stand before God. One set of books was opened and the dead were JUDGED by what was written in the books ACCORDING TO THEIR WORKS. And another book was opened, which is the Book of Life.

> Verse 13: And the sea gave up the dead which were in it along with those in death and hell. They were judged every man ACCORDING TO THEIR WORKS.

> Verse 14: Death and hell were cast into the Lake of Fire. THIS IS THE SECOND DEATH, DEATH OF THE SPIRIT.

Verse 15: And whosoever was not found written in the Book of Life WAS CAST INTO THE LAKE OF FIRE.

In the first coming, we had Satan bound and cast into the bottomless pit for a thousand years, the martyrs WERE RESURRECTED to rule with Jesus for a thousand years and the remaining Chosen and unchosen remained dead for a thousand years, to await the second judgment. These Chosen have achieved righteousness at the cross, so their names will be in the Book Of Life opened at The Great White Throne Judgment. Now we see Satan released to gather his troops for the second tribulation period. The focus of Satan's efforts will be to mirror those used in the first tribulation. Satan is/was under the control of Jesus during both tribulation periods. Satan will be allowed to harass the Chosen of God within limits set by Jesus. This provides the final screening test of the living Chosen of God. The facts of the two Great White Throne Judgments include:

1. Jesus was the Judge of both courts -- the first court mentions 'thrones' and the second court mentions 'throne!' Since we realize the "Unity of the Trinity" must be maintained, we can assume all three members of the Trinity were present for duty on both courts. In any case, the Father gave Jesus all power and authority to rule; Jesus was the judge. Based on the unity of the Trinity, Jesus' judgments were in the perfect Will of the Trinity.
2. In both courts, only the Chosen whose names were in the Book of Life would be accepted as the Father's children. Only the beheaded of the Chosen facing the first Court were resurrected to rule with Jesus for a thousand years.
3. All chosen remaining after the first court judgment and all martyrs and chosen from the second court judgment would be granted access to the Father's family.
4. Only the names of the chosen, that survive erasure from the Book of Life for work's righteousness, will be in the Book of Life considered by the court.

THE FATHER IS ASKING HIS CHOSEN TO HELP FIND AND COUNSEL MISSING CHOSEN UNAWARE OF THEIR BEING CHOSEN OF GOD.

The interest in the subject of 'end times' is generating fervor, excitement and many wild prophecies. There is an overabundance of books and more recently movies, that are competing for recognition and monetary reward. With a little searching, you stand a good chance of finding information that fits in your comfort zone but consists of false doctrine. I am just "A Layman Crying in the Wilderness; Where are my Father's Children? It looks like I am just another one, running with the crowd, seeking recognition and reward. Since I was commissioned by my Father to get into the Word and learn the truth from the Holy Spirit, I have already received my rewards in revelations received and serving in fellowship with the Trinity. Any royalties received will be used to support ministries actively engaged in the mission field. RECOMMENDATION: The books (mine also) you read, including movies you see, require Spirit counsel to determine the veracity of their truth content. The Father sent the Holy Spirit to His chosen to reveal biblical truth.

So our future is awaiting the Great and Terrible Day of the Lord when Satan will be defeated and cast into the lake of fire. Just prior to the battle, angels will be sent all over the world to gather the Elect (Chosen) for the battle. There is no seven year warning to escape the tribulation for those who don't want to suffer or be martyrs. It blows my mind that anyone would think they deserve to be spared the pain of tribulation when church history is replete with martyrs giving their all in witness. If the Father chastises those whom He loves, it would be reasonable to assume that those praying for a pre-tribulation rapture serve a different father.

In response to John's question on who will be included in the first resurrection, John was told that only those who would not take the mark of the beast and were beheaded. The rest of the dead would be taken up in the second resurrection. For the pre-tribulation rapture hopefuls, be prepared to go through tribulation and understand that only the Chosen/Elect will be taken up (raptured) in time to join Jesus' battle with Satan.

Now is the time for your spirit to ponder your chosen status by examining your spirit to Spirit channel to insure you are walking in one accord with the Spirit. If you have read his far, you are aware of the importance of walking under Holy Spirit power.

The chosen who died before the battle, will reside in paradise, the place where Jesus told the thief on the cross "Today you will be with me in paradise." There we will await the angels gathering of the saints, to join Jesus for the battle with Satan. Following the victory, Jesus will convene the Great White Throne Judgment.

The Father' Plan:

1. Reveals a step by step process to identify, draw, teach, baptize, counsel and select chosen that will give glory to the Father.
2. Introduces a plan to screen His Chosen to separate the wheat from the chaff.
3. Satan is picked by the Father to be the Great Deceiver of the Chosen.
4. Satan's action's would be within constraints established and controlled by Jesus. Consider Job, The Father's only constraint on Satin was taking Job's life and Job's faith was rewarded with twice the amount of wealth he lost. We can contrast Job's experiences with Jesus and His martyrs who lives were given to honor the Father. The Father's martyrs were blessed with salvation and eternal life and Jesus was blessed with his return to glory after setting the example of total obedience to the Father. OBEDIENCE TO THE FATHER/TRINITY IS DEMONSTRATED BY ACCOMPLISHING WORK'S RIGHTEOUSNESS TO GAIN ACCESS TO THE CROSS AND SALVATION. THE SPIRIT WILL EVALUATE YOUR WORKS TO SEE IF THE FATHER RECEIVES GLORY.
5. You must be under and embrace the counsel of the Spirit to display obedience acceptable to the Spirit. Your obedience to the Spirit is the same as obedience to the Father.

6. The beginning of God's Grace started with the Book of Life's listing of the names of God's Chosen, who will be given the opportunity to qualify for salvation via the Spirit. These are the names given to the Son, who will die for their sins. This means that the remaining souls in the pool were not under John 3:16's Grace and destined to be eternally cursed by Adams's sin.

WARNING! There are hundreds of denominations, in our country, championing their unique brand of doctrines. Most are based on ego controlled intellectual decisions in application of their designed hermeneutical exegetical principles. BOTTOM LINE: EXEGESIS, THAT IS NOT SPIRIT LED, IS EXEGESIS LED BY ANOTHER MASTER. It did not take long for my spirit to realize biblical exegesis error is rampant in the church and to conclude that Satan's Weapon of Choice is to use the same plan that worked so well in the garden: COUNSEL MAN'S EGO TO SATISFY MAN'S FLESH. Working on the church's intellectual control through sermon and bible class material, it appears that Satan had little difficulty in showing that the truth of the bible was detrimental to church enrollment and support. It appears that they don't want what happened to Jesus in John 6:66, happen to them when hard truth is proclaimed - Verse 66 "From that time many of his disciples went back, and walked no more with him." John 6:66! You have got to love the way Jesus flags a scripture that causes discomfort to church clergy and bible teachers. Most churches have grown to be an anathema to Christ by the blasphemy in exegesis found in their doctrines. This Record will expose many of them. IMPORTANT GUIDANCE FOR ONE OF THE FATHER'S CHOSEN:

1. Find out if you are among the Chosen.
2. If you are one of the Chosen, evaluate the security of your relationship?
3. Fellowship with Christians that show a hunger and thirst for righteousness.
4. Actively pursue spiritual fellowship with each member of the Trinity.

5. Actively engage the Holy Spirit to lead you into truth. The Father sent the Spirit to be the only reliable source of counsel and teaching on the Word. The Spirit is multilingual. He speaks any language in perfect understanding to the recipient. Communication is between your spirit and the Holy Spirit. Thoughts that come into your mind, with a sense of peace, may be considered coming from The Spirit. What you need to develop is a gift of discernment to ascertain what is and what is not of the Spirit. Seeking the gift of discernment in the early 70's provided my first contact with the Father in 1974, when He gave a scripture: Matthew 6:33 "Seek ye first the Kingdom of God ..." and told me I would never worry about my salvation. I have never worried!

6. Ask your pastor to compare your church doctrines with those found in this record. Most pastors do not want to get into a serious discussion on biblical doctrines such as God's Elect/Chosen, God's sovereignty, God's will, Divinity and John 3:16. This record will deal with all of these issues and more. Most of today's biblical truth is put through a blender to confuse and provide a false understanding of scriptural exegesis that can seriously affect anyone's salvation.

RECOMMENDATION: Read this Record several times asking the Spirit for feedback to your spirit. There is a good chance the pastor will question my theological qualifications. My credentials involve a six year walk with the Holy Spirit who was sent to counsel and teach me biblical truth. I have a Trinity that loves me, supports me and provides me with an abundance of peace and joy. I am committed to being a living sacrifice for the return of Jesus. I HAVE FOLLOWED JESUS' ADVICE TO HIS DISCIPLES TO WAIT ON THE HOLY SPIRIT WHO WILL LEAD YOU INTO ALL TRUTH! This advice and a personal desire to serve my Father. These are my theological qualifications.

If you are one of the Father's chosen, you can possess the same theological qualifications I have, if you have a hunger and thirst for righteousness and adopt the Matthew 6:33 starting point the Father gave me. The Father commissioned me to write this record for use as a guide to His unknown chosen. This Record starts with 6:33 and shows my walk with the Trinity. I would be blessed by each Chosen, following my path to the Cross, knowing their victory at the cross would please each member of the Trinity. Remember you are walking in the Power of the Spirit and Jesus is in control of any and all of Satan's chastisements.

EXEGESIS I

"GOD BREATHED"

8-31-2014 (Sunday) The word "breathed" caught my attention when the Pastor mentioned Jesus "breathed" on His disciples to receive the Holy Ghost. I thought about the garden and where the Father breathed Spirit Life into Adam's soul. The garden, where God breathed life into Adam, was the location of the beginning of all human life.

Genesis 2:7 "And the Lord God formed man of the dust of the ground, and breathed into his nostrils "the breath of Life." This included a spirit of the flesh and the Holy Spirit because Adam, at this point in time, was without sin. After sinning, the Holy Spirit was removed, leaving him with his flesh spirit and all of his seed condemned to hell. This condemnation affected all seed, chosen and unchosen, from birth to death. At this point we need to understand there are two deaths; one of the flesh and one of the spirit. The unchosen die twice; first by the death of the flesh and later the spirit at the Great White Throne Judgment (GWTJ). The chosen's spirit death will be determined by whether their names are still recorded in the Book of Life at the GWTJ.

Genesis 2:7 clearly states that the Father's breath was required for the start of life in man. We know that the Word teaches that there are two forms of human life: one for a spirit led flesh and one for spirit led spirit. When the Father breathed in Adam's nostrils, Adam was provided a Spirit counselor for his spirit and flesh. Adam received the Holy Spirit of God to initiate life, with an opportunity to fellowship with his Father. At this point there was no sin in God's holy garden.

Genesis 6:17 "And behold, I am bringing flood waters on the earth, to destroy from under heaven all flesh in which is the breath of life." Here, we need to distinguish between the spirit-led (Chosen) and spirit-led flesh of life. All will be recorded in the books Jesus ordered opened during the GWTJ. Those Chosen, whose names are recorded in the Book of Life, will inherit eternal life. The rest of those named, including former Chosen, whose names were erased from the Book of Life and written in the book of death (Rev 21: 12) for lack of work's righteousness, were cast into the lake of fire. Now consider:

Genesis 7:15 "And they went into the ark of Noah, two by two, of all flesh, which is the breath of life." The difference between 6:17 and 7:15 is that all flesh died in the flood, except selected chosen, who were offered sanctuary in the ark. It is clear that the Father considered Noah's servant attitude as work's righteousness and the best available candidate, to continue His salvation plan for the family He desired. It's like going back to the garden for a new start, except with the burden of Adam's sin hanging over Noah and his family. It is awesome to consider the power of the Father's will that is enforced by Jesus. The whole scenario of human history was set by the Father before the foundation of the world. The entire soul pool was established and the chosen selected and named in the Book of Life before creation.

John 19:22-23 "And when he had said this, he breathed on them, and saith unto them, Receive ye the Holy Ghost: Whosoever sins you remit, they are remitted unto them, and whosoever sin ye retain, they will be retained." As I considered the small "j" in he (Jesus), I had to step back to see if it conflicted with my earlier comments about the Father breathing "life" into Adam. I quickly realized that my comments dealt with the first member of a species. What's special about this verse is that the disciples were given the power to forgive sins, which they did in Jesus' name. Couple this with Jesus telling the disciples, that could perform even greater miracles than

He had performed suggests that the Holy Spirit would be resident with their spirits.

Confused? Let's step back and establish who Jesus was as True Man. A Divine Jesus had to divorce His divinity to become Jesus as True Man, since the Unity of a Divine Trinity can't be violated. To give Jesus a divine crutch is to drag divinity down to the level of a sinful true man. When the Father gave His seed to Mary, He was providing the seed of a second Adam beginning without sin. The only difference between Jesus and true man was Jesus starting without sin. THERE WAS NO DIVINITY! The bible does not hang God nor Divinity on a cross. Jesus was described as a sacrifice without blemish, who shed his sinless blood to cover the blood of the Father's sinful chosen! To equate a True Man of divinity to a True Man of Sin displays the efforts of churches to bring divinity down to the level of man and makes Jesus' passion, a hoax of the Trinity. Saying Isaiah 53 describes Divinity, rather than the Father's True Man son crucified, will reap the judgment of Revelation 22:20 "And if any man shall take away from the words of the book of this prophecy, God shall take away his part out of the book of life, and out of the holy city, and from the things which are written in this book." This scripture is applicable to the use of dispensationalism, as an intellect driven vehicle to generate false doctrine, favoring prosperity theology, which is evident in most, if not all denominational doctrine.

Jesus as True Man was empowered just as we are empowered as true man after Pentecost. This means that, as true man, Jesus functioned under the guidance of the Trinity. His ministry was managed, directed and supported by a Devine Trinity as a personal counselor. Since the Trinity was divorced from him, the bible indicates he sought guidance through daily prayer. This is akin to our spirit going through our resident Spirit to access the Trinity within us.

Chosen must serve as a vessel of the Spirit, who lends His righteousness to all approved counseled actions that bring glory to the Father. Vessel actions failing to follow Spirit counsel do not bring glory to the Father.

A Father pre-ordained works, for a chosen who does not submit to Spirit counsel, will not bring glory to the Father and risks name erasure from the Book of Life joining the ranks of the unchosen. Your will must accept the fact that serving the Trinity is through submitting yourself as a living vessel, acceptable for use by the Holy Spirit. Since only the righteous can give glory to the Father, the Spirit passes your qualifying actions to the Father, while depositing earned credit to your work's righteousness account. You, like all old and new testament chosen, must earn work's righteousness credit approved by the Spirit, to access the cross for sanctification. Only earned credit, that reflects Glory on the Father will be credited to your account. YOUR RIGHTEOUSNESS FOLLOWS SANCTIFICATION.

The functional areas of each Trinity member determines lead responsibility for oversight. The Father has the lead over the Salvation Plan and establishing His will. Jesus has the lead, as controller, in enforcing the Father's will. The Spirit has the lead for counselling and teaching the chosen, from the narrow gate to the Great White Throne Judgment and serves as the communications interface between a chosen and the Trinity.

As I was finishing the preceding paragraph, I began to wonder about the clarity of my comments on the interaction between the Chosen and vessel role with the Spirit and the Trinity. Consider:

+ When called righteous, Jesus said "There is none righteous, no, not one, only the Father in heaven. Jesus did not consider himself righteous as True Man." Many churches link righteousness with baptism. They don't seem to realize there is no righteousness this side of the cross, because your pardon or sin cleansing is accomplished on the cross. Since all flesh contains sin until death, we can conclude that the Spirits AYE-NAY decision follows death and who will access the cross.

+ As True Man, Jesus received his power through the Spirit. This is the same Spirit that the Father sent us as our counselor, to lead us into all truth. When you walk in the power and counsel of the Spirit, our vessel is in a position to give glory to the Father and earn work's righteousness points for your salvation account.

+ The Trinity is a SPIRIT DIETY, characterized by UNITY and MAJESTY COEQUAL, that cannot be compromised in any manner. For example, Jesus had to leave his deity with the Trinity to become TRUE MAN. While True Man, he had to look to heaven for Trinity Spirit counsel. Remember that the Trinity is the unity of three Spirits, in one accord. The Holy Spirit is the Spirit channel through which the Trinity responds to man's requests. The Spirit planted the seed in Mary and provided the power for the resurrection.

It is interesting to compare a family Trinity in heaven with a human trinity on earth. The Father and Son are bound together by the Spirit and act as a Divine Trinity. The chosen trinity consists of man, spirit and Spirit and only exists, until the last of the Chosen access the Cross. John 3:16 provides a salvation opportunity to demonstrate a work's righteousness path to the cross approved by the Spirit. The Spirit's primary task is to screen and qualify a chosen to access the cross. As I was considering this issue, I was reminded by the Spirit that those who are sanctified by the cross become the Bride of Christ. I have wondered about being called a Bride of Christ but I am confident it all falls into the Father's master plan. Consider the scenario of the Father sending His Son to gather His grandchildren. I believe that bride could be interpreted as the Father's grandchildren. It works for me. Following the Trinity model, the Father used the Holy Spirit to bind the new Spirit of man (received at the cross) with His Son. Jesus told his disciples that when He returned He would be in them as He is in the Father. Can you see the pattern? We have an interlocking of a Jesus-Spirit-man trinity with a Father-Spirit-Son Trinity. While I don't believe the divinity of the first trinity will be shared with me, I will still be in absolute awe of being one with the Trinity, by being linked through the Spirit.

Think of what the Father promised us in John 3:16. As one of His Chosen, we received the Spirit at birth, were drawn by the Spirit through the narrow gate and taught the Word, were baptized in the Trinity and equipped with a measure of faith, were provided Spirit counsel during adversity encountered during the faith walk to the cross, and being honored with an all-in-one trinity victory.

Denominations, seminaries, pastors, bible teachers, evangelists, commentaries, plus video and audio presentations account for the primary platforms for dispensing good and bad doctrine. How does a lay person address this problem? The purpose of my Record of being a Spirit scribe, is to locate and share biblical truth from the Spirit with the unknown chosen. My commission is to share the truth that I believe was revealed to me. The veracity of my truth will be determined by the Spirit confirmation of the Chosen. If the Chosen's receiver spirit is quickened by the Spirit, we have spirit to Spirit confirmation.

Since the Trinity is omnipresent with a Unity and Majesty Coequal, it's one God Divinity that can't be violated. This the reason Jesus, as True Man, had to divorce Himself from the Trinity.

I believe each of the functional Trinity members would take a lead in their area of responsibility, while maintaining Trinity unity.

When I first started seeking God, I wondered which member of the Trinity was responding. I quickly realized that the Spirit, sent by the Father upon a request by Jesus, was my companion, counselor and teacher. He was the one charged to lead me into all truth. The church has to guard against perverting lay persons with false Gospel that has eternal life consequences.

Maybe because of my love for the Father, I would, on occasion, discern that my Father was speaking to me. The Spirit just reminded me that the unity of the Trinity is the role model for His new family to follow. Because of Jesus sanctification of our soul, we now have Spirit life linked to the Trinity. Let's Look at John 14:20 again "At that day you will know that I am in my Father, and ye are in me, and I in you." What does this mean?

+ Our spirits are linked to the Triune God.
+ Our wills are linked to the perfect will of the Father.
+ Our desires will manifest acceptance of the Father's sovereignty with an acclamation of joy.

+ We will enjoy the awesome glory of the Trinity within.
+ We will savor the magnitude of God's gift, as it engulfs our spirit and soul.
+ We will celebrate the gift of eternal life.
+ We will understand why we had to have an account of actions of work's righteousness, before accessing the cross and sanctification through Jesus.
+ As we consider the price paid for our salvation, we can gain an understanding of the Father's love and desire to share creation with a family, that demonstrates a hunger and thirst for righteousness.
+ John 15:26 "But the comforter, which is the Holy Ghost, Whom the Father will send in my name, He shall TEACH YOU ALL THINGS AND BRING ALL THINGS TO YOUR REMEMBERANCE." To reject this gift of the Spirit is a guarantee of a request to appear before the Great White Throne Judgment.

These scriptures paint the following scenario:

+ The Father randomly chose the names written in the Book of Life before the foundation of creation.
+ A Salvation opportunity is offered only to those whose names are written in the Book of Life. These are the Father's ELECT or CHOSEN
+ Only those Chosen, who received the Spirit Baptism can receive the faith to engage the Counselor as a vessel, draw on Spirit power to acquire 'work's righteousness points" for his or her salvation account.
+ Like Abraham, the Chosen will have an account of earned "work's righteousness points" awarded by the Spirit, that demonstrates their hunger and thirst for righteousness. The Spirit will use their accounts to weigh the condition of their hearts toward the Father. If He finds weakness, their names will be removed from the Book of Life. The holiness of sanctification demands complete commitment to the GLORY of God. James claim, discounted by most denominations, 'that faith without works is dead' stands as a great stumbling block to truth and salvation.

For those who reject James' position on works, deny the Father's Word about being created in Christ Jesus for good works. No works mean you were not named in or removed from the Book of Life.

The Father set up a Soul Pool with the number of souls needed to cover the period from the Garden of Eden to the Great and Terrible Day of the Lord. Then, He randomly selected (choose) and recorded their names in His 'Book of Life.' These Chosen represent the total number of souls eligible to receive the Father's gift of grace. These are the souls given an opportunity to demonstrate work's righteousness approved by the Spirit. Spirit approval provides access to the cross and salvation.

IMPORTANT: The exegesis of John 3:16 has created church divisiveness over the understanding of "WORLD." The Father's Will limits a salvation opportunity to those He has named in His Book of Life, written before creation. Most churches offer an open invitation to all who would apply. Those churches sponsoring an open invitation, will be in conflict with the Father's Will! Being in conflict with the Father's Will is akin to refusing the Spirit's counsel, which can be an untenable position for one seeking salvation.

John 3:16 "For God so loved the world, that He gave His only begotten Son, that whosoever believeth in him should not perish, but have everlasting life."

The following scriptures are important to the understanding of 3:16. As you read them, it is helpful to keep in mind that the Trinity is all knowing and all powerful when dealing with man.

John 3;17 "For God sent not His Son into the world to condemn the world; but that the world through him might be saved." FACT: ACCESS TO A SALVATION OPPORTUNITY IS ONLY GRANTED TO THE CHOSEN. As Jesus prayed in the garden, he Told his Father that he did not pray for the world but only for those whom He had given him; God's Chosen are listed in the Book of Life.

John 3:18 "He that believeth on him is not condemned: but he that believeth not is condemned already, because he hath not believed in the name of the only begotten Son of God." Jesus is the Way, the Truth and the LIFE, no one comes to the Father but through him. Only those led by the Spirit have access to the salvation path. Access is offered only to those named in the Book of Life. Belief in Jesus is an act of righteousness controlled by the Spirit.

John 3:19 "And this is the condemnation, that life is come into the world, and men loved darkness, rather than light, because their deeds were evil." These are Adam's seed of sin that lies in all of his descendants, including those in the Book of Life. However, under the Father's sovereign act of grace, for those in the Book of Life, a salvation opportunity was provided to demonstrate work's righteousness and gain the right to access the cross.

John 3:20 "For every one that doth evil hateth the light, neither cometh to the light, lest his deeds should be reproved." Today, evil is openly flaunted with little fear of reproach. A sign of the end times. Only the Chosen who accept the Spirit's invitation to enter the narrow gate are offered a path to the light.

Recently, I was thinking about the intended audience of the Word when, thanks to the Spirit, my spirit began recalling (bringing into remembrance) scriptures for consideration. Consider "world" being defined as "Creation." Can we rationally argue that God loved every one regardless of sin and offered a salvation option to everyone who asked? Why did the Father, before creation of the physical world and man, put the names of His Chosen in the Book of Life? Jesus said "There is none worthy, no not one, only the Father in heaven. It is ludicrous to say that God loves all sinners when He designed His salvation plan to cleanse only those in His Book of Life, who prove worthy. As I keep repeating, Jesus told His Father, he only prays for those He had given him. IF THE FATHER HAD DENIED FREE WILL TO MAN, MAN WOULD BE UNDER GOD'S WILL, THERE WOULD BE NO SIN AND JESUS WOULD NOT HAVE BEEN CRUCIFIED.

IMPORTANT: SIN COUPLED WITH FREE WILL IS A KEY TO UNDERSTANDING THE FATHER'S SALVATION PLAN.

I recall asking the Father why he loved David so much, considering the sin of arranging the death of his general, to make his wife available for marriage. His response opened another example of His sovereignty by using GLORY as a major key to His Purpose and Glory. David had brought much glory to the Father. Now compare this with sin. Sin is linked to lack of righteousness and we all sin daily. "There is none righteous, no not one." Since the Father does everything to satisfy His Purpose and GLORY, what role does sin play?

A MAJOR REVELATION ON GOD'S GLORY

"THE KEY TO SALVATION IS WORK'S RIGHTEOUSNESS."

Following the lead of the Spirit, here are my revelations:

1. The Father designed a Family Plan that takes His assets and sets His Will to provide a family for His new creation.
2. The Plan assets included:
   + Satan, as an accuser of the brethren, would be used as a chastiser of the Chosen from Adam to the Day of the Lord.
3. Based on His free will experience with Satin, the Father provided free will to Adam and His descendant which would guarantee their sin nature and establish His sovereignty.
4. Placed Satan in the garden to chastise Adam by providing counsel that Adam could be like God, if he ate of the fruit. This locked in sin to all of Adams's descendants, which included both the Chosen and the unchosen.
5. The plan then introduced the gift of John 3:16, to provide a salvation opportunity for the Chosen. It covered the sin of the spirit. This was sin covered by Jesus' ransom.
6. The Father then set up a series of screens to separate the Chosen wheat from the chaff. The Spirit has functional control of the

screens: The Narrow Gate, the Word of God to qualify for Baptism and the Faith Walk to the Cross.

It is the faith walk that establishes 'GLORY' as the key to salvation. There is no salvation without the Father receiving GLORY. Sin is used as a tool to evaluate works that give the Father GLORY. Here, we join hands with the Chosen, of the Old Testament, in linking Sin to work's righteousness resulting in glorying God.

IT IS REALY NEAT, THAT THE OLD AND NEW TESTAMENTS FOLLOWED THE SAME PATH TO SALVATION. THE ONLY DIFFERENCE IS THE SPIRIT COUNSEL INVOLVED. IN THE OLD TESTAMENT, COUNSEL WAS RECEIVED FROM THE TRINITY IN HEAVEN, WHILE IN THE NEW TESTAMENT, COUNSEL WAS PROVIDED BY AN INDWELLING HOLY SPIRIT. Now reconsider:

1. Ephesians 2:10 "For we are His workmanship, created in Christ Jesus for good works, WHICH GOD PREPARED BEFOREHAND THAT WE SHOULD WALK IN THEM."
2. Hebrews 13:6-8 "6: For whom the Lord loveth he CHASTENED, and SCOURGETH every son whom He receiveth . 7: If ye ENDURE chastening, God dealeth with you as with sons; for what son is he whom the Father chasteneth not? 8: BUT IF YE BE WITHOUT CHASTISEMENT, whereof all are partakers, then ARE YE BASTARDS, AND NOT SONS.

It all comes down to the faith walk under the counsel of the Holy Spirit. Note in Ephesians 2:10 above, that the Father had prepared beforehand the works that we are to walk in. Here is the scenario:

The Chosen acts as a vessel to the Holy Spirit. The Spirit introduces and provides counsel on works the Father had prepared beforehand. Failure to follow Spirit counsel, in work performance, will result in denial of works righteousness credit. A series of work's righteousness efforts will form the basis for evaluating access to the cross. The decision is based on the GLORY received by the Father. Remember, it was not sin the made David great, it was the glory he provided the Father. The Father has set up a series of works for a Chosen to accomplish while under chastisement by Satan. The Spirit will provide counsel to and critique the Chosen on the merits of his/her performance regarding work's righteousness.

I believe the Father wants a family that emulates the unity of the Trinity, wherein the unity of the family spirit mirrors the Trinity in thought, word and deed bound by the Father's love. It could be called a divine Trinity in unity with a chosen unity family quickened by the Father's love and desire.

I believe, when the Father talks about long suffering, He is referring to completion of cleansing the sins of His Chosen. His plan was formulated before creation, implemented in the garden and reached fruition during the Great White Throne Judgment.

I don't understand why the Father's plan took so long, other than to demonstrate His Patience during the evolution of His salvation plan. I do know that I will always desire the protection, peace and joy of His WILL.

3. The John 3:16 world is limited to the Chosen. The intent was to provide His Chosen exposure to the "narrow gate." Matthew 7:14 provides a salvation insight not readily accepted by most churches: "Because narrow is the gate and difficult is the way which leads to life, and there are few who find it." 'Narrow' suggests the restricted access of the chosen and 'difficult' suggests being chastised by Satan during performance of the Father's preordained works during a walk of faith.

Scripture tells us that many are called but few are chosen to enter the narrow gate. This is the first screening of the Chosen. Access was limited to those Chosen who accepted the Spirit's invitation. We don't know how many of the Chosen would yield to the desires of the flesh and bypass the "narrow gate," but scripture declares "few will enter therein." Considering a scenario of conflict between Satan and the Spirit, controlled by Jesus, chastisement is not a cake walk that awaits the Chosen. The Father uses Satan, as a screening tool for the Spirit, to chastise the Chosen in the salvation pipeline. The Father did say that "He chastises those whom He loves." Jesus insures that Satan's application of chastisement is within the Father's Will. Satan's weapon of choice is DECEPTION. This was the first Spirit screening of the Father's Chosen from His soul pool. We don't know the number or their location, but the Great Commission (Mark 16:15-16) charges us to go into the entire world and find them.

Continuing with 'that whosoever ...'

4. Only the Chosen can be drawn by the Spirit through the narrow gate.
5. Only those Chosen baptized by the Spirit can start the walk of faith to the cross.
6. Only those Chosen, given the faith to be Spirit Led, are given the opportunity to earn work's righteous points, to access the cross for cleansing of their sin.

Another thought came to mind earlier today that causes me worry about church clergy and leadership. Based on the confusion evident among denominational doctrines, I fear that many church intellectuals responsible for doctrine are not among the Chosen. Their application of hermeneutics would be "Satan-led" versus "Spirit-led," yielding a myriad of competing church doctrines. Lacking Spirit Counsel, they would be exposed to Satan's weapon of choice for feeding the egos of purveyors of false doctrine. THE CHURCH MUST UNDERSTAND THAT "NO ONE KNOWS THE MIND OF GOD!" ONLY HIS CHOSEN ARE GRANTED ACCESS TO HIS EXEGESIS.

Consider the dilemma of the Father's church!100's and 100's of denominations with 100's and 100's of doctrine, providing a thick catalog of truths tailored to your every whim. Footnotes are provided to counsel a pastor on denominational trappings of 21st century feel good theology. The problem today is that there is little challenge to what is being taught or preached. The norm is that congregations accept church doctrine without knowing what it is. Today's churches operate in a spiritual malaise that permits denominational control through seminary teaching of pastors and bible study material. THE CHURCH HAS BECOME A PAMPERED

CHILD AND NOT A CHURCH TRIUMPHANT. I believe most of today's living chosen are unaware of their Chosen status. It is my prayer that you are among the chosen and will be blessed by my record. As a layperson, you may have a pastor or Sunday school teacher sharing bad doctrine. This record provides Spirit led truth in layman terms. Use this record as an example of a layperson's walk with the Spirit.

EXEGESIS II

DIVINITY

4/1/13: Sunday school class, John Chapter 1 on Divinity! The teacher began his discussion by establishing his belief that, as man, Jesus possessed Divinity. I said one needs to address several issues in a doctrine of divinity based on scriptural exegesis. I mentioned several from the following list I later compiled.

1. Can Divinity sin?
2. Can Jesus be TRUE MAN and Divine at the same time?
3. Was the Trinity guaranteeing a sinless sacrifice by virtue of a Divine true man?
4. Did Jesus consider himself righteous as true man?
5. How do you explain divinity and righteousness hanging on the cross as a sin bearer?
6. Can Jesus be Divine and unrighteous at the same time?
7. Can Jesus be true man and righteous at the same time?
8. Can the unity of the Trinity be violated if the divinity of Jesus takes up residence in True Man?
9. Why did Jesus tell Mary not to touch him because he had not ascended to the Father to receive His Glory? Can Jesus be divine without possessing glory?
10. Do you even think that the Father, or the Trinity (Jesus included) would consider, even for a moment, lessening the magnitude of the gift of His Son? If so, you do not know the Trinity or

the mind of God! The awesomeness of the Trinity displayed by this unified gift of love would not allow a crutch of divinity to overshadow the depth of Jesus' pain and suffering. GOD DOES NOT PROTECT "TRUE MAN" BY PRECLUDING THE POSSIBILITY OF SINNING WITH A "DIVINE TRUE MAN!" A DIVINE TRUE MAN SAVIOR IS A TRAVESTY TO BIBLICAL EXEGESIS!

Regarding the Divinity issue, my personal sense is that Jesus did not operate under his personal divine power, but Trinity approved power administered by the Spirit to satisfy Jesus' requests. The Unity of the Trinity and its Three in One doctrines demands the presence of all three members. I believe that when the True Man Jesus made his prayers to the Father, the response was a Trinity response which included a Divine Jesus. Jesus, as True Man, provides an interesting departure from the Trinity's standard mode of operations. Jesus was the only Trinity member to divest Himself of His divinity, to carry out a Trinity decision to be TRUE MAN, absent the sin of Adam. It is interesting to note that in this arrangement, a divine Jesus took part in the Trinity response to His True Man needs. This gift of GRACE to His children provides insight into a FATHER'S LOVE being above human understanding. Think about the Father's Grace, defined by the sacrificial gift of His Son, when you are tempted to exercise the oft expressed question "How could a loving God do this!"

10/18/15: During a church service, the pastor said Jesus could have decided not to die on the cross, which may be true if He was divine. But based on the unity of the Trinity, which is also a unity of Divinity, the Trinity was not resident in Jesus. The Trinity did not become resident in True Man until Pentecost. AN EXAMPLE OF HERMENEUTICS THAT LED TO FALSE EXEGESIS.

Trashing the image of the Father's Sovereignty with the Church's saying Jesus was a Divine True Man, denigrates the magnitude of the Father's love displayed by their Sacrificial Gift. The Father's pain was so great that He could not look at His son on the cross. And yet the Father said it pleased Him to offer His son. How a True Man can equate to a Divine

True Man can only be understood in terms of applying a hermeneutical dispensation to in their exegesis designed to drag Divinity into the mire of man's sin. It raises the issue 'Can Divinity sin?' The Trinity would not and did not provide a Divinity crutch. Satan counseled church doctrine provided the crutch. Fact: Today's church Intellect/Elite staff employing dispensational theology for their doctrines are subject to Revelation 22:19 regarding messing around with the word.

DISPENATIONAL THEOLOGY IS COMPLETELY DEVOID OF ANY UNDERSTANDING OF THE FATHER'S LOVE THAT IS CLEARLY DEFINED IN ISAIAH 53 AND THE NEW TASTEMENT WITNESS OF HIS SON ON THE CROSS. TO SAY THAT THE SON HAD A DIVINITY CRUTCH, COULD ONLY HAVE ORGINATED WITH A CHURCH THEOLOGIAN FOLLOWING SATAN'S COUNSEL.

We all deserve hell, but grace provided an option to battle the power of sin controlled by Satan. This battle graphically illustrates the Trinity commitment to pay the sin ransom for worthy chosen. Whenever we entertain a thought to question or judge God, we all need to take a deep breath and reflect on our legacy going back to the dirt in the garden, the value of minerals in our flesh, and realize our souls are the battle ground for Satan and the Spirit. THE RANSOM PRICE PAID FOR OUR SALVATION WAS JESUS HANGING ON HE CROSS.

Can linking Divinity to True Man be a deliberate attempt to bring Divinity down to the quagmire of man's depravity? Man can't accept the Fathers total sovereignty without accepting man's total depravity. Man needs to go back to the garden to understand his legacy denies him any rights to mess with the Trinity's Divinity and Sovereignty. We must not expose any member of a Divine Trinity to man's attempts to make them a more palatable and acceptable provider of His desires and needs. Don't honor the Trinity with false worship and praise but strive to present your hearts as a living sacrifice acceptable to God.

NO ON KNOWS THE MIND OF GOD
SOME PERSONAL THOUGHTS!

Holy scripture observes that no one knows the mind of God. (I love these little thoughts that are frequently popping into my mind urging my spirit to draw on what the Spirit shared with me during my exposure as a scribe.) Let me share the thoughts that come to mind as I consider the "Mind of God!" I would like to begin with a thought that just popped into my spirit.

+ Throughout my walk serving as a scribe, I have often pondered the Prince of Peace. My spirit was quickened, as I considered the prevailing Satan counseled doctrine of the Divinity of Christ as True Man. If church doctrine can be such an abomination to the Lord, they are probably out to lunch in understanding of Jesus as the Prince of Peace. They love to preach about the coming Prince of Peace ignoring the Book of Revelation and other end times eschatology. The Peace that Jesus brings, doesn't come until after the tribulation and the Great and terrible day of the Lord, leading to Great White Throne Judgment. The Books of the Dead were all judged on their works and cast into the Lake of fire. Those chosen in the Book of Life were all prejudged on their approved work's righteousness granting access to the cross and salvation. The Prince of Peace is Prince only to the Father's chosen who will inherit eternal peace.

+ The first consideration is the Bible! I would suggest that the Word provides much insight in God's mind.

+ Can we conclude that the treasure of His Word Spiritually discerned is the Father's gift to His chosen, that they may know the path to salvation. The greatest gift of the Father's mind is a Grace that provides the Spirit counselor as a faith guide to the cross and salvation. IMPORTANT: The gift of Grace is not a guarantee of salvation - it is a gift of the Spirit to counsel you on your faith walk to the cross. The Spirit's counsel is to convince your free will on issues that arise that could precipitate a fall from Grace. The Spirit will be evaluating the condition of your heart toward the Father and can pull the plug on your salvation. The idea of once saved, always saved is ludicrous and can cause a chosen to fall by the wayside, if not conditioned with righteous works that displays a heart eager to bring glory to the Father.

+ Now we know that the Word represents God's truth and this truth is His road map covering everything from creation to the great white throne judgment. Man's historical response to God's commandments, warnings, prophesy etc., clearly establishes the sin nature of man. The Chosen are granted the Father's GRACE providing a salvation option requiring steadfast compliance to the counsel of the Spirit. Grace does not guarantee salvation, only the opportunity to receive and follow Spirit counseling qualifies one for the Trinity's greatest gift. The Word includes the warning set forth by James: "Faith without works is dead. Show me your faith without works and I will show you mine with works!" THE WORD DOES NOT SAY THE FREE GIFT OF GRACE IS SALVATION.

+ Proper exegesis MUST BE Spirit led exegesis for man to open up the mind of God! One of the most significant issues that the church fails to understand or accept is the counsel that Jesus gave his disciples, when he said that it was the Holy Spirit that leads us into all truth.

The Holy Spirit was not providing the apostles with scriptures for unchosen theologians. The scriptures were designed for layperson consumption. It is evident that today's churches were led by unchosen intellectuals.

11/20/13: A typical sauna (Prayer closet) fellowship with spirit to Spirit interaction. During sauna times, either I or the Spirit bring up subjects for consideration. I had the Divinity issue with Christ on my mind when the soul for Jesus surfaced. I introduced the issue of the soul and raised the question of the soul's source. My conclusion is that it had to come from the Father's soul pool if he were to be declared True Man. When I first entered into dialog with the Father, the first thing that my spirit discerned was His desire for a family who loved Him without question. This was was one of the first and most important insights I had about my Father.

IT IS THE QUESTION OF THE HEART THAT HAS TO BE SATISFIED BY THE HOLY SPIRIT, BEFORE GRANTING ACCESS

TO THE VICTORY OF THE CROSS. THE HEART CONDITION IS LINKED TO WORK'S RIGHTEOUSNESS AND ACCEPTANCE OF THE FATHER'S WILL.

The Father's soul inventory includes elect and non-elect souls in the Father's warehouse with all souls provided free will. Compliance with the counsel of the Spirit weeds out chosen members, whose works of salvation do not meet the high standards of a heart condition acceptable to the Father. Get used to the idea that James was right in suggesting salvation without works is dead. Understand that the faith walk follows Spirit Baptism and that man still has free will. Blasphemy is the unpardonable sin that threatens an elect's salvation by denying the counsel of the Spirit. There is no back door or free ride to salvation! You must go through the narrow gate!! THE FATHER DOES NOT PLAY GAMES WITH HIS CHOSEN. THERE IS NO EASY WAY - YOU MUST BE FOUND WORTHY WHEN RESPONDING TO THE COUNSEL OF THE SPIRIT, TO PARTAKE IN BEING CLEANSED BY THE SAVIOR'S BLOOD - THE ONLY ACCEPTABLE SIN OFFERING. We need to keep in mind that the prize of the Father's creation is not the mind or the body of man, it is the SOUL of man. Often I have heard Christians express confusion over the difference between man's soul and spirit. Jesus did not die for man's intellect/mind nor his spirit. Our spirits are being counseled by Satan's Spirit and the Holy Spirit. Whose counsel you accept determines where your soul will end up. Your souls will be listed in one of two books; the Books of the Dead or the Book of Life. Think about and ponder:

+ The soul is the essence of man.
+ Do members of the Trinity have souls?
+ Where did the soul and seed of Jesus come from?
+ Does the soul issue impact our understanding of "True Man?"
+ What is the purpose of a soul?
+ What is the reason for Satan's battle engagement with the Spirit?
+ Finally, do the Father's random selections include family groupings of His CHOSEN, for man's legacy of a family unity that mimics the unity of the trinity?

As we consider these questions, we need to keep in mind that everything the Father does is for His PURPOSE AND GLORY, PERIOD! These are the thoughts that I would like to share based on scripture and discernment of the Trinity's nature during my walk with the Spirit.

+ In True Man, one can be of the seeds of Adam and Abraham but not their souls. The significance of the seed is that it propagates the sin the of first Adam. When this seed joins with and infects the soul from the Father's soul Pool, original sin lives on. This is why the seed of Jesus had to come directly from the Father to provide a sacrifice without blemish.

+ Ezekiel 18:4 "The soul of the father as well as the soul of the son is Mine: the soul who sins shall die." Ezekiel 18:20 "The soul who sins shall die." The son shall not bear the guilt of the father, nor the father bear the guilt of the son. So we can conclude that the soul of all who follow Adam is the subject to Adam's sin at their birth and not the intervening progeny of their father's sins from Adam. In effect, both chosen and non-chosen souls are subject to the sin of Adam. God's elect must overcome that sin with a faith walk under the counsel of the Spirit.

10/17/15: A Family sharing of scriptures included a DVD discussion of David's broken spirit. The pastor began with David's sin of sending his general to the front lines to get killed so he could marry the general's wife. The pastor noted that it took David a year to break down and repent of his sin. He quoted Psalm 51: "The sacrifices of God are a broken spirit: a broken and contrite heart, O God, thou wilt not despise." He went on to describe the role of brokenness when dealing with sin in our lives. It was a powerful sermon! I just wanted to add:

THIS IS AN EXCELLENT EXAMPLE OF THE FATHER'S CHASTISEMENT POLICY THAT BLESSED DAVID.

+ '.. sacrifices of God...' We are called to be living sacrifices!

+ '.. a broken heart spirit: a broken and contrite heart...' This is the goal of chastisement that prepares you to accept and walk in the Father's Will.

+ The highest form of brokenness is martyrdom. When linked to Jesus, it is the greatest form of living sacrifice that honors Him, as He honored only beheaded martyrs to join Him in the first resurrection and ruling with Him for a 1000 years.

EXEGESIS III

CHRISTIAN FANATIC?

As I considered the revelations in this Record, I thought it would be helpful to provide an up-front testimony, wherein you can base your judgment as to the state of the author's mind. I offer one way you can define 'Christian Fanatic.' He is 'One who loves Jesus more than you do!' There were many times in my early Christian walk that I judged without this definition. I have been an active Christian for many years. I even had a nursing home ministry for 35 years, before the Father commissioned me in 2009 to be a Christian Fanatic, by being a scribe to the Holy Spirit to search the bible for truth. At the age 80, the past six years of walking in the Spirit have been the greatest years of my life.

IF YOU ARE AMONG THE CHOSEN, THIS RECORD WILL PROVIDE YOU ACCESS TO THE KINGDOM OF GOD, BY SIMPLY FOLLOWING THE COUNSEL OF THE HOLY SPIRIT.

The Father's December, 2009 Call: "You need to get into the Word! You can't preach the truth if you don't know the truth!" The Lord spoke those words shortly after He provided a replacement for my 35 year nursing home ministry. Implicit in this call was the assurance that the Holy Spirit would be actively engaged since the Father sent Him as our source for all TRUTH. My testimony will establish my desire to bless Him and an eagerness to understand His truths. In effect, I will be a student and a scribe led by the Holy Spirit searching for the truth in God's Word. The

Lord first commissioned me for His service in the fall of 1974 when He quickened my spirit to Mat 6:33 (Seek ye first His Kingdom …) and promised that I would never worry about my salvation. At the time, I did not connect the "promise" with being "Chosen/Elected" because at the time I viewed "Chosen/Elected" as unfair. After my second Call, I quickly became acquainted with God's "sovereignty" and understood His right to elect/choose whomever He desires. I am now convinced that I was chosen from the beginning of time, even though I did not understand the link between election and salvation until after the Father's second December 2009 Call. I recognize that many will question my saying I was commissioned by my Father. I guess I was thinking of Jesus' Great Commission' call. I am sure the Father is not offended! IN FACT, THE INTENT OF THIS RECORD IS TO GATHER THE CHOSEN FOR THE SON'S GREAT COMMISSION.

Does the Father really speak to me? Also Jesus and/or the Spirit? YES, but while we think of 'speaking' as audible, our spiritual communication is spirit to Spirit. Members of the Trinity can also speak to us verbally, visually and by actions affecting our lives. Herein lies the reason for seeking fellowship with each member of Trinity; most if not all communication is processed through the Spirit based on your ability to discern the Spirit. The greater your discernment, the greater will be your ability to walk in the Spirit and the greater will be the Spirit power of your servant witness to the Trinity. The degree of discernment you possess, is measured in terms of the amount of time spiritual thoughts occupy your mind.

Do I think the Father considers me special because He talks to me? Yes, but not based on merit. I was an inanimate soul when He randomly selected me to be one of His CHOSEN /ELECT! This is why I get excited at being commissioned to find the unknown Chosen all over the world, so that they too, may know they are special to the Father and are being called into His service.

I believe there is one indisputable fact and it is Adam's sin, that condemned all of us to eternal punishment. There is none righteous - no not one! There is a second indisputable fact that all of the Father's actions support His

Purpose and Glory. ENTER GRACE: I believe it is the Father's desire to share His creation with a family. ENTER ELECTION: For His elect, the Father controlled the lineage of the elect, from Adam through Abraham to the Great White Throne Judgment of Jesus and insuring a salvation opportunity to cover the sin of Adam to the second coming of Jesus.

My Father considers all of his ELECT as special, since they were offered the opportunity to be counseled by the Spirit on their walk to the cross and salvation. When I look at my election in light of the Cross and my sin, I feel guilt and wonder at being "elected" to be blessed by the Father's GRACE.

How do I know it is the Father speaking to me and not the Son or the Spirit? Following my call, it was a question I asked myself and have tentatively accepted it as an issue of discernment. In the early 70's, when my friends were actively seeking the gifts of the Spirit, I requested the gift of discernment so I could sense, who and who was not, of the Father. When the Father speaks to my spirit about a personal issue, I feel/sense/discern it is the Father. The doctrine of the Trinity was one of my first Spirit led doctrinal searches of the scriptures. I believe that anyone searching the scriptures, without establishing a Spiritual relationship with the Trinity, is denying himself access to the Spirit of truth. You will be like a member attending a common Christian bible study, wherein members share their individual understandings of a scripture, under a Christian bible study standard practice of never challenging differing understandings and agree to disagree, without applying proper exegesis to the scripture. Searching scriptures without engaging the Spirit is an invitation for Satan to get engaged and control your scriptural understanding.

Once again, do I think I am special? Yes, because I believe anyone granted the GRACE of the Father's ELECTION is special. No one deserves an election based on the grace of a Divine Sovereign God. To be included is a sovereign act of the Father. Only the ELECT are given an opportunity for salvation through GRACE. HEREIN LIES THE GRACE OF GOD; NO ONE HAS EARNED A RIGHT TO SALVATION. THE FATHER SELECTED A RANDOM NUMBER OF INANIMATE SOULS AND PLACED THEIR NAMES IN THE BOOK OF LIFE. The Father's soul pool from which He selected His ELECT were all, except Jesus, subject to the legacy of Adams's sin. I believe this testimony will provide ample information on which to judge my ELECT status. I suggest that you ask the Spirit to lead your spirit, as you weigh the veracity of my Spirit led exegesis of God's Word. Understand that these are my words without outside editing. It is me that the Father commissioned, not me and John Doe! If you can't accept my layman's Record of exegesis and believe you have a Spirit led exegesis that is at variance with mine, you are spiritually obligated to discard my Record. Shades of church history past! Our disagreement echoes the continuing impact of the Father's chief chastiser employing his favorite weapon of mass confusion, through the church's purveyors of false doctrine. The church continues to wallow in the mire of misguided false doctrine, crafted by the great Deceiver!

Considering the rampant invasion of false doctrine in main line denominations, church leadership of biblical truth is suspect. They have rejected Jesus' counsel to His disciples to await the arrival of the Holy Spirit, who would lead them into all truth. There are two spirits vying for control of the truths entering your mind; Satan and the Holy Spirit.

This is why you can't compromise any of your truths provided by the Spirit. Couple this, with the fact that you are personally responsible for your salvation based on truth as you know it. You must stand on the truth you have received from the Spirit. Your spirit needs to discern the counsel of the Spirit when embracing any source of truth. I believe only Spirit filled elect would share my truths. With so many church doctrines, lay persons like me prior to the Father's December 2009 call, had little or no concern over pulpit oratory on truth. We sing about the 'Church Triumphant' ignoring the key to "Triumphant" is TRUTH. It is God's TRUTH that is triumphant. We need to expand comments on "TRUTH" by going back to the basics. Consider:

> John 14:17 "even the Spirit of TRUTH, whom the world cannot receive, because it neither sees Him nor knows Him."
> It is the Spirit that draws the chosen through the "Spirit Gate" for an opportunity to grow in the Spirit of Truth.

A word of caution: Spiritual growth in truth requires due diligence in studying the Word and a hunger and thirst after righteousness. The only avenue to God's truth is through submission as a vessel to the Spirit.

John 15:26 "But when the helper (Spirit) comes, whom I (Jesus) shall send to you from the Father, the Spirit of Truth who proceeds from the Father, He (Spirit) will testify of Me (Jesus)." Notice the Trinity in action, the Spirit proceeds from the Father to testify of Jesus to the elect after Jesus returns to His Father. Again, submission as a vessel to the Spirit is the only access to truth.

John 16:13 "However, when He, the Spirit of truth has come, He will guide you into ALL TRUTH." He, the Holy Spirit, will open up all biblical truths. When it comes to biblical truth, there is only one unimpeachable source. Today, we find ourselves in a world with a conundrum of doctrines and creeds in churches whose members, for the most part, do not know the doctrines and creeds of the church they attend. I have never heard a sermon tailored on a specific church doctrine that defines and compares it with other denominational doctrines. Are church members being led by the nose from cradle to grave, fed by pot lucks and social, feel good Gospel or have they been set free by a good dose of truth? Jesus said He was the Way, the Truth, the Life and no one comes to the Father but through Him. In 35 years of nursing home ministry, I can only think of a handful possessing the joy of their salvation and they stood out like a happy thumb. Churches have failed to instill a hunger and thirst for righteousness that generates excitement, joy and peace over the prospect of a living God.

I believe it would be helpful to establish my credentials as a LAYMAN, who has been blessed to be one of God's elect. This can best be accomplished with my testimony since you will be challenged to accept my witness of a walk with the Trinity, under the counsel of Holy Spirit. What I share will likely not be readily accepted or respected and certainly not sanctioned by many in the organized church. However, what I share will be a layman's hunger and thirst for righteousness as the Father directed in Mat 6:33 "Seek ye first the Kingdom of God and His righteousness ..." What I present is my desire to please my Father, by trying to satisfy His Purpose and Glory in service to the Trinity. I invite all "CHOSEN/ELECT" readers to allow the Spirit to be resident with their spirits, to quicken their spirits to each truth contained in my record of a walk with the Spirit. My walk with the Trinity, since my 2009 Commission, opened my future to the greatest adventure of my life. My prayer is that all clergy and lay persons will challenge the veracity of my record with an open mind and Spiritual guidance.

TESTIMONY

I have been blessed of God by His grace and mercy. I have a Savior that died for my sins and a Spirit that serves peace, joy and counsel, as He provides a compass for Christian service. In my testimony, I will trace the Lord's interventions that surfaced during my look-back at life. You will see that there is nothing special about me or my family other than the involvement of the Trinity in our lives. In Rom 2:10-11, Paul nails it: "As it is written, there is none righteous, no, not one. There is none that understandeth, there is none that seeketh after God." As I shared above, it goes back to GRACE! Only those who are invited through the Spirit Gate (the ELECT), vetted for the "born again" experience, committed to pursue the faith walk as a vessel of the Spirit, and receives work's righteousness credits can be children of God. So, as individuals, WE ARE NOT RIGHTEOUS DURING OUR LIVES BUT as long as we allow the Spirit to lead us, we have a righteous Trinity within us that includes a Savior to cover our sins. "ONCE SAVED - ALWAYS SAVED" is not valid even for the chosen. Salvation is available only to those who access the cross.

1935 to 1957

+ Born in the middle of the depression in Hancock, a small Northern Michigan town of 5000 residents.

+ Baptized and confirmed in a Swedish Lutheran church in 1946. Lost interest in church after confirmation.

+ Moved to a farm when I was eleven where chores began a 6:00 AM and ended 7:00 PM milking cows. As a growing boy, I enjoyed the strong work ethic I learned on the farm.

+ Graduated as an average high school student, 36 out of 73, in June 1953.

+ Graduated with an average 2.62 GPA with a BS Degree in General Science with a Geology major in September, 1957. I worked hard to achieve average recognition.

+ FIRST INTERVENTION (August 1956): Introduced to my future wife (Joan) on a blind date. I was invited to spend a week at her dad's cottage, after completing my Air Force ROTC Field Training Camp.

+ SECOND INTERVENTION: After completing my training, my brother drove me out to Joan's cottage, but we were unable to recognize her cottage since it was dark when dropping her off after our blind date. After driving down roads for over an hour including the road Joan lived on, I finally asked my brother to drive down one last road (Joan's) a second time and, if no luck, call it quits. Since I would be spending my senior year in college 600 miles away, I viewed the chances of continuing a relationship based on a three-hour blind date as irrational. The Lord arranged for Joan to be standing on the side of the road saying goodbye to family friends when we drove down the road, sparking a relationship that lasted over 57 years. During our week together, I vividly recall her positions on religion and abortion. On religion, she would only marry a Missouri Synod Lutheran Church member and I agreed to become a member since I had no church association. (Talk about sacrifice!) She also said that if, during pregnancy, there was ever a need for choosing between her life and a baby's life, the decision must be for the baby. At the time, abortion was not the serious issue it is today!

+ Prior to my graduation, during a review of my records, my adviser said that, while I had more than enough hours, I lacked one required course (blowpipe analysis) which delayed my graduation by one term. Following my graduation from the Michigan College of Mining and Technology in September of 1957, I was commissioned a Second Lieutenant in the Air Force and moved to Dearborn, Michigan to look for a job and be near Joan.

+ THIRD INTERVENTION: Like an act of providence, a manager from a steel company across the street from Joan's dad's drug store stopped in for lunch. He offered to see if he could find me a job with his company. I told him I had just been commissioned in the Air Force and could be called to active duty in the near future. Within a week, he gave me an application for a position as a project engineer. His company was considering a pilot program to hire some new college graduates as project engineers. I suspect that my sponsor may have recommended the pilot program to upper level management. It should be noted that I was not an engineer and could be called to active duty in the near future. I was offered a job as a Project Engineer assigned to Great Lakes Steel Corporation's Blast Furnace Division on Zug Island in Ecorse, Michigan. I was a geologist, raised on a farm, charged to study and make recommendations to improve operational procedures associated with Blast Furnace and Coke Oven operations. After performing in a respectable manner and providing a well-received project report, I had concluded that it is not what you have learned in college that is important but how you apply the skills learned that separates the student from the performer. I love the Lord's interventions!!

1958 to 1974

+ In January 1958, I received orders to report for pilot training at Lackland Air Force Base, TX in April 1958. Faced with the issue of Joan being in college for four years while I was on active duty in the Air Force, we quickly decided on marriage.

+ FOURTH INTERVENTION: Joan's parents had high hopes that Joan would go to college before getting married. Their acceptance and strong support of Joan's marriage decision leads me to believe that comfort provided by the Holy Spirit was involved in their strong support of our marriage.

+ We were married on Easter Sunday, April 6, 1958. The date was suggested by the church choir director. Wonder if the Holy Spirit was involved in the date selection!? There was one added plus about Easter Sunday, it only occurred every six years which opened the option of reduced celebration costs. NO THIS WAS NOT A SPIRIT INTERVENTION!

+ After our honeymoon, we drove to Texas with an 8ft X 29ft house trailer.

+ I failed my flight physical for allergies and sitting height. After considering my career options, we decided to accept an offer extended by the Air Force Institute of Technology to enroll in a one year course of study in meteorology at the University of Texas. I enrolled in June 1958.

+ FIFTH INTERVENTION: After completing the meteorology course in the summer of 1959, I was assigned as a Staff Weather Officer at Otis Air Force Base (AFB) on Cape Cod, MA. So we hitched up our house trailer and headed for Michigan to visit Joan's family. Joan was driving along Hwy 60 in southern Michigan when the trailer started swaying back and forth, before flipping itself over with the car on its roof. The roof of the car was crushed down 4 to 5 inches with our new son cradled on the back window. The back window did not break and there wasn't a scratch on our son. We flipped our car back over on its wheels and, as we were getting set to go, the wife of a couple who had stopped to help demanded that the police take us to their office and provide a room for Joan to nurse our son. She followed us to the station to make sure Joan was provided a room. As I driving crouched down continuing our trip, I was stopped by a deputy sheriff of a no stop light town at 3:00 AM. He told me I couldn't drive a car with the roof crushed down. When I asked him for my 3:00 AM options, he let us go!

+ SIXTH INTERVENTION: In September, 1961, the Lord opened up a six month TDY (Temporary Duty) assignment to Toledo Express Airport, OH to provide weather support to a National Guard Fighter Squadron called to active duty for the Cuban Missile crisis. This provided an opportunity for Joan to help her mother who was fighting cancer. While I was on my TDY assignment, I was alerted for a three- year tour in Germany. Since Joan needed to be with her mother, I requested a 12- month isolated tour and was alerted for a Korean PCS (Permanent Change of Station) tour beginning in May 1962. We returned to Otis AFB from our TDY tour in Ohio to process my PCS move to Korea (me) and Dearborn, MI (Joan and Family). We drove to Dearborn arriving shortly before Joan's mother died, giving her a chance to see her grandchildren. Joan and children stayed with her father while I was in Korea. We saw the Lord intervening on behalf of our family through this very difficult time in our lives. We began to sense a growing awareness of His presence that would allow us to steadily grow in His grace and mercy. Years later we would understand that we indeed were blessed of God because we were chosen of God from the beginning. We began to accept that, while in our lives there will be tribulation, our Father would never leave us or forsake us. We were being led by the Holy Spirit, without fully understanding the degree of His involvement in our lives! It was only after my Father's Call in December 2009, when we began an active engagement with the Spirit of Truth.

+ 7/14/62 EMERGENGY LEAVE to Chassell, MI for my father's funeral. To get the news that my father had died, I had to suffer through a lengthy interview by a social worker asking juvenile touchy/feely questions, about my relationship with my father, as if I was an adolescent. I have never forgotten the anger I felt, as I am sure many others have endured under an exercise of such pomposity. I suspect such anger was not righteous but, at the time, self- righteousness came easy - it is so easy to let the flesh control.

+ 12/20/62 60 DAY TDY ORDERS to Don Maung (Bancock), Thailand to temporarily replace a forecaster rotating back to the states until his PCS replacement arrived. On the flight to

Thailand, there was a stop in Saigon where my bags were taken off of the plane. I told the baggage handlers to put the bags back on the plane because my TDY orders were for an assignment to Don Maung, Thailand. When I arrived in Thailand, I was told that my duty assignment had been changed to Vietnam. I flew back to Vietnam where I provided weather forecast support for Danang Air Base in the north and an Air Support Operations Center in the South Vietnam delta area. During my 60 days in Vietnam, Joan thought I was in Thailand because I did not tell her my assignment had been changed. When writing, I would refer to changes in my location with respect to the "city" which she understood "city" to be Bancock. TID BIT: When I returned to Vietnam, I stayed overnight in a Saigon hotel built by the French. The room was large with a triple size bed and a bathroom with two toilets - concluded the second one that spurted water up was a woman's privy or water closet. I guess you would call such a room "very continental!"

Korea Remembrances:

1. The Five Man Shovel: I was driving along a road leading to the Kimpo Int'l Airport when I saw a construction crew operating a five-man shovel. One man was on the end of the handle controlling the shovel with two men on each side with ropes connected to the shovel. Korea in the early 60's, like our depression in the 30's, had cheap manpower.

2. TV Weatherman: A Lt General commanding the United Nations Command in Korea and his English PhD professor friend decided our Weather Detachment should provide weather forecasters for a TV Weather Show on the Armed Forces Korean Network. I and two other forecasters were chosen to do the show. Within a week, the General told us he wanted only one forecaster to do the show and he selected me. The General and the PhD would, on occasion, provide critiques of my show. The one critique that stands out was my use of "pretty," like pretty cold, pretty hot, etc.

3. A One in a Million Forecast: I was working the swing shift (4:00 to 12:00) when the weather hot-line rang asking that I provide a personal briefing to the General on when the rain would stop. It had been raining heavily for more than a day and I had issued my forecast for the rain to stop at 8:00 PM. I briefed the general on my forecast which was based on a low level wind trough (called disturbance or energy source on weather TV) that was over China three days earlier and based on upper atmosphere steering currents, I forecast that the rain would be ending by 8:00 PM. What makes the forecast "a one in a million" is that I was working with three day old data from an unreliable source. Later, after the briefing, the (SWO) staff weather officer, who normally briefs the General and was off-site at the time of the weather briefing request, stopped by the weather station. He was apprehensive about my forecast and extended the rain period another 12 hours. The rain stopped a little before 8:00 PM. The SWO apologized the next day. Looking back, I believe it was a Spirit blessed forecast - In all the humility I can muster, I must confess that I was good but not that good!

+ June 1963 Air Force Institute of Technology (AFIT) Application. The Air Force advised me that I would have to extend my 13 month Korean tour from May to September (4 Months) to allow fall term university enrollment. I elected to withdraw my AFIT application.

+ 7/4/63 PCS ORDERS to Lockbourne AFB, OH. Served as a Staff Weather Officer to a Strategic Air Command B-47 Bomber Wing. Reapplied to the AFIT program to get a Masters Degree in Meteorology.

+ 6/28/65 PCS ORDERS to the University of Michigan, Ann Arbor, MI. Worked on a MS in Meteorology. At the time, the meteorology department was working on a six-level model of the atmosphere to develop a numerical weather prediction model to generate computer techniques for weather forecasting. You see the results of these and similar efforts on TV weather programs. I enrolled in one of the numerical weather prediction classes which included the use of imaginary numbers. I dropped it like a hot potato recognizing my limited "imagination." As an example of my intellectual prowess, I would like to share a meeting I had with Head of the Department of Meteorology, to review my records. He told me that he had reviewed my records before assigning my grade for the course I took with Him. He said "Congratulations! You made on your own!" I blasted through the 3.00 GPA graduate degree requirement with a booming 3.01 GPA!! The way I looked at it, anything over a 3.00 GPA was overkill. I can live with a .01 overkill! Was I happy? To me, graduate school was a survival program which meant that, if you survive, you are happy the alligators didn't get you. I accept all such gifts from my Father with joy and thanksgiving. I view the MS as a gift! In all humility, I must admit that I was good at forecasting weather but must pay tribute a warrant officer and several sergeant forecasters who taught me real forecasting at Otis AFB on Cape Cod.

+ 9/30/66 PCS Orders to Norton AFB, California to provide Staff Weather Officer support to the Air Force Ballistic System Division (BSD). Duties included determining the environmental impacts during rocket motor testing and target environments during application of one or more multiple warheads and their impact on missile accuracy. Earned a "Pocket Rocket" for providing support for missile defense.

+ Spring 1968 PCS ORDERS to Anderson AFB, GUAM. Served as Chief Weather Forecaster, Temporary Detachment Commander, and Staff Weather Officer to the Third Air Division later renamed 8th Air Force.

"GUAM IS GOOD - BY ORDER OF THE BASE COMMANDER." A sign that greeted our arrival at the base terminal on Guam. The Base was a kid's paradise with an ocean beach, swimming pools, free outdoor and indoor theaters, and free shuttle bus rides.

Remembrances include:

1. Living in a house trailer while waiting for Base Housing. Neighbor was Charlie Corn who ran the Army Post Exchange for General MacArthur during WW- II. Charlie had a large home on a cliff

overlooking the ocean. We were told that there is an old Chinese proverb saying 'once you finish your home, you die' Charlie always had a new addition under construction. When one was completed, he invited more family members from Japan to join him and he would start a new addition. What our three boys liked was trick-or-treating. Charlie always handed out large bags of small Hershey chocolate candy bars.

2. On one occasion, our 6-year old son decided to go for a walk down town. The guards at the gates saluted him going out and coming back. Good security always gives one a warm feeling.

3. Roadside Property Sign: "No trespassing! - Violators will be Persecuted!"

4. Annual Base Celebration: Full day of a free luau, games, including a greased pole, drinks and athletic games. As acting Weather Commander, I was invited to the General's home for a reception. While we were talking to the General, the General's Aide interrupted us saying there were three boys at the front door saying they were hungry. Joan and I laughed and excused ourselves. Can't remember why they didn't eat the outstanding luau provided.

5. Going first class: When we were alerted for Guam, we were told to buy a "clunker" automobile because of the salt air. I bought a $200.00 Plymouth and shipped it to Guam. While on Guam, I had to place plywood on the back seat floors because they were rotten clear through. However, it served us well and I sold it for $200.00 when I left Guam. But I digress! Joan was driving home from shopping on base when she was pulled over for speeding. When she was told she was driving over the 25 MPH. Joan argued the car couldn't go 25 MPH. I guess the Air Policeman agreed and didn't give her a ticket. During our two- year tour on Guam, we were blessed with three R&Rs (Rest and Recuperation) vacations:

   1. Japan: Attended the World Fair, rode the Bullet Train and sight- seeing.

   2. Taiwan (Formosa): Landed in Taiwan and boarded a China Air Lines flight to an interior village while enjoying warm tea and warm fragrant face towels. We took a bus tour through Taroga Gorge. The gorge was a series of tunnels and bridges

cut through some 50 plus miles of mountains taking many years and 100s of lives to complete. Also enjoyed chair rides supported by two poles carried by four girls.

3. Hong Kong: Landed right down town on a runway built over the bay giving you the idea of expensive real estate. Driving to the hotel, you are impressed with all of the laundry hanging from 20 to 40 floor housing units and the number of people living on boats, tied to city moors and discharging sewage into the bay. When we landed, we were greeted by a driver who provided free escort service during our stay. The driver was paid by the businesses we visited. We visited Hong Kong when it still was a crown colony of England so we were able to visit the border and look into Red China. Our driver invited us to his home for snacks and drinks including Chinese beer. The poverty was real and wide spread with kids asking you to throw coins in the filthy water. They would return with the coins with big smiles on their faces. Highlights included: 1) a dinner with a burlesque show featuring men dressed as women and my youngest son asking if they were really boys, 2) Going to an ivory factory and buying an ivory chess set, an ivory ball with a dozen separate hand carved ivory balls inside and a carved ivory tusk bridge - it was a treat to see ivory craftsmen at work (sale of ivory was made illegal within a year of our purchases, 3) going to a Furniture factory and buying a six foot folding carved wooden screen that caused a customs headache getting it back to Guam and 4) an emergency landing in the Philippines to fix an engine problem with our C-97. Just about broke at this point but managed to buy some serving dishes made out of wood called monkey pod.

+ 7/31/70 PCS orders to Michigan State University, East Lansing, Michigan as an Assistant Professor of Aerospace Studies, Assistant Detachment Commander and Instructor of the senior class of Air Force Reserve Officer Training Corps (AFROTC) students. Remembrances included:

1. A student group of war protesters visited our offices to discuss the Vietnam War. They must have liked the Air Force because they were very polite and respectful. Most of their ire was directed toward the Army ROTC program.

2. Vietnam War Teach-In. The ROTC Programs were invited to attend. My Commander asked me to respond to Air Force questions. The Teach-In opened with a movie on napalm bombing in Vietnam. After the movie ended, a number of discussion groups were set up with large number of students attending the Air Force and Army ROTC discussion group. Most of the rough questions dealt with our involvement in the war. In spite of the movie on napalm bombing, the Air Force was treated with respect. The meeting was civil and controlled.

3. Death Notifications: As an additional duty, I was responsible for notifying families of a service member's death. I remember being called to do a death notification. Shortly after leaving to visit the family, my wife received a call to cancel the notification. Without a means to contact me of the change, I drove over a hundred miles to learn from the parents that they had been notified of their son's death in Hawaii about a week before. We chatted about the Air Force for a few minutes and they thanked me for coming.

4. High School Recruiter: Another additional duty of mine. When schools requested a recruiter visit, I would go and discuss Air force opportunities for 30 minutes to an hour. It was a pleasant break from the work routine and a personal blessing to me.

5. Big 10 Foot Ball Games: As part of the Michigan State University faculty, we received free football tickets and also hockey tickets. Prior to the game, the AFROTC students always fixed a lunch in the AFROTC building which was located about 100 feet from the stadium.

6. In 1966, when we were stationed at Norton Air Force in California, I talked Joan into enrolling in college courses offered on base by the University of Southern California. In

1968, she continued her studies at the University of Guam during our two-year tour. In 1970, we moved to Michigan State University for a 3 year AFROTC assignment. Joan completed her B.S degree requirements in Psychology, graduated with Highest Honors!

SETTING THE STAGE

From our blind date in 1956 to our move to Maxwell AFB, Montgomery, Alabama in 1973, I was an active Christian engaging in church services, bible studies, teaching Sunday School, neighborhood witnessing, delivering food to the poor and church council activities. I was baptized and confirmed but not "born again." I was a go-with-the-flow Christian man, who attended church more to please my wife than the Lord. I was not cognizant of the "interventions" cited earlier. They were a look-back from my Father's intervention in 2009.

My engagement with the Trinity began in 1974 while managing the AFROTC College Scholarship Program. We were assigned housing on base and, being still of the Lutheran persuasion, joined a Missouri Synod Lutheran Church.

7TH INTERVENTION: Shortly after joining, I was asked to join a bible study course called the Bethel Bible Series, a study of the New and Old Testaments that leaned heavily on scripture memorization. This intervention provided an invaluable asset in later communication with the Holy Spirit in post 2009.

8TH INTERVENTION - A BIGGIE! Fall of 1974. The Father gave me Matthew 6:33 "Seek ye first the Kingdom of God and His righteousness, and all these things shall be added unto you." and told me I would never worry about my salvation. Later, while growing in His grace and mercy, I experienced a growing appreciation of this scripture as the preeminent starting point and goal for my salvation path. It is a promise to provide for all of my needs, if I focus on serving and blessing Him and not on blessing myself. We are to worship Him in Spirit and Truth, if we are to acquire His blessings. The more I get immersed in His Word, the more I sensed that there is little thought given by the church to the seriousness of His warning in Matthew 7:14 "Because narrow is the gate and difficult is the way which leads to life, and there are few who find it." At this point, we need to understand that Grace intervenes and conditions eligibility to enter the narrow gate (Spirit Gate), on being one of God's Chosen (Elect). The Spirit just introduced a new understanding of Matthew 7:14. The Spirit is the Trinity's gate keeper that allows entry only to the chosen of the Father. This narrow gate is an opportunity walk for the chosen only; all others are denied entrance. Prosperity Theology is at odds with Matthew 6:33 by focusing on the goodies and not the 'giver.' It begs the question of the church's adverse impact of church doctrine on the elect's ability to remain Spirit led, during their faith walk from the Spirit Gate to the cross and salvation.

My initial response was to consider resigning my Air Force commission and going into the mission field. However, I was invited to join a visit to a nursing home. After several visits, I sensed that the Lord had quickened my spirit for a nursing home ministry. I started out teaching weekly bible classes in the 70's and began Sunday church services in the early 80's, continuing until the Lord provided a replacement in November 2009.

The five years spent in Alabama were the formative years of my Christian walk. I would like to share some remembrances. Joan introduced me to "remembrances" which her father used and I adopted it, because it was classier than memories.

+ Bill Bright's Campus Crusade for Christ Visit: A massive effort which attracted great Christian involvement up front and during the crusade, with after crusade involvement for almost non-existent. Crusade excitement generated a large turnout for pre-crusade home witness visits while only a handful reported for the follow-up visit witness. There was box after box of index cards filled with requests for follow-up visits. This was a stark condemnation of Christian values. The excitement of the crusade ended when the crowd departed and a damper was put on the

Great Commission - only a few laborers for the harvest! Such "crusade Christians" don't seem to understand that when the Lord says the path to salvation is "difficult," "few" find the gate and the only other path leads to the Great White Throne Judgment. The Lord we serve operates from a position of Sovereignty, which put simply, His purpose and glory. Jesus did not suffer and die on the cross so we can gather at the Father's storehouse to receive blessings. We are told that the harvest is ready and were given the guidance of the great commission, to serve as gatherers for God and not servers of self. Frankly, I do not feel I serve a "Let the good times roll" God. We need to remind ourselves that we are unrighteous and don't deserve salvation. Get to understand that it is GRACE that provides the key to salvation and start to show your respect to an awesome God, by a demonstrated desire to SEEK FIRST HIS KINGDOM AND RIGHTEOUSNESS. Get out of the "bless me mode" and get into the "hear am I, send me mode." Last time I looked, "the greatest in God's kingdom is the servant."

+ There was one pre-crusade visit I'll never forget with an 88-year-old Jewish man working in his front yard. As I introduced myself and shared Jesus with him, he said he had three Catholic daughters and they never shared Jesus with him. He cited his neighbor as an example of a Christian that you would never know was a Christian, except for his attending church on Sunday. To paraphrase a biblical admonition: "You honor me with your lips (on Sunday) but your hearts are far from me (on Monday through Saturday)."

+ Pentecostal Experience: Many Christians aggressively seek to be touched by the Holy Spirit. I can remember going to many such meetings, getting up on stage looking for a touch from the Spirit and watching everyone around me falling on the floor, leaving me the only one standing. After a while, I began seeking the giver for a servant's heart and the gift of discernment. I wanted to discern the involvement of the Spirit in my life.

+ The Fortune Teller: A small group of us decided to share Jesus with a fortune teller located near the base. When we entered the living room of her home, we noticed a podium with a large bible.

175

The fortune teller was very pleasant allowing us to share Jesus and offered us some coffee. When I picked up a cup to get it filled, the saucer came up with the cup like it was glued together.

+ Praying in The Dark: As a member of the church council, I had a key to the church. Several times a week, I would drive to the church and kneel and pray in the dark. You would be surprised at the number of sounds you hear in a big dark room.

+ Witnessing in The Mall: A friend and I would go down to the mall on weekends to witness. On one occasion, I was witnessing to an officer from the base and the word was out in the headquarters that there was a crazy major in the mall talking about Jesus. When witnessing, you quickly learn that the person being witnessed to is the one that is embarrassed.

+ Witnessing in a hospital: On occasion, I would use my lunch hour to visit patients in the base hospital. One of my visits was with the dying wife of a senior officer. The visit was a real blessing to me as we shared Jesus; especially her lack of fear, her peace, and her spirit that was filled with excitement and anticipation of seeing her savior in the near future. I was honored at her request that I be one of her pall bearers.

+ Starting Nursing Home Bible Study: Within a month of the Father's calling in 1974, I contacted a local nursing home and started a weekly bible study which continued until going to Illinois for my final Air Force assignment. It was a growing scriptural experience and an eye opener, the lack of personal understanding and assurance among the patients. It left me with the feeling that Pastors and their social gospel focus on goodies and happy church life was creating seniors that are lacking exposure to doctrinal truth based on Spiritual exegesis of the Truth. Jesus is the Way/ TRUTH/Life. The Spirit is responsible for leading us into truth (Jesus). The Spirit is the comforter. If the Church's seniors are apprehensive, they lack an understanding of the Trinity and biblical truths, based on an understanding of God's sovereignty and a Comforter, to provide joy and peace until the greatest day of their lives. Pastors need to understand that they are responsible for the truths they are teaching their flock. Couple a pastor's false truth teaching with a church members individual salvation responsibility (me only) and we have a recipe for disaster.

9TH INTERVENTION: Not all interventions are comfortable! In late 1974, Joan called me at work to say the base hospital had called with results of blood tests for our son, Wayne. Wayne's white blood count suggested Acute Lymphatic Leukemia (ALL). What followed was multiple hospital visits, spinal taps, experimental drugs, and bouts with nausea. I will never forget seeing my son in a bath tub full of water and ice cubes, in an attempt to get his body temperature down. The Lord allowed it all which triggered an avalanche of prayers and a Spiritual inspired cohesion, that served our family, as an anchor to the Father's grace. From the beginning, Wayne had never questioned his Father and, later in this testimony, you will be able to understand the blessings of a Father, that walks with you and strengthens you in your walk through the valley.

Why do bad things happen to good people? It is a question that challenges the elect and non-elect! Maybe we should ask why bad things happen to THE single sinless person. Why did Jesus go to the cross? EVERYTHING THE FATHER DOES IS FOR HIS PURPOSE AND GLORY! If we can't accept the Father's will, we have no part in Him. This is the real LOVE OF GOD. A LOVE that is not fully understood or embraced. Look at our Christian heritage of suffering! Bottom line; we are called to present our bodies as a LIVING SACRIFICE, holy, acceptable unto God, which is our REASONABLE SERVICE (ROM 12:1). Yes, the rain falls on the just and unjust but God's GRACE and mercy is reserved for His elect. The elect led by the Spirit, will walk in the Father's will, being counseled by the Spirit, while being tested with Father ordained works chastised by Satan. If the chosen's vessel accepts and performs under Spirit counsel, the Father will be glorified and the chosen will be granted work's righteousness credit. Those elect, who choose to follow a different path, lose the protection of the "Comforter" and their names will be erased from the Book of Life. Wayne walked under the power of the Spirit to salvation in Jesus. Wayne's walk through the valley of cancer was an adventure that glorified the Father.

In 1978, we were assigned to Scott Air Force Base (AFB) in Illinois, approximately 60 miles east of Saint Louis where Wayne went for spinal taps to check his spinal fluid white blood counts. Wayne went into remission and enjoyed a normal life during our second and final year at Scott AFB. I retired from the Air Force on 7/1/80 and we moved to Chattanooga, Tennessee for a new career as a civilian.

Shortly after our arrival in Chattanooga, Wayne came out of remission and spent the rest of his life battling cancer until the Lord called him home four days before his 18th birth date.

10TH INTERVENTION: The Father continued to use Wayne in his hospital visits and final stay in Emory hospital in Atlanta. While in the hospital, one of the Doctors came in every day, when he was working, to give Wayne a word from the Lord. When the Doctor came in with His final word from the Lord, he was quiet and Wayne asked if he had a word, and the doctor said yes, but was not sure what it meant adding that the word was "Wayne, my son, be prepared to die tomorrow!" Wayne responded with "He probably means die to self!" Two days later, a Doctor came into Wayne's room and told me Wayne was on the verge of his systems shutting down and asked if I wanted measures taken to prolong his Life. I told him to ask Wayne. Wayne responded "Why? I can't lose, the Lord would either heal me or take me home. After the Doctor left, Wayne said he should get a pair of boots so he could 'Kick the bucket! NOTE: He was referring Jimmy Durante, in a Mad, Mad, World movie scene, kicking the bucket. Then he told his brothers about some things that needed to be corrected, in order to please the Lord, and his parents that his sister needed to attend a Christian School. He dropped off into a disturbed sleep, suddenly he spoke saying "Satin you are defeated!" He settled down in a quiet sleep for a couple of hours, when he started repeating hallelujahs, until the Lord took him the paradise. We praised Jesus all the way back home for the way He had treated one his precious servants.

While in Chattanooga, I worked and suffered a Reduction in Force twice as a program manager, after which I took a crack at truck driving. In less than a year and several accidents, I accepted my boss' recommendation to quit while I could still do so with a clean record. My depth perception was terrible! While my driving record was less than stellar, I still enjoyed the experience and left with a great admiration of the truck drivers I met. I will never forget driving on an Atlanta by-pass, nestled between and keeping pace with two 18 wheelers while going 80 MPH.

11TH INTERVENTION: I can also remember making a delivery in Macon Georgia. I tried to make a right turn from a center lane, to allow a greater turning radius and because of the narrow lanes, but still didn't have the room for a clean turn. There was a light pole right on the curb that I brushed enough to cause the glass fixture fall. I called to report the accident and, while waiting of the police, I told the Lord if I get a ticket, I quit. The officer looked over the damage and said he would turn it in as a maintenance request. It wouldn't surprise me, if my Father wanted me to get my fill of truck driving. Looking back from a 2009 encounter with the Father, I am convinced that it was just another example of His controlling my path with the SPIRIT.

12TH INTERVENTION: Shortly after arriving in Chattanooga, I was invited to join a nursing home visit. Within a few weeks, I assumed responsibility for the ministry. After preaching with notes for several weeks, I felt the desire to try preaching without notes. The first few weeks were exciting! I would start a sentence without knowing how it would finish and the finishing words were always added. Looking back from 2009, I can only conclude the Spirit was engaged in my ministry without my discernment. Reflecting back on my 35 years of nursing home ministry, I realized I had been mimicking what I had heard from the pulpit, bible study classes, evangelists, etc., except for two issues that really bugged me:

1. Isaiah 53: 5, 10, 12 "But he was wounded for our TRANSGRESSIONS, he was bruised for our INIQUITIES: the chastisement of our peace was upon him; with his stripes we are healed; an offering for SIN; bare the SIN of many and made intercession for the transgressors." PLEADING THE BLOOD OF JESUS IS FOR COVERING SIN ONLY - PERIOD! All other prayers are requested in Jesus' name!

2. John 3:16 "For God so loved the WORLD, that He gave His only begotten Son, THAT WHOSOVER BELIEVETH IN HIM should not perish but have everlasting life." Contrast John 3:16 with John 17: 9 and 12 "I pray for THEM: I pray NOT FOR THE WORLD, but for THEM which thou hast GIVEN ME; for they are thine.' and 'While I was with them in the world, I kept THEM in thy name: THOSE THAT THOU GAVEST ME I have kept, and none of them is lost, but the son of perdition; that the scripture might be fulfilled." JESUS DIED FOR THE FATHER'S ELECT (CHOSEN).

Even as a struggling layman, I could not buy the heretical application of Jesus' shed blood. I cringed every time I heard someone, especially pastors, bible teachers and evangelists plead the blood of Jesus. Crucifixion and stripes were a Holy covering for sin, PERIOD! All other prayer requests are to be offered in Jesus' name and the answers are conditioned on the Father's will. My personal feeling is that to plead the blood of Jesus, for other than covering sin, is blasphemy against the Trinity!

I could never accept the position of most churches that the grace offering of John 3:16 was open to anyone. From where I stood from confirmation to today, such a position makes a mockery of the Trinity. It amazes me how the church, beginning with the introduction of Darby's new wine in circa 1630, quickly embraced a new theology called "Dispensationalism." This "new wine" introduced the "rapture of the church" and a system of bible footnotes by Schofield, that has led to today's prosperity theology embraced by the majority of the churches. It is my layman's personal opinion that dispensationalism is a despicable use of dispensations to bastardize the meaning of truth in the scriptures. The vast majority of today's denominations have gorged themselves on the application of personal bias inherent in dispensational freedom to mold church doctrine. How does a lay person know the efficacy of the truths being routinely spewed from the pulpit, a bible teacher, an evangelist or a pope? Dispensationalism is a scourge on exegesis and the layperson that hungers and thirsts after righteousness. When you are playing games with scriptural truth, you are playing games with Jesus who is the Way, the TRUTH, and the Life. There is a price to be paid for leading the Father's children astray! Denounce your practice of accepting of intellect and ego interpretation of doctrine, no matter where acquired and go back to what Jesus told His disciples: "It is important that I return to the Father so that He can send the comforter, the Holy Spirit, He will lead you into all TRUTH. In November 2009, the Father told me to get into the Word and admonished me with "You can't preach the truth if you don't know the truth." This was after 35 years of teaching and preaching in nursing homes. I knew that if I were to seek the truth, I would need to be a vessel of the Spirit, the source of all truth. Not only did the bible come alive, I became addicted to the excitement of a living Word and a developing relationship with each member of the Trinity. The truth that sets the captive free is found only in the Bible and since we are dealing with Spiritual Truth, it has to be revealed by the Spirit.

I will deal with this issue in more detail later when I will show you that it impacts the key doctrine of the Father's sovereignty. You don't want to mess with my Father's sovereignty by questioning His right to any action that promotes His PURPOSE and GLORY!!

The rapture of the church: I have never bought into the idea that the church would be taken out before the start of "tribulation." I could only accept a rapture that occurs as a means to escape a great and terrible day of the Lord. 1Thessalonians 4:16-17 "For the Lord Himself shall descend from heaven with a shout, with the voice of the archangel, and with the trump of God: and the dead in Christ shall rise first: Then we which are alive and remain shall be caught up together with them in the clouds, to meet the Lord in the air: and so shall ever be with the Lord." 1Thessalonians 5:9 "For God hath not appointed us to WRATH, 'but to obtain salvation by our Lord Jesus Christ." The "dispensationalists" don't seem to realize that the church has an extensive history of tribulation that continues today. Our Lord allows tribulation of the saints but will not impose His WRATH on His elect. I believe the wrath described above occurs at the last trump when God's wrath will precede the great white throne judgment. In my opinion, those playing the feel good, pre-tribulation rapture game and its denial of tribulation for Christians, may find themselves in a sticky wicket trying to justify their ignorance of biblical truth before Jesus at the great white throne judgment. How can you justify seeking the goodies and the good times of prosperity theology and ignoring the guidance of Mat 6:33 'Seek ye first the kingdom of God and His righteousness, …,' If you think the two are compatible, then you are not Spirit led elect, whether or not attending church, know one thing: If you are of God's elect and don't embrace Mat 6:33, you are vulnerable to having your name removed from the Book. It is time to get rid of platitudes from the pulpit, bible classes, etc., and start seeking the Holy Spirit, who the Father provided as our only source of truth.

THE 13TH INTERVENTION: It was during the first week of December 2009, when the Father spoke to me for the second time. On the prior Sunday, I was surprised to find a family, including two retired Baptist ministers, talking to patients. They told me they were looking for a nursing home ministry. I suggested we take turns conducting services for a few weeks and, if convinced they would like to continue, I would look into serving in a nursing home near my home. They accepted my ministry, and since it was near Christmas, I decided to wait until January to check out a local nursing home. During the first week in December, the Father made it clear I needed to get into the Word because I couldn't preach the truth if I didn't know the truth. With the emphasis on "truth" in the Father's commission, I recalled Jesus telling His disciples that it was important that He go to the Father so He can send the Comforter, the Holy Spirit who will lead them into all truth. As an elect, like Jesus' elect disciples, I am blessed with the comforter and Spirit. The command was clear; submit to the Spirit to open the truth and share it with the Chosen.

EXEGESIS IV

PONDER TIME

I am approaching the 6ᵗʰ anniversary of my Father's 2009 visit telling me to get into the Word saying I couldn't preach the Truth if I didn't know the truth. Recently, my spirit began entertaining the idea of trying to describe the Grand Scheme for execution of the Father's will. Describing the Father's Master Plan for Creation and Salvation, as a scribe for the Spirit, would provide a venue to compare doctrinal differences with prevailing church doctrines. This venue would allow the Holy Spirit to quicken the spirit of those who are among the Chosen, because they have a spirit to Spirit relationship based on John 3:16's gift of grace. Participation in such a venue would have to be initiated by those who have read this Record and feel drawn by the Spirit to check out his or her being among the Chosen. What the Father brings to the table is Satan as the chastiser of the Chosen, Spirit counsel for the walk of faith, chastisement control under Jesus and an opportunity to earn work's righteousness credits that brings Him glory. If you are among the Chosen and agree to subject yourself to the counsel of the Spirit, you will learn what the scripture means about being "Created in Christ Jesus for good works." YOU WILL HAVE TO DEMONSTRATE WORK'S RIGHTEOUSNESS THAT GLORIFIES THE FATHER BEFORE BEING GRANTED ACCESS TO THE CROSS."

The Chosen are called to lay up their treasures in heaven. Jesus' recognized our greatest treasure as life, when selecting only martyrs to accompany Him in the first resurrection and to rule with Him during the millennium.

The faith walk to the cross is not a cake walk. This record will clearly show that James was right: "Faith without works is dead!" If your faith walk is judged by the Spirit to be unworthy, you lose your Spirit life access, access to the cross will be denied and your name will be removed from the Father's Book of Life. REMEMBER YOU ARE RESPONSIBLE FOR YOUR SALVATION WHICH IS LINKED TO THE TRUTH YOU EMBRACE.

Considering we are living in an age of hundreds of denominations, promoting their brand of biblical truths in their doctrines, ignoring any unity of truth with other denominations, we have a formidable task before us. It is to set the captives free from controlled denominational bias. The captives are the Father's Chosen listed in the Book of Life. (John 8:32 "And you shall know the truth, and the truth shall make you free.") I believe that most churches shy away from or water down the Doctrine of Election, out of fear of having to explain who are the Elect or Chosen. I believe that most of the Chosen do not know that their names are written in the Father's Book of Life. In 1974, my Father gave me Matthew 6:33 and told me that I would never worry about my salvation. It wasn't until 2009 that I linked the 1974 "worry" to the 2009 "Chosen." That's 35 years of ministry without exposure to election doctrine.

The truth I will share is designed to compare a Layman's Spirit led exegesis with intellect led exegesis of major denominations. TO PUT IT BLUNTLY, THE EXISTING DISUNITY IN DENOMINATIONAL DOCTRINE HAS TO BE AN ANATHEMA TO THE TRINITY. My record will describe my walk as a scribe, recording exegetical revelations of biblical scriptures. In my Father's 2009 commission to seek truth, I immediately knew where to begin. I recalled Jesus told his disciples, when they wanted him to stay with them: "It is important that I return to the Father so that He could send the Holy Spirit, to would lead them into all truth." For centuries, the organized church has been arguing over doctrines displaying disunity in hundreds of competing doctrines. We must be concerned about the number of the Father's chosen that may have been lost because of disunity evidenced by doctrinal differences. I pray churches will graciously receive all who would seek a comparison of this record with their doctrines. Any effort seeking biblical truth will please the Trinity. I have experienced a lot of love in the many churches I have attended during my lifetime! I am confident of church love. We need to insure that this love is bolstered by solid doctrinal foundation. SOMETHING TO PONDER!

Accepting the "whosoever" of John 3:16 as limited to the Chosen, there is evidence in the word to show that there would even be attrition among the Chosen. Consider what Jesus told the Father "I do not pray for the world, I only pray for those you have given me" adding that He had lost only one - the son of perdition - for an eight plus percent attrition rate. I have often wondered about the attrition rate for the Chosen! SOMETHING TO PONDER!

Please understand this about John 3:16. Accepting Jesus dying for all the people in the world is a crucial weapon for prosperity theology, to increase church membership by downgrading sin's importance and cheapening love's greatest sacrifice. We all deserve to go to hell. The Trinity has to be disturbed by exegesis malfeasance of the church, as it witnesses the moral and theological decay of righteousness. Has the church ever considered the magnitude of the penalty, for Adam's sin of eating an apple? "Katy bar the door, the flood gates of grace to cover virtually anyone and everyone's sin has been opened, by simply changing from a "a required service" to a "right to be blessed" theology. Consider the millions of martyrs from Jesus' time and ongoing today, and try to justify the rampant bless me theology of today, that is designed to fill church coffers by selling a religious bless me source, for all needs and desires of members. We can live to bless and serve the Trinity or we can live to gratify the Flesh. It depends on what you do with your treasures. You can lay them up in heaven or let the flesh consume then on earth. It is a Spirit life vs Spirit death decision. SOMETHING TO PONDER!

Most churches teach that Jesus was True Man and True God. The statement, as it stands, is true. But if you accept it to mean "at the same time," it is bad theology. The God head is a UNITY of three divine persons of majesty coequal. For example, we are baptized in the name of the Father, Son and Holy Spirit to maintain the UNITY of the Trinity.

The Holy Spirit is the member in a functional role as our go-to person of responsibility for our interface with the Trinity. THE UNITY OF THE TRINITY CAN NOT BE COMPROMISED. To proclaim Jesus' divinity is to cast aspersions on his performance as True Man. Such a doctrine drags Divinity down to man's level and denigrates Jesus' suffering with the crutch of being a Divine True man. SOMETHING TO PONDER!

Denominations lack the courage and conviction to compare doctrines with other denominations providing total doctrinal disunity. Accepting a universal right of churches to develop their own set of doctrines is an act of Spiritual appeasement. It is an act of dispensationalism, that routinely uses hermeneutics to supplant scriptural exegesis with intellect driven exegesis. It is epitome of a theology that satisfies the flesh rather than the spirit. The disunity found, in the doctrines of most churches, stigmatizes the Trinity which is based on truth. A problem when you consider Jesus is the way, the TRUTH and the life. To be discussed further. SOMETHING TO PONDER!

Today's theology includes a blanket promise of salvation for the asking, coddled by a Trinity guaranteeing salvation with a "once saved, always saved" policy covering all of your sins in perpetuity during our walk to the cross and salvation. This is the Hallmark of Prosperity Theology that has filled the coffers of evangelists and mega churches and, to a lesser degree, sustained survival of some smaller churches. Prosperity theology, coupled with political correctness, is particularly onerous in today's mega churches, who have used their prosperity theology programs to feed their growth, at the expense of less fortunate small church memberships. Prosperity theology is based on selling the Trinity, as a storehouse of blessings to be tapped for personal use and not a theology of service to the Trinity. The bible cautions us to lay up our treasures in heaven that serve the Trinity. The Father has already provided the Pearl of Great Price as your service goal to achieve salvation and the Spirit counsel to assist you as you serve. Jesus, as a disciple, was sent to serve the Father. We, as disciples of Jesus, are sent to serve Jesus as ambassadors to the Chosen in their faith walk to glorify God. Matthew6:33 provides clear guidance: "SEEK YE FIRST THE KINGDOM OF GOD, AND HIS RIGHTEOUSNESS; AND

ALL THESE THINGS SHALL BE ADDED UNTO YOU." This prime directive tells us to focus on righteousness in His service and He will provide for all of your needs. Many of today's churches focus on personal needs satisfaction and pays lip service to work's righteousness. As the Lord observed: You honor me with our lips, but your hearts are far from me. SOMETHING TO PONDER!

We readily agree that "the God of the New Testament (NT) is the same as the God of the Old Testament (OT)" and "God does not change!" How do churches advocating Prosperity Theology, change God's OT image as a task master of righteousness into a NT image of compassionate giver of all things good, that meets all desires. I will clearly demonstrate how self- righteous church leaders have twisted God's Word to control management of the church through disassociation of Spirit led exegesis. As I was completing this entry, a smile came across my face as I thought about what the Spirit had revealed about salvation. I can't imagine how any servants of my Father could ignore the concept of the Father's WILL. Every action in creation will be accomplished in accordance with the Father's will to satisfy His Purpose and Glory, enforced by His Son. His Will for today's church has been set in place before setting the foundation of His creation. Remember the scripture that says He knew us before creation. Your life has been laid out for you before creation. He has Willed every action in every person's life using Jesus as the enforcer of His will. Every evening as Joan and I prayed for her dementia, we understood that His decision was made before creation, acknowledge and accept His Will and remind Him that our lives are totally committed to witness His Will. SOMETHING TO PONDER

This record's intent is to locate the chosen and provide a copy of this Record sharing a personal walk with the Trinity to the cross, revelations of truths received from the Spirit and feeling the personal excitement of a growing fellowship of our spirits with the Spirit of the Trinity. A spirit to Spirit communication channel can grow into a two way sharing of information on an as needed or desired basis. Since the Spirit was assigned by the Trinity to counsel the Chosen, He is the only one that can confirm the veracity of one seeking spirit to Spirit confirmation. Only the Father's

Chosen, who feel drawn by the Spirit, will qualify to receive spirit to Spirit confirmation of the truth shared in this Record. SOMETHING TO PONDER!

BUT FIRST YOU MUST PREPARE YOUR HEART TO SEEK THE KINGDOM OF GOD AND RIGHTEOUSNESS (MATTHEW 6:33). I firmly believe that if you are one of The Father's Chosen and allow yourself to follow the counsel of the Spirit, you will experience a hunger and thirst for righteousness, that will sustain you through any and all chastisement the Father allows Satan to use, to deny you the victory of the cross. If you do not experience a sense of peace and joy in your spirit upon completion of this record, there are only three conclusions you can reach: 1) You are not one of the Chosen; 2) You are a Chosen who desires the pleasures of his current life over the offer of eternal life, or 3) I am a heretical Christian fanatic. You spirit will make the decision as to the conclusion you will reach. This is the most important decision in your life - IT CAN BE A LIFE AND DEATH (SPIRITUAL) DECISION - that deserves a serious search for truth. The best approach to make your decision is to understand the applicable biblical truths. They Are:

+ Jesus is the Way, the Truth and the Life. Without Jesus, there is no salvation.
+ Holy Spirit is your interface with all three members of the Trinity.
+ The Spirit knows and controls all actions of the Father's elect.
+ The Spirit knows who and where the Chosen are.
+ The Spirit draws all Chosen to the narrow gate and screens the desires of their heart to judge worthiness to access the narrow gate.
+ The Spirit teaches the Word of God and judges those eligible for Spirit Baptism.
+ The Spirit, through Baptism, provides faith and counsel for the walk of work's righteousness to the cross.

To seek your Chosen status, you will be under the control of the Spirit who knows who and where you are, DRAWS YOU THROUGH THE NARROW GATE and judges whether you get to access the gate. If, after studying the truths provided in this Record, you would like to determine your status as a possible Chosen of the Father, the recommended way is to assume you have the Holy Spirit resident with your spirit and ask Him to confirm your chosen status. The very fact that you are interested and sense within yourself a hunger and thirst for righteousness, you may have the heart qualities the Spirit desires for access through the narrow gate. The spirit will acknowledge your Chosen status with sense of peace and joy in your spirit. You need to actively promote this Spirit to your spirit relationship in your daily life. HE IS YOUR COUNSELOR AND YOUR CLOSEST FRIEND. "Those who walk in the Spirit shall be known as Children of God. As you increase the time you spend with the Spirit, you will increase your gift of discernment, which is a bonding with the Spirit, providing real time Spirit counsel on all issues in your service life. This source of power is only available to the Father's chosen. Romans 8:16 "The Spirit Himself bears witness with our spirit that we are children of God." It is my prayer that this record will awaken your spirit to receive counsel from the Holy Spirit. To be led by the Spirit, you must seek the Spirit in prayer requesting His counsel to share revelations of the Word. SOMETHING TO PONDER!

There are four categories of people who may read this Record:

1. A Chosen, who has received the Spirit baptism and is demonstrating work's righteousness that brings glory to the Father. Upon completion of the walk of faith, there will be a Spirit review of work's righteousness performance to determine access qualification to the cross and salvation. Those denied access by the Spirit will have their names removed from the Book of Life. THIS IS THE FINAL STEP TO THE CROSS AND SALVATION!

2. The Chosen, who have accepted the Spirit invitation to access the narrow gate and being taught God's Word (Truths), will be granted gate access. Upon completion of instruction, the Spirit will review the condition of the heart in making His decision for or against Spirit baptism. Those rejected by the Spirit will have their names removed from the Book of Life.

3. The Chosen who refuse the Spirit offer to access the narrow gate in favor of remaining in the world of sin. Their names will be removed from the Book of Life.

4. Those not selected for the Book of Life, during the Father's random selection in the soul pool, will be subjected to the sin of Adam. They do not receive the Spirit Life opportunity provided the Chosen under John 3:16's Grace.

NOTE: The Book of Life contains the names of chosen whose souls would have physical and spiritual lives plus in dwelling Spirit of Life at conception. The remaining souls will have physical and spiritual lives without an indwelling Spirit of Life at Conception. Adam and Eve had an indwelling Spirit of Life which departed when Adam sinned. Adam's sin condemned all of his descendants, chose and unchosen, to physical and spiritual death. Including His chosen under the consequences of Adam's sin that included spiritual death, the Father established the need for a salvage plan. The Father's Salvation Plan to address the spirit death consequences included:

+ Placing Adam's spiritual death consequence for the chosen in abeyance.
+ Providing Jesus as a sin sacrifice without blemish.
+ Set up a screening program to separate the wheat from the trash among the chosen.
+ Establish John 3:16's Grace opportunity for the Chosen.
+ Install the Spirit as overseer of the Salvation program to identify, teach, guide, counsel and critique chosen from access to the gate to access to the cross.
+ Pay the sin ransom with Jesus blood.
+ Erase from the Book of Life, the names of chosen denied access to the cross. Their status will change to unchosen and their names will be included in the Books of the spiritual dead.

The four listed categories comprise the entire inventory of souls in the Father's soul pool to cover the period from the Garden of Eden to the Great White Throne Judgment. This scribe's Record targets the chosen who are currently living. I believe the Father's random selection of souls for His Book of Life is a Chosen distribution that includes all of His creation. Since we do not know the location of the randomly selected souls, we can't place any limit in our witness plan as to race, religion or national origin. This is why the Great Commission charges us to GO OUT INTO THE ENTIRE WORLD! I believe that all, who serve under the edict of Jesus' Great Commission, serve in a continuing desire to share their hunger and thirst for righteousness with the missing chosen.

The Father's truth must be preached to all peoples, if we are to reach all chosen. We are called to witness to the truth. It is the Spirit who is responsible to draw, screen, teach, counsel and critique all chosen. As chosen, we know that the Father's Will is going to be enforced by His Son guaranteeing the Father's purpose and glory will be satisfied. I am reminded how this distribution would fit like a glove to Jesus' commission to be witnesses to all nations. The Word tells us that the end will not come until the Word is preached to all the world. Today's communication's technology can open up vehicles for explosive growth in church doctrine. Think about the potential of a church possessing chosen witnesses, filled with a hunger and thirst for righteousness, strengthened with incorruptible biblical doctrine and serving under the counsel of the Holy Spirit. As I was typing these words, I recalled John's words regarding souls in the book of revelations. Churches promoting salvation without works should consider the role of works, presented in the Book of Revelation's judgment of souls cited in the Books of the Dead. Their spirits were judged on their works.

> John 20:4-7, 12,15 "And I saw thrones, and they that sat upon them, and judgment was given unto them, and I saw the souls of them that were beheaded for the witness of Jesus, and for the Word of God, and which had not worshiped the beast, neither his image, neither had received their mark on their foreheads, or in their hands; and they lived and reigned with Christ a thousand years. (5) But the rest of the dead lived not again until the thousand years were finished. This is the FIRST RESURRECTION. (6) Blessed and holy is he that had part in the first resurrection; on such, the second death

had no power, but shall be priests of God and of Christ, and shall reign with Him a thousand years. (7) And when the thousand years are expired, Satan shall be loosed out of his prison."

(12) "And I saw the dead, small and great, stand before God; and the books were opened, and another book was opened, which is the BOOK OF LIFE: and the dead were JUDGED out of those things which were written in the books, according to their WORKS.

(15) "And whosoever was not found written in the BOOK OF LIFE was cast into the lake of fire."

Verse 20:4 tells us about the chastisement the Father allowed Satan to inflect on the martyrs - up to and including death. The martyrs of Jesus' time considered martyrdom as a thank offering to the Father for the gift of His son. Jesus gave them the special honor of resurrection and reigning with Him.

Verse 20:5 tells us that the remaining dead will not be judged for a thousand years. Following the Great and Terrible Day of the Lord and defeat of Satan, the Great White Throne Judgment convenes and the books are opened, including the Book of Life.

Verse 20:6 tells us that achieving the first resurrection was Jesus' final judgment for the martyrs. If you achieve a positive judgment for Spiritual Life, you are in the Father's Kingdom!

There is no physical life in heaven. Our physical life ended when we died our first death.

Verse 20:7 releases Satan for the tribulation period, leading to the great and terrible day of the Lord. Satan will chastise the church in agreement with the Father and controlled by Jesus, as Satan's last actions to separate the wheat from the chaff.

Verse 20:12 Here we see books of the dead opened, and the Book of life. That all of the dead's works were judged by what was written in the books, ACCORDING TO THEIR WORKS.

Verse 20:15 "Those whose names weren't found in the Book of Life, were cast into the Lake of Fire.

The Spirit reminded me role of thecrucifixion in the Judgment. Access to the cross means access to Jesus' salvation judgment. Until the cross, a chosen's spirit residency was held in an abeyance pending the decision to access the cross. Then under John 3:16's grace option, access to the cross provides a sin ransom paid for by the blood of Jesus. Access to the cross is based on your record of works righteousness that pleased the Father. At this point, your residency was moved from being in abeyance to the Book of Life because your works had already been judged by Jesus. YOUR VICTORY OF ETERNAL LIFE WAS CONSUMATED ON THE CROSS BY THE JUDGE, BEFORE HE CONVENED THE GREAT WHITE THRONE JUDGMENT. This is an example of how the Spirit clarifies previous revelations that link revelations into a web of supporting revelations, that reveal the truth of the Father's salvation plan, with John 3:16 as the focus of His grace.

Matthew 12:25 "Every kingdom divided against itself is brought to desolation, and every city or house divided against itself will not stand. The church includes chosen and unchosen members. The body of Christ, represented by Chosen lay persons and Chosen clergy, are called to labor in the field to harvest the 'wheat' of unidentified Chosen. To participate in the harvest, the Chosen need to heed the counsel of:

+ Luke 12:1-5 "In the meantime, where there are gathered together an innumerable multitude of people, in so much that they trod one upon another, he began to say unto his disciples first of all, beware of the leaven of the Pharisees, which is hypocrisy. (2) For there is nothing covered, that shall not be revealed; neither hid, that shall not be known. (3) Therefore, whatsoever ye have spoken in darkness shall be heard in the light; and that which ye have spoken in the ear in closets shall be proclaimed upon the housetops. (4) And I say unto you my friends, be not afraid of them that kill the body, and after that have no more they can do. (5) But I will forewarn you whom you should fear: Fear him, which after he hath killed hath power to cast into hell: yea, I say unto you, Fear him." These scriptures speak to today's reality of most churches preaching false prosperity doctrine that has squelched the voicing of Spirit led truth. But the day is drawing near where the Chosen shall put on the full armor of God and speak the truth from the House tops. We are told not to fear for our physical death, but the power of false doctrine that can send our spirit and soul to hell. As I was typing this paragraph, I realized I was typing an end times scenario of tribulation and the second coming. Our future end times event begins with the release of Satan after his thousand-year captivity.

Increase in martyrdom, widespread acceptance of false church doctrine, promotion of prosperity theology, weakness of clergy kowtowing to political correctness, all lead to the birth pangs of an end times scenario.

+   Verse 1: Beware of the clergy who are teaching false doctrine.
+   Verse 2: All truth will be revealed!
+   Verse 3: When forced into covert witnessing groups, the truth will be revealed by group members in one on one witness sharing. Church history is strewn with millions of martyrs that were engaged in witnessing to the truth of Jesus. Martyrdom is also rampant today. We need retraining of our church mice, who were neutered by prosperity theology, political correctness and lack of chutzpah in many male members. I can remember, in the mid 80's while watching an all-male choir of church members sing on mother's day, turning to my wife and saying that there was no one in the group with whom I would want to share an end times ministry. I should add that the church believed in pre-tribulation rapture. I always found it repugnant for anyone wanting to escape an end times ministry, knowing what Jesus went through in providing a salvation path to God's kingdom.

+ Verse 4: Salvation is the gift of Spirit life to the Chosen under John 3:16. Every one dies the physical death. The battle with the Trinity is centered on the soul. Before the foundation of the world, the Father's Will ceded, without objection, the right of all souls to Satan except His Chosen. In addition, Satan was given the right to chastise the Chosen within limits controlled by Jesus. In effect, Satan was the Father's winnower to separate the Wheat from the chaff. The Chosen, who displayed a work's righteousness that glorified the Father, were given access to the cross and salvation. Upon salvation, they became spirits in union with the Trinity and other chosen who preceded them.

+ Verse 5: The only ones, who escape hell, are those chosen whose names were in the original Book of Life, who glorified the Father during Satan's chastisement, awarded the salvation gift and withstood erasure from the Book of Life opened at the Great White Throne Judgment.

NOTE: In the Book of Revelation, all souls not listed in the Book of Life are subjected to judgment based on their works and cast into the Lake of Fire. Only the chosen pre-judged on the cross, based on retaining their name in the Book of Life, join the Father's family for eternity.

Since the Chosen target is spread out across the world, we have the gigantic task of the Great Commission before us and chosen laborers are needed for harvest. The coming tribulation will provide ample opportunity to lay up your treasures in heaven.

From 1958 to 1974, I was active in church; teaching Sunday school, serving on the council, witnessing, etc., without feeling spiritual involvement. In the 1974 commission, the Father arranged a 35 year nursing home ministry; again without distinguishable Spirit activity. In 2009, the Father told me that, if I wanted to preach the truth, I needed to get into the Word. WELCOME HOLY SPIRIT! The Bible came alive, my spirit experienced fellowship with the Trinity and I became a servant filled with power, peace and joy. The only clue I received from the Father, of anything special, was in 1974 when He gave me Matthew 6:33 and told me I would never worry about my salvation. I didn't connect the salvation worry with being one of His Chosen because I had a problem with abortions and other tragedies going on in the world, without correction by the Father. My understandings of the Father's attributes cleared up these issues, which I will address later. I believe the Father was well aware of my commitment to Him before Spirit baptism in 2009. I also believe that He was aware my opposition to the misuse of Isaiah 53 and John 3:16. Pleading the Blood of Jesus for anything other than the soul and passing out free gifts and salvation passes upon asking is not Spirit led exegesis.

NOTE: For the unknowing chosen: Take this record seriously. I spent 16 years as an active church member, without any awareness of my chosen status. I spent another 35 years in a nursing home ministry with continued ignorance of my chosen status, even after being told by the Father I would never worry about my salvation. That's over 50 years of church membership wherein the Doctrine of Election was not taught. Don't ignore Election, more commonly referred to as 'Chosen.' Seek the Holy Spirit and you may find yourself accessing the narrow gate with the Spirit welcoming you as one of the Father's chosen.

Over the past five years, I have recorded a lot of spirit to Spirit discerned notes from the Trinity and have considered many options of format. Since I am a layperson, I wanted the language to be my language without professional editing services. This makes sense to me, because I believe the bible was written for the lay person, not the clergy. The Spirit just reminded me of the organized church's problem with scriptures since there is very little or no unity in denominational doctrines. Given the bible reflects the mind of God, no one knows the mind of God, and lack in spiritual unity of biblical exegesis, the church turned to man's intellect tarnished ego and church politics in establishment of church doctrine. Apparently the church ignored the SPIRIT who was sent specifically to share what is in the mind of God.

DISUNITY OF DOCTRINES – AN ISSUE WITH ETERNAL CONSEQUENCES THE CHOSEN'S DILEMMA

February 16, 2016: Yesterday, while conducting my final review before publication, the issue of 'DISUNITY OF DOCTRINES' began to weigh heavily on my spirit. I was having a hard time organizing my thoughts as the significance of this issue started to take root. It was late in the day, so I decided to ponder this issue with the Spirit and start fresh the next day. I would like to share the thoughts that entered my spirit providing new perspective that has rearranged my thinking regarding the roles various Christian church members in the Father's Salvation Plan.

+ 'IN THE BEGINNING GOD! We have to go back before creation to understand who we were. From not existing in any form, we began with the Father forming our bodies from the dirt in the garden and breathing in the breath of life. With that breath, Adam and Eve were born in the Father's image received a soul, spirit, free will and a Spirit counselor. They began life, like Jesus, without sin. The Father's Salvation Plan, designed before creation, sent Satan to the Garden providing him with authority to chastise Adam, Eve and their descendants. This authority was exercised under limitations set by the Father and enforced by Jesus. As we know, Satan's form of chastisement was to counsel Adam's ego to be like God. This chastisement authority continues through the centuries and will continue until Satan's Lake of Fire destiny. While Satan is serving his 1000-year sentence in the bottomless pit, his surrogates continue chastisement activities in his absence. The Father uses chastisement to enforce His will which introduces the need to establish important understandings of the Father's attributes.

+ SOVEREIGNTY: We need to recognize that the Father is the Potter and We are the Clay. He has the right to control our every action, word and deed. He has total control over us by providing an environment of actions affecting the decisions made by our mind. While no one knows the Mind of God, He knows and controls every mind. All of His divine sovereignty actions are enforced by Jesus to insure the Father's Purpose and Glory are satisfied.

+ TRINITY: It is a God head UNITY of three Divine Gods with Majesty Coequal. They can function as the Trinity (in the beginning) or individually over assigned activities while linked to the Trinity. For example, we are baptized in the name of the Father, Son and Spirit (Trinity), while the Spirit is assigned to nurture the chosen, from the narrow gate to the cross.

+ DIVINITY: It is an attribute of unity confined to the Trinity that establishes sovereignty. This is one reason you can't attribute divinity to the definition of True Man.

+ OMNISCIENCE: All knowing. The Father knows and controls all knowledge which complements His will to satisfy His purpose and glory. He controls all thoughts and actions entertained by your mind including Satan's chastisement actions and counsel.

+ OMNIPOTENCE: All powerful. Working in concert with the Father's Omniscience, to insure His will and purpose. Omnipotence and Omniscience complement each other as the dynamic duo insuring satisfaction of the Father's Will.

+ DOCTRINE: A church's expressed understanding of scriptural truths, based on man-designed science called hermeneutics used in defining scriptural exegesis. Most denominations have integrated dispensationalism principles into their hermeneutics. These new principles, allowed the denomination to use a dispensation to replace a scripture they didn't understand or fit into their prosperity theology. It appears that 'dispensationalism' is the culprit for total collapse of Unity in denominational doctrines. Christians need to understand that doctrinal disunity makes selecting a Spirit revealed doctrine, if one exists, is like finding a needle in a hay stack or pinning a tail on a donkey. You have to be a chosen, led by the Spirit to have access to biblical truth.

Since the Father uses Satanic chastisement as a screening tool to separate the wheat from the chaff in congregations, it is rational to conclude that all denominations are subject to Satan's chastisement resulting in doctrines of false exegesis. These doctrines are based on Satan's counsel to satisfy the flesh with prosperity and political correctness, which is the antithesis of glorifying the Father. Since only the Father's chosen have access to Spirit led revelations and denomination doctrines lack Spirit led exegesis, then we are faced with the Question: ARE THERE ANY CHOSEN AMONG THE CHURCH THEOLOGIANS RESPONSIBLE FOR THE EXEGESIS REFLECTED IN THEIR CHURCH DOCTRINES? The evidence supports the Church's widespread pollution of faulty doctrine. It is time to put the King of Kings and Lord of Lords back on the throne and show respect and awe for the majesty of our Trinity.

WARNING: WHAT I SHARE WITH YOU WILL BE FOREIGN TO WHAT YOU HAVE BEEN TAUGHT ABOUT THE FATHER, THE SON AND THE HOLY SPIRIT. THE TRINITY-MAN RELATIONSHIP HAS BEEN REVERSED, TO A GREAT EXTENT, BY A TRINITY THAT IS NOW THE SERVER, INSTEAD OF THE ONE SERVED. THIS IS EVIDENCED BY A PROSPERITY THEOLOGY AND A SALVATION POLICY OPEN TO ALL WHO ASK. NOTE: SATAN'S HARVEST OF CHAFF FROM AMONG THE CHOSEN IS DOING WELL.

TAKE NOTICE

+   YOU ARE CALLED TO SERVE - NOT TO BE SERVED!
+   YOU ARE CALLED TO BLESS - NOT TO BE BLESSED!
+   YOU ARE CALLED TO WITNESS TO THE TRUTH!
+   YOU ARE NOT CALLED TO COWER IN POLITICAL CORECTNESS!
+   YOU ARE CALLED TO PICK UP YOUR CROSS AND FOLLOW JESUS!
+   YOU ARE CALLED TO WALK IN THE COUNSEL OF THE SPIRIT!
+   YOU ARE CALLED TO BE A LIVING SACRIFICE!
+   YOU ARE CALLED TO WORSHIP HIM IN MIND, BODY AND SPIRIT!

+ YOU ARE CALLED TO WALK IN THE WILL OF THE FATHER!
+ YOU ARE CALLED BY THE FATHER TO PARTAKE IN SATAN'S CHASTISEMENT, WHILE PERFORMING WORKS RIGHTEOUSNESS TASKS.
+ PREORDAINED BY THE FATHER, TO ESTABLISH WORTHINESS TO BE ONE OF HIS CHOSEN CHILDREN.

Chastisement can take many forms, up to and including martyrdom. The form of chastisement each of the Father's chosen receives, was preordained before the foundations of the world. Here is where you lay up your treasures in heaven based on the glory the Father receives from your chastisement. The Father presented His Son as a martyr to cover our sins. After the resurrection through to today, Jesus' apostles and countless Christians honored the Father's gift with martyrdom. As a Christian, we should be honored to be martyrs for the Devine Trinity's gift of Salvation. The significance of martyrdom in the eyes of Jesus was dramatically evident when He selected the martyrs to rule with Him during the millennium.

WHAT CAN A CHRISTIAN AND A CHRISTIAN CHURCH DO?

1. Accept the fact that your every thought, action, and desire conforms to the Father's will with Jesus controlling the environment that insures your will reflects glory on Father's will. The Father's Salvation Plan identifies, selects, and trains His chosen to instill a desire to totally accept His will. The Father restored righteousness to His Kingdom when He cast Satan and his angels into the Garden. The unity of the Trinity means being in accord in thought, action, and desire PLUS WILL. The Father's chosen who are granted access to the cross have demonstrated work's righteousness that rejected Satan's chastisement in a manner giving glory to the Father.

2. Remember the Father chastises those whom He loves. In fact, He says that if you are not partakers of His chastisements, you are not one of His chosen sons. The Father's Salvation Plan (FSA)

was designed to screen His chosen to separate the Wheat from the Chaff. Allowing Satan to Chastise His chosen is the final and most difficult screen for measuring the worthiness for an aye-nay decision to access the cross and salvation. The Father allowed Satan to chastise His son to provide the ransom payment for our sin. Eleven of the apostles were martyred under Satan's chastisement. Martyrdom has been rampant since the resurrection through to today. If you treat the Father's chastisement lightly, you can plan on a nay decision for access to the cross. It is not the sweet Jesus of prosperity theology that will sit in judgment of your access to the cross. He is the King of Kings and Lord of Lords who rules with righteousness on those whose names end up among the unchosen in the Books of the Dead.

3. Be ever conscious of the presence of two spirits engaged in the battle for your soul. This battle engages your will and spirit desires of the flesh by Satan vs the will and desire to seek the righteousness counsel of Spirit to spirit. The bible is very clear on the desire of the flesh to allow sin on our lives. In fact, Paul said he was the greatest sinner of all. So we need to understand that in the battle for your soul, it is a battle between the flesh and the heart. Does the flesh or the heart dominate spirit desires? The ransom paid on the cross was for your spirit. This is why the spirit should reflect a hunger and thirst for righteousness complemented with repentance of sin. WHICH SPIRIT DOMINATES THE COUNSEL YOU RECEIVE? THE ANSWER CAN REFLECT THE CONDITION OF YOUR HEART. If your heart reflects a desire to glorify the Father, you are OK!

4. The CHOSEN is a big issue. They must accept the fact that the Father has the right to select, before creation, a number of souls from the soul pool and placing their names in a "Book of Life." The proclamation of His CHOSEN is an anathema to mainline Christian theology. It limit's the definition of 'world' in John 3:16 to the chosen. Jesus was with the Father during His random selection of the chosen from the soul pool. Jesus knew who the chosen were when He told the Father that He did not pray for the world but only for those He had given him. Basically, the church

ignores preaching on the Book of Life and uses dispensationalism to assist their hermeneutics to cloud true exegesis of 'world.' Their promotion of prosperity theology is based on selling salvation to everyone in the world who asks and ignoring the Book of Life which lists the names of salvation candidates. Without these two deceits, the churches would fall into demise, being no longer relevant. As I was typing this last sentence, the Spirit quickened my spirit to an understanding, of why the Father's Plan included chastisement, in the form of the church's acceptance of Satan's counsel for these deceits. Consider the following revelation as an example of 'No one knows the mind of God!' to which we can add 'unless led by the Spirit!'

A NEW HOLY SPIRIT REVELATION

THE FATHER'S WILL INCLUDED THE REQUIREMENT TO ATTRACT HIS CHOSEN TO A VENUE THAT WOULD PROVIDE EXPOSURE TO THE HOLY SPIRIT. IT WOULD PROVIDE AN ENVIRONMENT FOR SATAN AND THE UNCHOSEN TO TEST THE HEARTS OF THE CHOSEN FOR A HUNGER AND THIRST FOR RIGHTEOUSNESS. THIS REVELATION PROVIDED A NEW WRINKLE THAT ADDED THE UNCHOSEN AS A MEANS TO TEST THE CHOSEN. ATTRACTING THE UNCHOSEN WAS PART OF THE FATHER'S PLAN TO COMPLEMENT SATAN'S EFFORTS DURING CHOSEN TESTING.

5. The Great Commission: Jesus charges us in Matthew 28:19-20 "Go ye therefore, and teach all nations, baptizing them in the name of the Father, and of the Son, and of the Holy Ghost: Teaching them to observe all things whatsoever I had commanded you: and, lo, I am with you always, even unto the end of the world. Amen." THIS COMMISSION IS ONLY FOR THE CHOSEN WHO ARE LED BY THE HOLY SPIRIT.
   + 'teach all nations' means everyone in the world, regardless of religious affiliation.
   + 'baptizing them' means baptizing of the chosen.

+ 'Teaching them' means Spirit led teaching.
6. Reaching the Church Chosen.
    + In church staff and membership. They include the chosen who acknowledge their status, closet chosen who don't acknowledge their status, and chosen unaware of their status. In over 55 years of church membership, I have never heard anyone say he was among the chosen. I did ask a Presbyterian once, if he was a chosen and he hesitantly admitted he was. I have never heard a sermon or bible class discuss 'chosen.' I did ask a bible class teacher once, if they ever discussed the chosen issue. He said the subject was considered by the class once and rejected after one class of intense argument. Prior to my second commission by the Father in December 2009, I would have been among those who believed being chosen was unfair. There may be churches that seriously preach the Book of Life and chosen but I have not experienced their open witness of being among the chosen, suggesting their status, as being among the 'closet chosen.'

A SPIRITUAL LIFE OR DEATH DECISION

We have heard that the difference between a believer and non-believer is that the believer dies once and a non-believer dies twice. I suspect that most Christians don't understand the Father's involvement in this scenario. For your edification of what awaits us in the final chapter of our lives, seriously weigh your spiritual condition as defined by the Father's scenario below:

1. The Potter makes Adam out of clay as True Man providing him His seed, a soul, spirit and free will. The Father then breathes on him the Spirit of Life and makes Eve from one of Adam's ribs. At this point, Adam is without sin and comparable to the second Adam (Jesus) who also received the Father's seed. Both Adam and Jesus were without sin and divinity as True Man.
2. The Father sends Satan, as the accuser of the faith, who counsels Adam to be like God and eat forbidden fruit. Sin entered Adam's

seed staining the seed of all of his descendants, including the chosen and the unchosen. When Adam sinned, the breath of the Father's Spirit of Life left him thereby committing all of the souls and spirits of his unchosen to purgatory.

3. The First Death is death of all flesh resulting in burial.

4a. The Second Death affects all of the unchosen, whereupon their soul and spirit go into purgatory to await the Great White Throne Judgment of the Book of the Dead, to be judged by their works and cast into the Lake of Fire.

4b. The Second Death affecting all of the chosen is held in abeyance pending the results of a John 3:16 grace option which offers the counsel and teaching of the Spirit for a work's righteousness walk of faith to the cross. The chosen accessing the cross will be prejudged for retaining their names in the Book of Life. The chosen denied access to the cross will join the unchosen and their names will be moved from the Book of Life to the Books of the Dead.

5. Jesus gathers his chosen and angels for the Great and Terrible day of the Lord.

6. Jesus convenes his Great White Throne Judgment and passes judgment on those named in the Books of the Dead, based on their works. They will be cast into the Lake of Fire.

7. The Book of Life will be opened to reveal the chosen judged on the cross. The cross judgment guarantees the chosen's name will be in the Book of Life.

The Father's salvation scenario involves the choice of two paths. One path follows Satan's counsel based on satisfying the flesh leading to the Lake of Fire while the second path follows the counsel of the Spirit leading to eternal life. Both paths are subject to Satan's chastisement which provides two options. One is to seek Satan's temporal relief for the flesh or to endure Satan's chastisement under Spirit counsel in a manner that glorifies the Father. One leads to the Books of the Dead and the Lake of Fire, while the other leads to the Book of Life and membership in the Father's family. BOTH DESTINATIONS ARE ETERNAL!

I have pondered often over Pastors embracing and teaching false doctrine. Considering the bible is very clear on Jesus being the truth that sets you free and no one comes to the Father but through Him. In addition, the last few verses in the Book of Revelation clearly states that anyone messing around with the truth contained in the Bible, will be denied biblical blessings and access to or removal from the Book of Life. I have met many fine pastors, over 55 years of church attendance, exhibiting great ministerial deportment but were in submission to false denominational doctrine. It is my prayer that they will read my record with an open mind while seeking Holy Spirit counsel regarding veracity. Every one of the Father's chosen, including me, is individually responsible for knowing the truth that sets one free and gains access to the Book of Life. I am excited about the truth that I received from the Spirit and this book reflects my witness to that truth.

CONCLUSION:

ANY CHRISTIAN CHOSEN EMBRACING DENOMINATIONAL DOCTRINE, WHOSE VERACTY HAS NOT BEEN TESTED BY THE HOLY SPIRIT, IS IN JEOPARDY OF ENDANGERING THEIR SALVATION AND ETERNAL LIFE. THIS IS A WAKE UP CALL TO EXAMINE THE TRUTH YOU EMBRACE, REGARDING EFFICACY BASED ON HOLY SPIRIT COUNSEL RECEIVED BY YOUR SPIRIT. FOR EXAMPLE, IF THERE IS NO SENSE OF HOLY SPIRIT CONFIRMATION OF REVELATIONS SHARED IN THIS RECORD, YOUR ONLY OPTION IS TO REJECT MY WITNESS. HOWEVER, IF YOUR SPIRIT WAS QUICKENED WITH A SENCE OF PEACE, SEEK REPENTENCE OF FALSE DOCTRINE AND ACTIVELY SEEK THE COUNSEL OF THE HOLY SPIRIT.

A FAMILY MESSAGE

Our walk with the Trinity since December 2009 has been one of experiencing the fullness of God's Kingdom in terms of Grace, Mercy, Peace and Joy. We had sensed a strong presence of the Trinity Spirit and fellowship during our valley experience with dementia. We were in total agreement that the Will of the Father, as it will always be a blessing of experiencing his presence. I had saved a short note Joan wrote and placed on my desk shortly after becoming aware of her ALZ/Dementia: "I may not know what the future holds but I know who holds the future!" The Father knows us well and has shown us a compassion that is overwhelming. We were especially pleased to sense the presence of the Spirit when experiencing a hunger and thirst for righteousness. As Joan and I continued to share the future, we found our love growing stronger as we walked in the Will of our Father. The Father exercised His Will, on September 25, 2015 by receiving her into Paradise to share in the joy prepared for her, by His Son. Joan is in Paradise awaiting the date of my Father's will for my victory, following completion of work's righteousness service. When I join Joan, we know we will share Paradise briefly and Heaven eternally. WE ARE MORE THAN OK! WE HAVE BEEN CHOSEN BY A FATHER WHO IS WELL PREPARED TO BLESS A FAMILY FOR WHOM HE HAS LONG SUFFERED. I pray that what I share in this message and my RECORD will bless the whole family.

AN ADMISSION: I have often thought about Mark 6:4 "But Jesus said to them, 'A prophet is not without honor but in his own country, and among his own kin, and in his own house." They all smiled knowingly and let

Dad do his 'thing!' However, I am confident when they read my Record, they will realize the unique Author-Ghost Writer arrangement between the Spirit and I is one of Scribe and Spirit. On occasion the thought would go through my mind about the wonder I feel, at being commissioned by Father to fellowship with the Spirit to open up His word for His Chosen. I know I am not qualified for this Record project but it pleases the Father to use my empty shell that would be receptive to Spirit counsel performing works the Father had prepared. I once attended a church that displayed a motto saying 'It is not I but Christ in Me!' In my case, 'It is not I but the Spirit in Me!' I admit, that every time Satan tried to dissuade me from my shell service to the Spirit, the Spirit provided a special revelation.

Walking through the Word with the Holy Spirit is an adventure of witnessing partial revelations of the minds of Sovereignty. There have been a lot of changes in my walk with the Lord and I am sure there are some among you that have wondered if I have gone over the deep end of Christian Fanaticism. Indeed, my walk with the Trinity has grown into a personal fellowship that blesses and amazes me beyond my wildest expectations. I will even admit to an excessive enthusiasm over the Trinity and Spirit led exegesis that may mark me as one of those fanatics. You can also be marked as one who hungers and thirsts after righteousness or a martyr who presents himself as a living sacrifice. Considering the fact that Jesus only selected martyrs to serve with Him in the current millennium, we can conclude that a church without Christian Fanatics is likely a bless me church that continues to seek, worship and milk the golden calf.

The excitement over Jesus is the blessing in fully understanding the legacy that starts with clay in the garden and reaches completion with the Gift of the Father's Son. If one can't get excited over a Father's love expressed on a cross, it is rational to suggest such a person is dead in Christ.

This will probably be my only Family Message. Since December 2009, I have been committed to serve the Father's Will, which began with my Record of Biblical truth and continues, at the Father's pleasure, until all of His chosen have been counseled by the Spirit. I believe I will be part of

Jesus' Great Commission that ushers in Hebrews 6:17 'For the great day of His wrath has come, and who is able to stand.

I wanted to share the most important event in my life - being commissioned to record a Spirit led exegesis for the Father's Chosen. The Father had been measuring my commitment to Him for 35 years as I served in a nursing home ministry. I believe my Father knew the commitment in my heart for His service when He told me, in 1974, that I would never worry about my salvation. He knew that I was His committed servant when He commissioned me to write a record of Spirit led doctrine for His Chosen. I believe He accepted my nursing home ministry, as one having demonstrated work's righteousness, worthy of fellowship access to the trinity for support of my Record.

This message shares my path to the cross in terms of encouragement, witness and counsel. It is important to understand that there is no standard access path to the cross. It is solely based on being led by the Spirit and following Spirit counsel. You must be able to weigh and discern the veracity of any teaching, preaching and sharing of biblical truth passages. The only guaranteed access to biblical truth is the Spirit. Access to the Spirit is only provided to the Father's Chosen. My record shows the greatest teaching of false doctrine comes from the pulpit. You are responsible for the truth in your soul and spirit - you stand alone at the Great White Throne Judgment. When the Book of Life is opened, our desire is that all family members have been found worthy to be part of God's Kingdom. Your salvation is too important to entrust to anyone but the Spirit. Only the Chosen can worship the Father in Spirit and in truth. Only two types of personal records will be opened during the judgment. One with a record of sins and one cleansed of sin by Jesus. My advice: Seek the counsel of the Holy Spirit, in an attitude of total obedience and repentance, for your faith walk to the cross. THIS IS AN ACTION DECISION POINT FOR SALVATION.

The Father commissioned me for His service twice. In the Fall of 1974, He gave me Matthew 6:33, told me I would never worry about my salvation and arranged a 35 year nursing home ministry. In December 2009, He provided a replacement for my nursing home ministry, told me I needed to get into the Word and admonished me with "You can't preach the truth if you don't know the truth!" I knew that the Spirit was the only God sent revealer of biblical truth. My thoughts turned to the three-in-one TRINITY with UNITY and MAJESTY COEQUAL. For a while, I wondered which God was talking to me. I finally concluded that in the unity of the Trinity there is no privacy and as His Chosen, we communicate as part of that unity. In the 1970s, when all of the super Christians of the day were seeking Spiritual gifts, I asked for the gift of discernment. Unknown to me, I believe the Father intervened with my spirit regarding which gift I needed. Over the past six years, this gift has developed into a frequent two-way spirit to Spirit dialogue. When initiated by the Spirit, it responded to an issue I'd been thinking about. I find myself becoming more and more comfortable with the idea that my spirit is hosting the Trinity. My sense of awe and humility is always overshadowed by the question "Why me Lord?" I don't deserve this blessing!" Then I remind myself that it was the free opportunity gift of the Father's grace that allowed me to host the Trinity during my faith walk to the Cross. I am fully aware that, as a random soul selectee for the Book of Life, I was no different nor deserving than any other soul in the soul pool. HEREIN LIES JOHN 3:16's GIFT OF GRACE - BEING CHOSEN FOR THE BOOK OF LIFE. IT IS NOT A GUARANTEE OF SALVATION! IT IS AN OPPORTUNITY TO DEMONSTRATE WORK'S RIGHTEOUSNESS, UNDER SPIRIT COUNSEL TO TEST YOUR WORTHINESS TO BE A CHILD OF GOD.

When I was commissioned by the Father to learn the truth, I had immediate access to the trinity, experienced a heightened sense of spiritual discernment and a bible that came alive. As the Spirit shared with me the false doctrines permeating mainline churches, it didn't take long to recognize that today's churches are being systematically neutralized by rampant social theology and political correctness. As the Spirit continued to expose errors in church doctrine, I began to link the exposed truths together creating a mosaic that showed the Father's Will beginning before creation, with the formation of His Soul Pool and random selection of His Chosen for the BOOK OF LIFE. This is the time He exercised His omniscience, omnipotence and free will to set in motion His Family Plan which included His Salvation plan for His handpicked Chosen. OUR LIVES ARE LAID OUT FOR US FROM THE SOUL POOL TO THE GREAT WHITE THRONE JUDGMENT AND ON INTO ETERNITY. THERE IS NO GUARANTEED SALVATION FOR ANYONE; HOWEVER, THERE IS AN OPPORTUNITY FOR THE CHOSEN TO PROVE THEMSELVES WORTHY FOR GOD' S KINGDOM.

The record of my scribe walk with the Spirit lays out, in layman terms, how church doctrine has ignored the Holy Spirit in the application of hermeneutics in their doctrine development. The disunity of denominational exegesis is rampant suggesting a dire future for anyone formulating, teaching or preaching false doctrine.

A GLARING EXAMPLE: The promotion of John 3:16's grace gift as a free salvation package to all who ask. This is the most serious and egregious of all doctrine violations. They are selling doctrine designed to promote the receipt of blessing from God rather than the serving God. Here are examples of serious truths not found in most, if not all, churches:

+ Only the Father's Chosen are included in His "World" of John 3:16's blessing.
+ Not all Chosen can access the cross and salvation.
+ Once saved, always saved exegesis of predestination theology, provides a primrose path to salvation and is illogical and easily debunked with Spirit defined exegesis.
+ Accepting a "divine" Jesus is to mock the Trinity's greatest gift of love. It provides a True man with backup help, if needed. It is an effort to drag divinity down to man's level which is morally repugnant.
+ Chastisement is the Father's most effective tool to separate the wheat from the chaff among His Chosen.
+ Satan's Weapon of Mass Diffusion is his counsel to intellectual hermeneutics.
+ Satan is always within the Father's will when he chastises the Chosen.

+ The first and second Adams were alike as True Man without divinity.
+ Adam's sin consigning all of Adam's descendants to hell was within the Father's will with one limitation. The second death of the chosen spirit was placed in abeyance determination of their right to access the cross to pay for salvation.

This sample of issues, and others, are addressed in detail in my Record. I share this to give you a heads up for the need to develop a serious Spiritual relationship with the Trinity. Keep in mind that the vast majority of churches are selling a feel good theology that is rarely challenged, in spite of rampant disunity in denominational doctrine. When I became aware of the proliferation of doctrines, I realized that if I was seeking sources other than the bible and the Spirit for exegesis, I would pollute my interface with the Spirit. This is the genesis of false exegesis used by Christian intellectuals and egos charged with denominational doctrine oversight. They weigh their hermeneutics, under Satanic counsel/chastisement, against many other sources in establishing their doctrines.

EPILOGUE

A QUICK REFERENCE SUMMARY

As I was completing my final review of this Record, I was apprehensive over the impact it's revelations are going to have on the church staff and members. I feel like one of the Father's whistle-blowers chastising the church for their false doctrine. After almost six years of walking with the Spirit receiving revelations of truth and sharing thoughts with the Trinity, I feel a sense of inadequacy and honor in presenting a State of the Church message. The message is clear with well documented truths. There are an unknown number of the Father's Chosen, denied the Truth of being named in the Father's Book of Life offering the only opportunity for salvation and eternal life. The church has been delinquent in teaching doctrines of truth impacting the salvation of many chosen. Debunking a couple of the serious doctrinal errors follow:

1. John 3:16! This is the most serious! You get this wrong and you lose all credibility for scriptural exegesis. Every church I have attended has offered a free "come to Jesus" enticement to boost the coffers and membership. They are offering salvation for the asking, without conditions. It is justified by a hermeneutics interpretation of the word "WORLD." Their interpretation is "everyone in the world." They ignore the Father's random selection of chosen from among the entire soul population needed to populate creation from the Garden to the second advent of Jesus. The names of the Elect were written in the Fathers 'Book of Life' for a salvation

opportunity under John 3:16. The remaining souls would enter life to be condemned under Adam's sin. This Book of Life will be opened during the Great White Throne Judgment, to reveal those chosen who had glorified the Father by demonstrating 'Work's Righteousness' during Satan's chastisement. While no new names will be added to the Book, names will be removed by the Father's screening operations to separate the wheat from the chaff.

THE CHURCH'S ARE SELLING A FREE BIRTHRIGHT AKIN TO THE SELLING OF INDULGENCES BY THE EARLY CATHOLIC CHURCH. The only difference is one of financial creativity. Today's church took the one indulgence payment price of the Pope and installed an ongoing gift offering program that uses scriptures in a seduced misapplication of tithing. This record provides an in depth discussion of John 3:16.

2. The Divinity of Christ as True Man. Most Christian hermeneutics support this Doctrine based on the scripture "Jesus is true God and True Man." It doesn't say 'Jesus is True God and Jesus is True GOD Man.' This is another flagrant use of hermeneutics to accept Satanic counsel to provide exegesis. The application of hermeneutics is a process wherein two opposing spirits, Satan and the Holy Spirit, are providing counsel. IF YOU EXAMINE THE DOCTRINES OF CHRISTIAN DENOMINATIONS IN AMERICA, YOU WILL FIND LITTLE OR NO UNITY OF TRUTH IN THEIR DOCTRINES. IN FACT, THE DIVERSITY OF DOCTRINES IS A DIVERSITY OF BIBLICAL TRUTHS COMING FROM THE SAME BIBLE! HOW CAN A LAY PERSON KNOW WHAT IS PREACHED FROM THE PULPIT IS TRUTH? It appears the church wanted to bring the Divinity of God down to make the trinity more relevant. Maybe it evolved with the church wanting a divine Pope to continue Christ's True man divinity after the resurrection. The idea of linking a pope to divinity is ludicrous because you are saying divinity can sin. Again, this record examines divinity extensively.

Here are a few examples that establish the divinity hoax.

i.   The unity of the Trinity cannot be violated.

ii. Divinity is the overarching power of binding three Gods into One.

iii. Divinity would not require Spirit help for the Father's seed to impregnate Mary.

iv. Divinity power would not need the Spirit power for the resurrection.

v.   Divinity cannot sin! This destroys the True Man option to sin.

vi. Divinity cannot be crucified!

vii. Satan could not or would not engage Divinity with temptation in the wilderness.

A clear example of the church trying to bring down Christ to our level by replacing a "True Man' with a 'Divine True Man.' Maybe it is the result of Satan's counsel on 'True Man' that Jesus would be more relevant or maybe we could have a Divine Pope. Can you imagine divinity residing in a Pope sinner?

3.   The church's need for a false doctrine on ELECTION was needed to support their false doctrine of John 3:16 dealing with the definition of 'WORLD.' Most churches practicing prosperity theology ignore or plays down the DOCTRINE OF THE CHOSEN, also called ELECTION, and opens their 'WORLD' of John 3:16 to all who desire salvation. If the truth of John 3:16 were adopted by a church, it would need to adopt the truths of the Book of Life and the Father's Chosen and implement strict Spirit controls over their invitation to an alter call. Obviously, the church membership and treasury would be markedly reduced. You may ask why the Lord would allow this to happen to the church? You will find the answer in this Record. It involves the sovereignty of the Father's Will and using the church as a screening tool to promote the Great Commission. This Record will show:

+   The thrust of the Father's salvation plan was to set up a program to IDENTIFY AND SCREEN HIS CHOSEN, WITH TEMPERED SATANIC CHASTISEMENT, TO IDENTIFY THOSE CHOSEN WITH A HEART THAT

DESIRES TO GLORIFY THE FATHER WITH WORK'S RIGHTEOUSNESS. He sent His Son to establish a living church for those interested in the salvation promise whether Chosen or unchosen. Some Chosen would be screened out for lack of interest in salvation and their desire for the world. The church would provide a venue to expose those interested, whether unchosen or Chosen. This allows the church to perform a membership candidate gathering operation and provide their biblical doctrine, of limited veracity, to their denominations. The Father used Satan's power as a Deceiver, to counsel the church's intellect responsible for Doctrine. There are two counselors available for development of Doctrine; Satan and the Holy Spirit. Satan attacked the ego of Adam to be like God committing his descendants to hell. Satan attacked the ego of the church's elite running their Doctrine program, with counsel promoting prosperity theology that focused on the social and physical needs of the church, at the expense of the Spiritual needs of the soul. NOTE: ALL OF THE CHURCH'S ACTIONS ARE CONTROLLED BY JESUS ENFORCING THE FATHER'S WILL. The Father's plan included Satan's chastisement of a chosen's spirit and soul during the faith walk to the cross. This walk of faith is a walk of work's righteousness that measures your hunger and thirst for bringing glory to the Father.

IMPORTANT: THE FACT THAT YOU MAY BE A CHOSEN IN A CHURCH PREACHING FALSE DOCTRINE DOES NOT MEAN YOUR NAME WILL BE REMOVED FROM THE BOOK OF LIFE. CONSIDER:

1. YOU HAVE SOLE RESPONSIBILTY FOR YOUR SALVATION!
2. YOU HAVE THE HOLY SPIRIT RESIDENT WITH YOUR SPIRIT. THE TRINITY LIVES WITHIN YOU. YOUR SPIRIT NEEDS TO SEEK THE INDWELLING HOLY SPIRIT.
3. IF YOU HAVE A DESIRE FOR KNOWING JESUS, THERE ARE MANY SCRIPTURE DEALING WITH 'SEEKING.'

During my first encounter with the Father in 1974, He gave me Matthew 6:33 'Seek ye first the kingdom of God and His righteousness ..." and told me I would never worry about my salvation. I had spent 35 years in a nursing home ministry, when I recalled the 1974 visit upon a second visit from the Father in a December 2009. He told me to get into the Word and record Spirit led revelations as a scribe. I knew that I had to SEEK a relationship with each member of the Trinity, especially the Holy Spirit. I have been walking with them for six years and they have been the best six years of my life! The Spirit will quicken your spirit WHEN YOU START SEEKING HIM. SEEK THE SPIRIT, HE IS WAITING TO WELCOME YOU.

These three examples are the tip of the iceberg. Jesus is charged by the Father to enforce His Will. Jesus was granted all power to control every aspect of the Father's creation, including thought word and deed. All of the church's actions, good or bad, are under Jesus's approval. The Father's Master Plan was established before creation.

ADVICE: MAKE IT A LIFE PRIORTY TO FIND OUT IF YOUR NAME IS IN THE BOOK OF LIFE. IF YOU ARE IN THE BOOK OF LIFE, SERVE THE TRINITY WITH A FERVER IN A HUNGER AND THIRST FOR RIGHTEOUSNESS.

Jesus made it very clear when He said: "If you love anyone, including self, more than Me, you are not worthy of Me." To love one member of the Trinity is to love every member of the Trinity.

11/13/2015 A Sauna fellowship with the Trinity, sharing thoughts on the Chosen's soul journey from being a soul in the soul pool before creation, to the Trinity's welcome home in the Kingdom of God.

A CHOSEN'S SOUL JOURNEY TO
THE FATHER'S KINGDOM

SOUL POOL: This pool provides the souls needed to cover a spectrum of souls from the Garden to the second coming. They are inanimate and named by the Father. They will be sequentially released based on conception requirements. At conception, the Father breathes life into the soul at which time the soul is given a spirit of the flesh and a Spirit of Life, that includes free will.

BOOK OF LIFE: Upon completion of the Pool, the Father randomly selects souls across the entire spectrum and writes their names in the Book of Life. This is the same book found in the Great White Throne Judgment (GWTJ). During the journey, there will be a separation of the Wheat from the Chaff from among chosen. There will be some chosen that prove to be unworthy, causing their names to be erased from the Book of Life

GARDEN OF EDEN: God's creation included the Garden where He breathed life into Adam. The Father then kicked Satan out of Heaven into the Garden and allowed Satan to counsel Adam to sin by eating the forbidden fruit. Adam's sin condemned the seed of all of his offspring to Spiritual and physical death, including the chosen and the unchosen. The First Death is the death of the flesh which both the chosen and unchosen will partake. The Second Death is the Death of your spirit. The Second Death for the unchosen will be when the books of the dead are opened and their spirits are cast by Jesus into the lake of fire.

JOHN 3:16 BLESSING: "God so loved the WORLD, that He gave His only begotten Son ..." Most churches view the WORLD as all souls. We have established above that only the chosen are named in the Book of Life. Since Adam's sin included a Second Death for the chosen's spirit, the Father had to grant a stay of execution until their sins of the spirit could be cleansed by a sacrifice without blemish, to pay a ransom for release from the Second Death requirement. The Father's Salvation Plan provided the chosen an opportunity to demonstrate work's righteousness that glorified the Father. If worthy, Jesus would pay the ransom for the chosen's spirit.

THE CROSS PAYS THE RANSOM FOR YOUR SOUL. YOUR JUDGMENT WAS COMPLETED ON THE CROSS BY JESUS PAYING YOUR RANSOM AND JUDGING YOU RIGHTEOUS.

The most sensitive word in the church's biblical lexicon: ELECT OR CHOSEN. Christian denominations have a hard time accepting the Sovereignty of the Father's right of choosing who will be in His eternal family. I was one of those having a problem with God arbitrarily selecting who could call Him Father in the new heaven. Subsequent to my 2009 meeting with the Father, the Spirit opened my eyes of understanding of the 'Potter and the Clay.' I realized my legacy went back to the dirt in the garden with father Adam receiving life from God's breath. It provides new comprehension to Jesus' word's 'There is none righteous, no not one, only the Father in heaven.' Understanding my roots, makes the realization that the Father honors me as one of His chosen. Extending my roots back to the soul pool, I am fully aware that there was nothing to distinguish me from the rest of the souls in the pool. All of us were inanimate and named by the Father. When the pool was complete, the Father made a random selection of souls from across the entire spectrum of the soul pool. He then established a Book of Life and wrote the names of those randomly selected in the Book. The Book is not a guarantee of salvation but a John 3:16 grace option to a faith walk to the cross under counsel and teaching of the Holy Spirit.

BEING ONE OF THE CHOSEN IS NOT A GUARANTEE. YOU MUST PROVE YOU ARE WORTHY!

A FEW SCRIPTURES DEALING WITH THE ELECT AND CHOSEN!

2ND THESSALONIANS 2:13 "But we are bound to give thanks always to God for you, brethren beloved of the Lord, because God hath FROM THE BEGINNING, CHOSEN YOU to salvation through sanctification of the Spirit and the belief of the Truth." Note: 'BEGINNING' means soul pool. Capital 'S' in Spirit signifies the Holy Spirit.

2ND TIMOTHY 2:10 "Therefore I endure all things for the ELECT'S sake that they may also obtain the salvation which is in Christ Jesus with eternal glory." 'endure' suggests that the salvation walk is an endurance course for the elect. Seems logical since martyrdom began with the first tribulation and has continued to today with an anticipation of increased martyrdom as the Father readies His Son for Satan's release from the bottomless pit to assume command of the coming tribulation. A word of caution: resist the false doctrine of pre-tribulation rapture and gird yourself with the full armor of God.

TITUS 1:1 "Paul, a servant of God, and an apostle of Jesus Christ, according to the faith of God's ELECT, and the acknowledging of the truth which is after Godliness." Notice the links among God, servant, apostle (Chosen), Christ, faith, elect, truth and Godliness which is righteousness. TODAY'S CHOSEN ARE JESUS' PRESENT DAY CHOSEN DISCIPLES

CARRYING JOHN, THE BAPTIST'S, BATTLE CRY IN THE WILDERNESS, ANNOUNCING THE 2ND COMING OF THE LORD. WE CAN EXPECT MANY MARTYRS DURING THE COMING TRIBULATION PERIOD.

2ND PETER 2:4 "The Lord knoweth how to deliver the GODLY out of temptations, and to reserve the UNJUST unto the day of JUDGMENT to be punished." The Chosen who follow the Counsel of the Spirit will be delivered from temptations while the unchosen will be delivered to the judgment seat of Christ and cast into the Lake of Fire. Notice how the Lord controls the actions of the just and unjust. Jesus judged the spirits of the Godly as righteous before the battle. The unjust spirits are held in purgatory for Great White Throne Judgment following the battle.

THE GREATEST TREASURE YOU CAN LAY UP IN HEAVEN, THAT GIVES THE FATHER THE GREATEST GLORY, IS MARTYRDOM. THE FATHER HAS PRE-ORDAINED THE CHOSEN TO BE SO HONORED.

PONDERING THE MIND OF GOD

After completing a six year walk as a scribe to the Holy Spirit, I am sending this Record of Spirit Led Revelations to a publisher. As I was considering the response to my book, I realized the Spirit was continuing to guide my thoughts. So I was led to include these final comments. I acknowledge that this Record reflects a special personal blessing for having the honor of a six-year fellowship with the Trinity. I recognize that when I share thoughts with a member of the Trinity, I need to keep in mind the Unity of the Trinity responds with one voice. So when I address the trinity, I address the member I feel has oversight as a functional lead for the topic being addressed: 1. Father as Designer, Planner, Trinity's Will and Purpose, plus Receiver of the Trinity's Glory. 2. Jesus as Savior, King of Kings and Controller to insure the Father's Will and Purpose is accomplished, and 3. Holy Spirit as Counselor and teacher to the Father's Chosen who draws, counsels, teaches, and critiques a Chosen's faith walk to the Cross, and determines worthiness to access the cross. We seem to overlook that we were baptized in the name of the Father, Son and Holy Spirit. Under the unity of the Trinity, each functional member's actions reflect total concurrence of the Trinity. For example:

1. As titular head of the Trinity, the Father provided the "Word."
2. Jesus received the Word and shared the "Word" with the disciples.
3. The disciples recorded and shared the "Word" with the Chosen.
4. The Great Commission commands the Chosen to share the "WORD" with unknown Chosen all over the world.

So the Spirit reveals the Word by revealing Jesus as the Written Word received from the Father of the Trinity. WHAT MOST MEMBERS OF THE CHURCH DON'T REALIZE IS ONE CAN NOT ACCESS THE WORD (JESUS) WITHOUT THE HOLY SPIRIT. The Father's Salvation Plan set the scenario of His Plan as:

1. Send the Father's Word to His Son who shared the contents, as received during his journey to the Cross, with the chosen disciples.
2. The disciples recorded Jesus' Word as received directly or later divinely inspired. They recognized Jesus and Word were synonymous.
3. Jesus told His disciples to wait until the Spirit is sent by the Father to be their counselor and teacher, who would lead them into sharing all truth in power.
4. The Father sent the Spirit to baptize the disciples in the Trinity, not just the Spirit.
5. The Spirit was sent as counselor to provide counsel and divine additions to the Word.

IT IS IMPORTANT TO UNDERSTAND AND EMBRACE THE TRUTH THAT ALL ACCESS TO ANY MEMBER OF THE TRINITY IS THROUGH THE HOLY SPIRIT. CONSIDER:

+ Romans 8:14 "For as many as are led by the Spirit of God, they are sons of God."
+ Luke 4:1 "Then Jesus, being filled with the Holy Spirit, was LED BY THE SPIRIT into the wilderness." This scripture suggests that Jesus' journey as True Man, reflects the importance of being led by the Spirit. Consider:
+ Galatians 5:18 "But if you are LED BY THE SPIRIT, you are not under the law." We are walking under grace.

THESE REVELATIONS HIGHLIGHT THE UNDERSTANDING OF WHY JESUS TOLD HIS DISCIPLES NOT TO DO ANYTHING UNTIL THEY HAD RECEIVED POWER FROM ON HIGH. Luke tells us that Jesus enjoyed Spirit power during his walk to the cross. He was continuously counseled by the Spirit to resist Satan's counsel to sin and He complied with total Spirit counsel. FAST FORWARD to the Chosen. Jesus knew that without Spirit counsel, we would be exposed to Satanic counsel only. THEREFORE, we need Spirit Counsel to combat Satan's counsel. Our salvation worthiness weighs on our source of counsel compliance which measures the glory received by the Father. Consider Matthew 3:8: "Therefore, bear fruits worthy of repentance."

While Jesus rebuked Satan's counsel 100 % of the time, the Father understands we are no Jesus. I believe that the Spirit knows the percentage of rebuking needed to demonstrate a heart that hungers and thirst for righteousness. It is your heart that tells Him you are worthy to be a child of the Father. In heaven there will be no Satan to impact total joy and peace.

IMPORTANT CONSIDERATIONS

I haven't finished my walk of faith, so access to the cross and salvation is still in the future. These means I am under chastisement by Satan but honoring the counsel of the Holy Spirit. It also means that I still have my free will. My intent is to withstand Satan's counsel and honor my Father by walking with the Spirit. However, you don't know me from Adam and need to seek and ask for Spirit discernment of what I am sharing. Keep in mind that Satan is the great deceiver. This why we are to test the two spirits providing our counsel. If your heart hungers and thirsts after righteousness and you sense a presence of peace, you are being quickened by the Holy Spirit and can ask about the veracity of revelations I have shared. If you believe your spirit was quickened by the Spirit but did not provide a confirmation of peace for the revelations in this record, I am not who I say I am or you are not one of the chosen. YOU MUST EVER BE VIGILANT OF SATAN'S SPIRIT OF DECEPTION COMPETING WITH THE HOLY SPIRIT, IN THEIR BATTLE FOR YOUR SOUL. INGRAIN IN YOUR SPIRIT:

+   THERE IS ONLY ONE ABSOLUTE SOURCE FOR BIBLICAL TRUTH. THE BIBLE!

+ THERE IS ONLY ONE ACCESS TO BIBLICAL TRUTH. THE HOLY SPIRIT!
+ THERE IS ONLY ONE GROUP ELIGIBLE TO BE LED BY THE SPIRIT. THE CHOSEN!
+ THERE IS ONLY ONE TEST FOR BIBLICAL TRUTH. SPIRITUAL DISCERNMENT!
+ THERE IS ONLY ONE ACCESS TO SPIRITUAL DISCERNMENT. NARROW GATE!
+ THERE IS ONLY ONE PERSON RESPONSIBLE FOR YOUR SALVATION. YOU!

VERIFY ALL TRUTHS REGARDLESS OF SOURCE.

The recommended first step is Matthew 6:33 "But seek ye first the kingdom of God, and His righteousness, and all these things shall be added unto you. THE PATH STARTS WITH SEEKING THE SPIRIT BECAUSE HE STANDS AT THE GATE.

A NEW RAPTURE WRINKLE.

While taking another look at the rapture of the church, I ran across Revelation 4:16-17 "For the Lord himself shall descend from heaven with a shout, with the voice of the archangel, and with the trump of God: and the dead in Christ shall rise first; (17) Then they which are alive and remain shall be caught up together with them in the clouds, to meet the Lord in the air: and so shall we ever be with Lord." Up until know, I believed that there was no salvation without cross access. You had to die for the ransom to be paid for your soul. It is the gift of John 3:16!

Now, Verse 16 says 'the dead in Christ shall rise first' followed by verse 17 saying 'they which are alive and remain shall be caught up together in the clouds.' We seem to have a conundrum!

This was on my mind last evening and I considered Jesus waving the cross approach to salvation, by providing a blanket salvation opportunity as part of the rapture experience. It was on my mind when I awoke this morning, As I was typing the word 'alive,' my spirit was quickened. We are talking about one group being 'dead' and the other 'alive.' I recalled when Jesus raptured only the martyrs and John asked about the remaining chosen, Jesus said they (the dead in Christ) would be in the second resurrection. At this point in time, we are talking about chosen who were in the Book of Life awaiting the Great White Throne Judgment. Subsequent to the first resurrection, the chosen who accessed the cross were judged by Jesus for Spirit life and transferred to be with Jesus in Paradise. The spirit of the chosen 'dead' will come alive at Jesus' call. They had accessed the cross and were in the Book of Life awaiting the second resurrection.

FINAL THOUGHTS ON THE NUMBER OF CHOSEN

The 2015 Census estimated 7, 256 490,000 living souls at the end of the year. Considering attrition over 6,000 years, we can conclude the Father had a real big soul pool. When we consider 'that narrow is the gate and few there are that enter therein,' we can conclude that 'few' souls compared to a multi-billion number of souls can be a large number – 1 % of 7.2 billion is 72 million. I have come to the conclusion that the number of chosen in the Book of Life in the beginning is not the important number. The number of chosen remaining in the Book of Life, when opened at the end of the Great White Throne Judgment (GWTJ), is the important number. Consider the following scenario.

+ The Father sets his Will and Purpose: He wants 5,000,000 children for His Family.
  ++ MANY ARE CALLED to access the narrow gate. FEW ARE CHOSEN.
+ The Father names Jesus as controller to insure His Will and Purpose are satisfied.
+ The Father appoints Satan as chastiser of His chosen to test their worthiness.
+ The Father appoints the Spirit to draw, teach, counsel and approve cross access.

+ The Father sets up chastisement screens to control access to the narrow gate, baptism in the Spirit, Spirit counsel through works He had prepared before the beginning of time, providing work's righteousness opportunities to bring glory to the Father.
+ The Spirit selects the chosen, that brought glory to the Father, for access to the cross.

Under this scenario, the Father provides Jesus with the number of chosen for the John 3:16 gift whose names were written in the Book of Life.

Jesus manages the screening action to control who survives each screening action leading to approval to access the cross.

The LINGERING QUESTION: HOW DID THE FATHER KNOW WHOSE NAMES WOULD BE WRITTEN IN THE FINAL BOOK OF LIFE? HE KNEW US IN THE BEGINNING!

Since my December 2009 commission from the Father, I have pondered the issue of the 'few' who entered the narrow gate and how many chosen there are. Prior to my commission, I could not accept the fairness of a chosen selected by the Father, before creation, Using the 2015 census, we would have 7.2 billion souls. Consider 1% or 72 million souls available for the first Spirit screening, to gain access to the narrow gate. If we added all of the dead souls prior to 2015, we would have a humongous number of souls, both chosen and unchosen. Like the cattle on a thousand hill, the stars in the galaxies and the sand on the beaches, we can only conclude that we are not privy to this information in the mind of God because it would not suit His Purpose. It is an example that no one knows the mind of God with one qualification; the chosen have access to biblical revelations of His mind shared by the Spirit. However, as I am now pondering how the number of the chosen could impact the Father's will and purpose, the Spirit quickened my spirit with a number of thoughts. The genesis of these thoughts was my six-year accumulation of biblical revelations. You have probably noticed that I mention my 'ponderings' on God's Word. Looking back, I recall the Lord's recommendation to 'think upon these thing.' It is commonplace during the day for my thoughts to be preoccupied with 'thinking upon biblical revelations' that have blessed my soul. In trying to explain the Father's purpose, I would like to suggest a plausible scenario:

+ The Father names 5,000,000 chosen for his Book of Life in the soul pool.
+ The Father sets his will and purpose for a family of 1,000,000 chosen.
+ The Father has provided man with free will and desire to satisfy the needs of the flesh and spirit. He knows it is in man's nature to sin.
+ The Father sets his screens for separating the chosen wheat from the chosen chaff.
+ The Father appoints Satan, as the Chastiser of the saints to counsel/deceive man into feeding the needs of his flesh and ignore needs of his spirit.
+ The Father controls church doctrine to provide false exegesis to attract both the chosen and unchosen.
+ The Father uses false doctrine to test the chosen as to which spirit counsel they will elect to follow: Satan's counsel for prosperity theology or the Spirit's call to present your bodies as a living sacrifice.
+ The Father uses unchosen church members as a screening tool to test the chosen, on whether they would prefer to buddy up with the unchosen and prosperity theology or Jesus who asks you to pick up your cross and follow Him.
+ The Father appoints Jesus to control the screens to provide 1,000,000 children. The environment of every chosen during the walk to the cross is controlled by Jesus. He controls how much chastisement Satan can apply and all activities that impact your quest to reach the cross. The Screening Basis for Separations of Chosen from Unchosen:
+ Soul Pool: Random selection of chosen.
+ The Narrow Gate: The chosen's desire for knowledge of God.
+ Spirit Teaching of the Word. A hunger and thirst for Righteousness.
+ Walk of Faith. Works righteousness that gives the Father glory.

5. An equal application of chastisement standards providing an equitable work's righteousness consideration for access to the cross.

JAMES WAS RIGHT: SALVATION WITHOUT WORKS IS DEAD!

THE FATHER WAS RIGHT: TO BE MY SON, PARTAKE IN MY CHASTISEMENT.

THERE COST FOR OUR SALVATION – UP TO AND INCLUDING MARTYRDOM!

Everything is under the Father's Will to serve His Purpose and Glory. Real time is measured from the Garden of Eden to the Great White Throne Judgment. The entire panorama is displayed before the beginning of time. This panorama attests to the Fathers omniscience in knowing everything about you and everyone else. He is also in control of the chosen program. It is all spelled out in His Salvation Plan and the chosen is the focus of His purpose and glory. His purpose is His chosen family and His glory is the ticket to the cross. We have no need to know the total number of souls and how many were among the chosen. We need to understand up front that 'Jesus did it all!' is a prosperity theology wherein Jesus is the only martyr. The Father's Plan for a path to salvation called for us to be a living sacrifice and to pick up our cross and follow Jesus. Jesus allowed only the martyrs to join Him in the first resurrection. The remaining chosen were told to await the second resurrection.

In this example, Jesus was tasked to screen out 4,000,000 chosen to arrive at a family of 1,000,000 chosen. The numbers presented above are not the focus of the Father's Plan.

What the Father wanted was a plan that:

1. Offered a significant number of chosen an opportunity to prove themselves worthy.
2. A worthiness test that glorifies the Father with a heart committed to the Father's will.

In his omniscience, the Father knew the number of chosen He would need to gain the number of chosen needed to fill the family size stipulated in His purpose.

IN CONCLUSION, THE FATHER PROVIDED THE NUMBER OF CHOSEN, WHO WOULD BE BLESSED BY THE JOHN 3:16 OPPORTUNITY TO EARN SALVATION. THE FATHER PREORDAINED THE WORKS THEY WERE TO DO UNDER CHASTISEMENT FROM SATAN. WORKS PERFORMED UNDER HOLY SPIRIT COUNSEL EARNED WORK'S RIGHTEOUSNESS CREDIT, GLORIFIED THE FATHER AND GAINED ACCESS TO THE CROSS. THOSE WHO YIELDED TO SATANIC COUNSEL WERE SCREENED OUT.

NOW HEAR THIS – YOU ARE RESPONSIBLE FOR YOUR SALVATION!

+ JOHN 3:16 WAS AN OPPORTUNITY GIFT TO PROVE WORTHINESS!
+ YOU MUST DEMONSTRATE A HEART THAT HUNGERS AND THIRSTS FOR RIGHTEOUSNESS AND A DESIRE TO MAKE THE FATHERS WILL YOUR WILL.
+ BE A PARTAKER OF CHASTISEMENT THAT BRINGS THE FATHER GLORY!
+ YOU MUST ENDURE THE FATHER'S CHASTISEMENT TO THE END!
+ THINK ABOUT YOUR SIN LEGACY AND THE RANSOM PAID FOR CLEANSING!

GUIDANCE FOR THE FATHER'S CHOSEN

LUKE 12:1-5

VERSE 1: "In the meantime, when there were gathered together an innumerable multitude of people, insomuch that they trod one upon the other, he began to say unto his disciples first of all, beware ye of the leaven of the Pharisee, which is hypocrisy." Leavening can be described as a process of adding to dough to changes acceptability. What Jesus is saying is that what the Pharisees are doing is adding to the law to put more burden on the people. This Record reveals that the Pharisee practice of falsifying the law is akin to the current practice of falsifying biblical truth to fill the coffers of memberships and/or bank accounts of churches and/or evangelists. Prosperity theology that focuses on satisfying social over spiritual needs is more lucrative.

VERSE 2: "For there is nothing covered, that shall not be revealed, neither hid, that not be known." I believe this record is one example of Jesus' revelation in this verse. I believe the 2nd coming is nigh and this Record plays a small part in the Father's plan for His Son's return.

VERSE 3: "Therefore, whatsoever you have spoken in darkness shall be heard in the light; and that which ye have spoken in the ear in closets shall be proclaimed upon the house tops." The Spirit will be quickening the Chosen to step forward equipped with the full armor of God to proclaim the return of the King of Kings. The tribulation period will provide an ample opportunity for God's Chosen, if selected by the Father's Will, to be a martyr. It is an opportunity to lay up the optimum treasure in heaven, honoring the Trinity.

Verse 4: "And I say unto you my friends, Be not afraid of them that kill the body, and after that have no more that they can do." This is the pep talk of all pep talks. Jesus is calling us friends and reminding us that we are joining in His battle for our SOULS. He set the stage and now He will take His army across the goal line for victory. WE ARE BATTLING FOR OUR SOULS AND NOT OUR BODIES!"

Verse 5: "But I will forewarn you whom you shall fear: fear him, which after he hath killed hath power to cast into hell: yea, I say unto you, Fear him. JESUS IS THE JUDGE WITH THE POWER TO CAST A SOUL INTO HELL. OUR CHOICE IS AN ETERNAL DECISION!

UNDERSTAND THIS!

THE FATHER, BEFORE THE FOUNDATIONS OF THE WORLD, HAD IDENTIFIED THOSE IN HIS BOOK OF LIFE, WHO WOULD BE TESTED FOR MARTYRDOM. BE PREPARED, IN YOUR SPIRIT, FOR BEING SELECTED AS ONE OF HIS MARTYRS.

Printed in the United States
By Bookmasters